W9-CCT-540

Passionate
Attachments

BOOKS BY SIGNE HAMMER

Daughters & Mothers: Mothers & Daughters

Women: Body and Culture: Essays on the Sexuality of Women in a Changing Society

Passionate Attachments

FATHERS AND DAUGHTERS IN AMERICA TODAY

Signe Hammer

Rawson Associates · New York

The author wishes to thank the following for permission to quote from the works listed below:

The Managerial Woman, by Margaret Hennig and Anne Jardim, Copyright © 1976, 1977 by Margaret Hennig and Anne Jardim. Reprinted by permission of Doubleday & Company, Inc.

My Heart Belongs to Daddy, by Cole Porter, Copyright © 1938 by Chappell & Co., Inc. Copyright Renewed, Assigned to John F. Wharton, Trustee of the Cole Porter Musical and Literary Property Trusts. Chappel & Co., Inc., Publisher. International Copyright Secured. All Rights Reserved. Used by permission.

Library of Congress Cataloging in Publication Data

Hammer, Signe.
    Passionate attachments.

    Bibliography: p.
    1. Fathers and daughters—United States.
I. Title.
HQ777.H26   1982   306.8′742   81-40265
ISBN 0-89256-182-3   AACR2

Copyright © 1982 by Signe Hammer
All rights reserved
Published simultaneously in Canada by McClelland and Stewart, Ltd.
Composition by American–Stratford Graphic Services, Inc.,
Brattleboro, Vermont
Printed and bound by Fairfield Graphics,
Fairfield, Pennsylvania

Designed by Jacques Chazaud

First Edition

Contents

DISCLAIMER

While the dialogue in this book has been taken from interviews, the names and circumstances of the characters have been changed. Any resemblance to any living person is entirely fortuitous.

Acknowledgments

As always, my first and greatest debt is to Dr. Marjorie Taggart White: analyst, therapist, mentor, friend. She read many chapters in draft and helped me sort out ideas in countless discussions. She provided unstinting emotional support and, on occasion, even the sheer practical advice I needed to get through the rough patches. Whatever clarity and validity this book possesses owe much to her wisdom and knowledge.

The project was conceived in discussions with Sandra Elkin, whose commitment to it went far beyond the range of the usual agent's interest. She read early, largely illegible drafts, talked over ideas and, when all else failed, provided milk and cookies. Her support was invaluable.

My editor, Eleanor Rawson, not only bought and believed in the book; she provided unflagging support through two years and a number of conceptual revisions. Her suggestions were crucial to its final form.

My manuscript editor, Sharon Morgan, worked with me on revisions with the patience, thoroughness, and sheer caring that have become all too rare among editors. The shape of individual chapters owes much to her clear eye.

And then, of course, there is the Writers Room. After a year of living and working in the same space, a desk in this oasis in Times Square saved my sanity and my book. I found more than space to work; I found the support and fellowship of other writers. Marjorie Iseman, at the next desk, read some early chapters, paid me the compliment of a positive response, and gave me the benefit of her wit and intelligence in innumerable discussions. She also worked late next to me more times than I can count. Bernard A. Weisberger, whose desk I inherited, read some chapters in draft and gave me a strong positive response at a crucial moment. Felicia Hirsch, Molly Haskell, Denise DeMong, Harry Maurer, H.B. Gilmour, Judy Rossner, Lucinda Franks, John Thackray, and others have all shared those moments of lightness or commiseration that help relieve the burden of a writer's essential isolation. This extraordinary combination of privacy and fellowship has been the greatest gift of the Writers Room, and it owes much to the work of Dey Gosse, the executive director.

Elaine Pagels read several early chapters and gave me the benefit of her comments, as did Karen Durbin. Robin Morgan blessed and encouraged my project even while deeply involved in her own. The writers' group Women's Ink gave me a reading from the manuscript; the response of fellow members was invaluable. Susie Orbach and Carol Bloom, co-founders of The Women's Therapy

Centre Institute, invited me to speak in their inaugural lecture series, thus allowing me to try out my ideas on an audience of professionals. Jean Detre showed me some unpublished material on Antigone.

Several psychologists and psychoanalysts gave me the benefit of their knowledge and experience in searching interviews and discussions. Dr. John Munder Ross of New York City, clinical associate professor of psychiatry at Downstate Medical Center and a noted psychoanalytic theorist and author of many articles on fathering, provided the clarity and insight that helped crystallize a number of my ideas. Dr. Lora Heims Tessman, a Massachusetts clinical psychologist in the private practice of psychotherapy with adults and children and at MIT and author of *Children of Parting Parents,* was also particularly insightful and helpful. Both their writings and their comments are cited in this book; any errors of interpretation or application are entirely my own.

Dr. Sylvia Brody of New York City, a psychologist noted for her psychoanalytic work with children and co-author with Sidney Axelrod of *Mothers, Fathers, and Children,* one of the few studies to deal directly with fathers, gave me the benefit of a productive interview. Together with her book, this helped me to understand the motivation for various paternal attitudes toward daughters. In addition, Dr. Leah C. Shaefer of New York City, a psychotherapist and author of *Women and Sex,* was very helpful, as were Peggy Papp of the Ackerman Institute for Family Therapy in New York City and psychologist Dr. Carol Beauvais of New York City.

For the concept of the Identity Triangle, I am indebted to a number of people. Dr. Ernest Abelin of New York City, whose work on the theory of early triangulation has become increasingly influential, was kind enough to send me a then-unpublished paper which was of great help. Dr. Nancy Chodorow of the University of California, Santa Cruz, discusses Helene Deutsch's theories of triangulation in the life of girls and women in her book *The Reproduction of Mothering.* This sent me to Deutsch's own writing, and ultimately helped shape my theory of the Identity Triangle as the central structure in which women's identity is formed. Dr. John Munder Ross provided usefully concrete elucidations of triangulation. But to the best of my knowledge (how can one finally be sure, when intellectual influences are so complex?) the term "Identity Triangle" is my own, as is the particular way I have extended and used the idea; most certainly, any errors I have committed in interpreting other people's ideas are entirely my own.

For the concept of reciprocal identification, I am indebted to the work of Dr. Michael E. Lamb, now of the University of Utah, and his colleagues Margaret Tresch Owen and Lindsay Chase-Lansdale, who described the idea of "reciprocal role learning" in a 1979 paper that also sent me to the work of others. Again, I have reshaped and extended the concept in a direction for which I take sole responsibility.

Helene Deutsch is a primary contributor to both these central ideas. It is high time to look past her "daughterly" adherence to Freud's ideas of masochism and passivity in women and recognize that in her clinical work she developed insights central to any coherent theory of women's identity.

After I had written the first drafts of the two biographies for Chapter Six, I became aware of striking similarities between the lives of these young women and those of the older corporate executives whom Margaret Hennig and Anne Jardim described in their book *The Managerial Woman*. The authors articulated a complex series of ideas with which I wrestled for a long time; in the end, Chapter Six became a kind of dialogue with their book. If I have failed in any way to do justice to their monumental achievement, the fault is entirely my own.

The computer reference librarian at Elmer Holmes Bobst Library, New York University, patiently helped me to select and key four data bases for computer bibliographies. Ms Katharine Wolpe, librarian, and Miss Jeanette Taylor, assistant librarian, of the New York Psychoanalytic Institute Library were also very helpful. Diana Tummons and her Typecasters service and Judy McCusker provided extraordinary services in speedy and elegant typing. Lydia Fabbroni provided some able research assistance.

Finally, I am indebted to the fathers and daughters who granted me their time, their insights, and their stories. They are, ultimately, the ones without whom this book would never have been written.

Passionate
Attachments

Introduction

... my heart belongs to Daddy—
'Cause my Daddy, he treats it so well.

—Cole Porter, "My Heart
Belongs to Daddy"

*I*n the 1970s, we discovered our mothers. When I wrote *Daughters &
Mothers: Mothers & Daughters*, the first book to look at the relationship
from the point of view of daughters as well as mothers, feminism was at
its height. With our new consciousness, we looked at our mothers and
ourselves and discovered a lot of rage, a lot of pain, and many new links
of identity.

We weren't thinking about our fathers.

Daddy. Maybe we only saw him at dinner. He gave us our allowance,
taught us to swim or ride a bike, tried to teach us to drive (we both ended
up in a rage). After dinner, he had a tendency to disappear—with his
newspaper, his book, to watch television—into the den, the family room,
the study, the basement workshop.

But we still loved him.

If we are successful in our work, we often credit our fathers' influence
more than our mothers'.

If we are successful in love, we also credit our fathers. Because they
were wonderful men, and adored us, we learned to expect love, adoration, protection, financial support from other men, from our lovers and
husbands.

It is not surprising that the father-daughter relationship is the last one
in the family to be explored. We haven't wanted to rock the boat.

Nevertheless, in the 1980s we have, finally, begun to think about our
fathers. For one thing, a lot more of us are out in the world, working.
There we must deal with the male boss, whose power derives ultimately
from the power of the father, and we find that in learning how to relate

to men at work we inevitably come up against our own, internalized fathers.

When we ask ourselves why—beyond immediate financial need—we are working, we arrive at Daddy. Did he want us to work? How would he feel about an ambitious daughter? Are we working to please him, or do we have our own goals in mind?

Money becomes a Daddy issue, too. Is it all right to earn my own money? Or am I supposed to let a man earn it for me? What if I were to earn more than my father?

Power and authority are Daddy issues. Daughters may fall relatively easily into a mentor relationship—after all, a male mentor is a father figure—but it may be much harder to give that up and become the authority ourselves. Daddies are authority, we learned while growing up. Even if our own father wasn't, there were all those others: George Washington, the Father of our Country; the Fathers of the Church; God the Father; the Founding Fathers of (pick any one) the country, the university, the town, the corporation.

Sons are supposed to grow up to become Daddy. But with whose voice, whose authority do we, the daughters, speak?

Thousands of us who got married, raised children, then returned to school, to work, have had to develop new relationships to husbands and to other men. We are also newly discovering the fathers who gave us our grounding in femininity—in how to please and nurture a man. And if we unconsciously duplicated that relationship with our husbands, when we break out of the pattern, there is Daddy, with whom we must, at last, come to terms.

Millions of women of all ages are trying to relate to men in new ways. But if we aren't going to fall into the habits and patterns set by our fathers and mothers, we have to know who our fathers are, what they are like, and why. We have to see how they related to our mothers, and how we identify with them as well as with our mothers.

My first source of information for this book was my own father, who died fifteen years ago of a massive aneurysm while walking back to work after lunch. He was only sixty-three, and when he died I felt an extraordinary mixture of freedom and depression; then I felt guilty because I felt free. Neither my anger nor my tears surfaced for years.

One of the reasons I wrote this book was to find out why it was so hard to get in touch with my feelings about my father.

I had to find him—and myself. It has been a painful journey; sometimes a frightening one.

And when I came to my second source, daughters and their fathers, I made a lot of discoveries. There was something at the heart of the father-daughter relationship that was not to be found in the sitcoms.

I found sadness, loneliness, wistfulness, a longing for understanding. I also found great love, support, and inspiration.

I found fathers who could barely bring themselves to talk about their daughters, so bound up were they in an involvement that remains a secret aspect of masculine identity.

I found fathers who denied any possible influence on their daughters, as though they were afraid, somehow, of what they might find if they admitted their emotional involvement, and their responsibility.

I found fathers who are full partners in caring for their small daughters, and who are extraordinarily alive and sensitive to the realities of their daughters' lives.

I found daughters who said the main thing about their fathers was that they couldn't *find* them—somehow, this kind of father had never been there at all, although he had certainly come home for dinner, slept under the same roof.

And I found daughters who were alive and full of energy in dynamic relationships with fathers who adored them, but who still spoke, wistfully, of how they hoped they had finally made their fathers understand what was really important to them, or who they really were.

I found Good Girls who had become good wives and mothers and Good Girls who had become good executives.

I found out what Good Girls need to go through to grow up.

As I listened to the fathers and daughters I interviewed (nearly a hundred of them in all), some unexpected patterns began to emerge. Very often, for instance, daughters described their fathers as both "passive" and "dominant," an apparent contradiction that eventually led to my discussion of the nature of Daddy in Chapter Two.

I also began to realize how powerful an influence fathers have on their daughters' identities. Daughters learn who they are as much from their fathers as from their mothers, so I had to move beyond the well-worn concept of role models to new ideas of reciprocal identification. And it began to be clear that sexuality cannot be split off from identity. Passionate attachments involve our whole sense of ourselves.

One of the most difficult things to deal with was the fact that women's lives and the shape of the family have changed in the last ten years at an unprecedented rate. The family and the role of the father as I knew them, growing up in the 1950s, seem already to be ancient history.

Whether I have been successful in charting some of these changes, only the reader can tell. The focus of the book is not primarily on how fathering is changing, though that is an inevitable aspect.

Rather, the focus of the book is on the structure of the relationship, and on the ways in which the identities of fathers shape it and the identities of daughters are shaped by it. I hope I have made some discoveries about the nature of American fathers, and about certain fundamental aspects of the American father-daughter relationship, that ultimately transcend change.

Signe Hammer
New York City
April 1982

Part One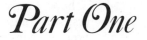

CHAPTER ONE

Passionate Attachments

*T*he second person I ever wanted to be was my father.

It was World War II, and he was away at war with all the other fathers. I was a baby when he left, so that by the time I was old enough to make memories I had a blank book named "Daddy" that I could fill with dreams and fantasies.

I dreamed he was God. My mother taught me to pray to God to bring Daddy home safely. He had flown to war on one of the big airplanes I saw at Baer Field when we shopped at the PX. I knew Daddy and God were both out there in the sky somewhere; probably they were the same person.

God had a lot of glamour. He was certainly a man. He looked down and saw everybody, while they waited for him to come home so their lives could start again. Who wouldn't want to be Daddy-God?

The second person I fell in love with was also my father. I dreamed he was handsome and blue-eyed like the sailor on the poster at the post office, flashing a snappy salute while the flag streamed out over his head. I learned to sing "Bell bottom trousers, coat of navy blue; I love a sailor-boy, and he loves me too." No one else knew my father was my secret love, steaming home to me on a battleship or flying in a plane with sharks' teeth painted on the nose, like the ones that buzzed our house daily.

To be God, to be adored by the Navy, to be rescued by the Air Force—what dreams of power were in my love and my identification! To love my father; to become him. These desires merged in a voluptuous dream of total fusion.

At the heart of the father-daughter relationship lies the mystique of perfect love.

For her, it is the first great love of her independent life.

For him, a daughter is, at last, a controllable female, one he can mold to his image of the ideal woman. In her eyes, he seems to be the powerful male he believes he ought to be—but which, the world being what it is, he knows he is not; at least not all the time. While his son may, briefly, adore him in a similar way, a son will soon challenge his authority, and will someday grow to be bigger and stronger than he. A daughter's adoration can go on forever. In her eyes, Daddy believes, his image will always be golden. He is Daddy, the paradigm of males.

The relationship is doomed, of course, and even while it lasts the dream is held in a delicate balance. On his side, it can tip easily into the darker regions of overseductiveness or incest, or it can go the other way, into rejection, neglect, phobic avoidance.

For her, it can become the last, as well as the first, great dream of her life. If he returns her love in the right way, she will be secure in her femininity forever. If he does not, she can spend the rest of her life looking, desperately, for acceptance and identity.

And if he does love her, the dream all too easily becomes the consuming one of her life. She is vulnerable to entrapment—with her father's and the world's entire collusion—into the permanent role of adoring daughter, which of course carries over, as it was intended to do, so naturally into the role of adoring wife or devoted secretary/aide/assistant.

It is the contradictions and complications of father-daughter love that make it so mysterious—and so compelling.

When my father came home from the war, I was three, the smallest one in the family. Everyone had been waiting for him—it was what gave my first awareness of life a strange tinge. He was not there, but he was still the center of all our lives. My mother wrote to him nightly. She threatened my brothers with his return, and punished them—when they would let her—in his name. They, in turn, liked to taunt me with their memories of a mysterious time called "prewar," a time that counted, as my time did not, because *Daddy was there.*

The first time I saw him, he was standing in the railroad station next to my mother. The first thing I noticed was that he seemed huge: bigger and bulkier than she was. He dwarfed my third brother, my tormentor, closest to me in age and unrelentingly jealous of my existence. Even my oldest brother, then thirteen and the closest thing to a father image in my family so far, was suddenly smaller, younger, softer. My father put everyone in perspective.

He had yellow-brown cat's eyes and he smelled of shaving lotion—an odor none of my brothers had yet acquired. He was the first grown man in my life. I counted on him for everything.

He broke my heart.

Perhaps your father never did. Some daughters move serenely from a doting Mommy to a doting Daddy, then go on to build their lives on the firm conviction that they are loved, honored, and valued. Since they start out that way, they go on demanding these things from the men in their adult lives, whether boyfriends, husbands, lovers, or bosses.

But even doting has its pitfalls, as we shall see. And the truth is that most of us have had a few holes punched in our dream of perfect love, because our fathers were people with their own problems. They came to us with their own dreams—only to find that, as likely as not, we didn't fit. We persisted in making angles where they wanted smoothness; in disappearing into our own lives just when they most wanted us to stay and comfort theirs.

The love affair between fathers and daughters is never quite in synch.

I was locked into an interminable battle with my three older brothers for possession of my mother. Being the youngest, and the only girl, was no real help, because my mother's heart had already been given to my third brother, four years older than I. He was born premature, and the first son to be blond and high-strung like herself. (The first two, dark-haired and stocky, obviously belonged to their father.)

My mother and I were not happy with each other. We were very close—too close for my pleasure. Because, while it seemed to me that she loved my third brother far more than she loved me (he certainly pointed this out to me often enough), at the same time she was possessive. Her sons were growing up, going to school, getting away. She wanted to keep me close.

I wanted to possess her, but I didn't want her to possess me. That was my dilemma, and the source of our struggle. She wasn't there enough for me when I needed her; but whenever I wanted to sail off into the world on my increasingly competent legs, she held me back. It was many years before I was able to realize that she was far too unhappy about herself to love a little girl in ways that were not either too fiercely possessive or too brusquely angry.

In my earliest memories, she was reserved, preoccupied. Although she wanted me to be near her, most of the time when I was with her she could not attend to me. I would play quietly, fearfully, near her while her back was turned, toward cooking or the letter she was writing. If I badgered her, her anger was swift. Too often, our encounters ended in tears, after which I would be put to bed.

My father was going to take me away from all of this, set me up with a new identity as *his* daughter, make me as powerful as my brothers, as big as my mother, as important as himself. He was King in our family, and he would certainly make me Queen.

He had no idea he was supposed to do all this for me. He had, of course, no objection to being a hero, but I don't think it would have occurred to him to consider what this meant to me.

To him, it meant putting in an appearance as Daddy now and again—

as Social Lion Daddy, for instance, when he came to my fourth birthday party and sat among my guests, with a paper hat on his head and a big smile on his face, blowing bubbles out of one of the tiny bubble pipes that were my party favors. The great joke of this being that he normally smoked a real pipe—and now here he was, Daddy Among the Children, the best bubble-pipe smoker of them all. He made huge bubbles, that hovered agonizingly on the rim of the pipe before sailing gently into space. He made cascades of small bubbles, flirting out of his pipe like tiny kisses, so that my girlfriends laughed and grabbed for them. He was the first father on the block to return, and I should have felt proud; but he was their hero, not mine.

That night, I dreamed a fat boy had usurped my place at the birthday table, sitting happily in front of a huge cake done in pink and white like the bedspread in my parents' bedroom. Things were not altogether what I had hoped they would be. Instead of rescuing me and setting me up above everyone else, my father had me thrown out of my mother's bedroom, where I had slept in my crib since his departure—my single claim to oneupmanship in the endless jockeying with my brothers for favor and advantage. To make things worse, I was ignominiously installed in my third brother's room, right in the thick of the battle!

Instead of a Rescuer Daddy, a hero who would single me out, make me feel special, he was looking disturbingly like just another competitor for attention.

That was partly how I saw it. But there was another picture—the one he, perhaps, saw most often—The Way Things Were Supposed to Be. This was the picture in the magazine advertisements, the textbook illustrations, the fantasies of America. Daddy in the bosom of his family.

He went to work, he came home: the high point of the day, the moment everybody had been waiting for. "Daddy's home!" The household, which has been in a kind of suspended animation all day, the life that went on not *real* life, just women's-and-children's life, pretend life, Waiting-for-Daddy life, springs into movement. After a quick kiss, Mother disappears into the kitchen to fix dinner. Brothers appear, as from nowhere, scrubbed and ready to eat. As future Daddies, they begin to have their own lives, out there in the world.

My father sits in his wing chair by the fire. Pipe and slippers—well, pipe, anyway. Cat on his lap instead of faithful dog resting its head on his knees. Sons strewn about the floor, playing with trucks, model airplanes, toy cars, mobility in their hands even at home.

And daughter. In her little smocked dress and black patent-leather Mary Janes, she runs to the door to greet him, is swept into a big hug, gives and receives a fat kiss. Smack. "Daddy!" Sits demurely next to him; gets to fill his pipe. Daddy's pipe. Daddy's Girl.

Who waits. Hangs on his words, his looks, hopes of his smile. Thinks of things to say that will please him. That will make him turn toward her, smile, approve. That will make him adore her.

I always believed in this picture, too.

Here a reasonable reader will probably point out that I expected far too much from my father, and was therefore doomed to disappointment.

This is true, but only partly so. Small children are not reasonable by nature. They need a lot; they demand everything.

And then, first love is always narcissistic. What I wanted from my father was quite simple: I wanted him to give me myself.

That is why in both these pictures of my father at home, what I am doing is waiting, waiting, for him to single me out.

"If her father shows affection for his daughter," wrote Simone de Beauvoir in *The Second Sex*, "she feels that her existence is magnificently justified; she is endowed with all the merits that others have to acquire with difficulty; she is fulfilled and deified."

To be Daddy's Girl would mean I was somebody; my place in the world would be assured.

To be rejected by Daddy would mean I was nobody and nothing: Zero. Wiped out.

Where does Daddy get this kind of power? Part of it comes, quite simply, from his scarcity. Mother is around all day—or she was, when most people reading this were small and the nuclear family was still intact. Even if she worked, we children were likely to be much more her business than his. Before and after work, she was the one who bathed, fed, and diapered us, just as she got his dinner.

He was hardly ever home. From the beginning, his presence seemed like a gift—at any moment he might go away. It was necessary to please him, to propitiate him, to make him want to come home and be with us. With me. He was a prize catch; his attention brought immediate prestige.

There is the mystery of his work. He works in a large building, full of other men. They all feel important there, as I can see when I am finally old enough to visit. Women do things to serve them, just as my mother does at home. My father makes long telephone calls, he goes away on trips, he is late for dinner because of his work. He lives for it; we follow, a sort of appendage.

Once again, Simone de Beauvoir writes of the father, "As a rule his work takes him outside, so it is through him that the family communicates with the rest of the world: he incarnates that immense, difficult, and marvelous world of adventure; he personifies transcendence, he is God."

It is clear to me early on that work is much more than a powerful competitor for his time and attention. It, like him, is much more important than we are.

Because of his work, we move east. We buy a certain kind of house in a certain kind of neighborhood, within easy commuting distance of the city where he works. It is a big house; for the time, he makes a good income. It is in a fashionable neighborhood, important for the rising executive.

My mother is happy with these decisions: she lives wherever he installs us, has waited out World War II in a dreary suburban tract house in Indiana, far away from her own family, just because my father was stationed at a field there before he left for the war. Now she thinks she can make something of us, of the family. She likes the status, and the good schools, and the big house. She has followed his work for fifteen years, often moving more than once a year, as he was transferred around the Pennsylvania Railroad, the corporate world in which he had chosen to live out his identity.

Now he has been called to Philadelphia, home base; she thinks we will settle permanently. She is not far from her mother, in New York, and her brother, in New Jersey. It is somehow perfectly normal that he, going on ahead, has chosen the neighborhood, the house. That is his right, his prerogative. She, like the rest of us, is on board his train.

It was a shock for me to realize, gradually, that although my mother had absolute power over me, with my father she was passive, seeming often to be as helpless as I was with her.

Little by little, I learn other things about my father. He controls the money—all the money in the house is his. He doles out small amounts in allowance, so he decides what our personal freedom to buy treats will be. When I am seven, he decides I can have a bicycle, a second-hand one I have located at the small gas station down the street. He makes me save up my allowance for it.

It is a mixed message. I get pride of possession, but does it really belong to me? He has been the one to make all the decisions about it—I would have preferred him simply to go to the store and buy me a new bike, a glorious maroon coaster bike with shiny fenders and chrome handlebars, like my friend Barbara's. The gas-station bike is small, dented, rusty, painted matte-finish blue—a homemade job.

He thinks that saving my own money to buy the bike will make me "appreciate it," and "take care of it." But earning the bike does not make me feel strong and competent and worthy—because he is Daddy, and because I know perfectly well he could afford to buy me a new one, his decision not to do so becomes a judgment on my worth to him. Rather than teaching me the value of a dollar, he has called into question *my* value—the value of *me* to him. It is a problem that will haunt me all my life. As I get older, my perception of his value judgment on me inevitably becomes part of my sense of my own worth.

But it may be that before a young daughter learns about a father's work, and his power over money, she learns about the sheer physical fact of him—his difference.

Consider what a father looks like to a small girl, still a toddler, maybe two feet tall.

He is hairy: the backs of his hands, his arms, are curly with hair. It sprouts fascinatingly from between the flaps of his partly unbuttoned shirt. Even if he hasn't much hair, the planes of his body are different— flat, angular, harder than Mother's. There is an absence of breasts; the swelling at the chest is liable to be muscle, but it still, confusingly, has these two nipples. He might invite you to do things like punch his stomach, which he holds rock-hard for your astonished fist.

His hands and forearms are thick, or thinner but still ropy with muscle. When he picks you up to swing, excitedly, above his head, you discover his strength.

He has, of course, a penis—an item you discover sooner or later—and it looks huge, possibly ugly, possibly interesting or even enticing. It seems to be a completely different animal from the tiny penises of your brothers, or of the boys on the block with whom you may already have played show and tell. Even erect, theirs are merely fascinating—his seems powerful, awesome, perhaps terrible. If you have ambivalent feelings about him, that erection can develop, in your fantasies, into a weapon.

On the other hand, if he is fairly casual about nakedness, perhaps takes baths or showers with you, and you find his penis enticing and give it a poke or pull, you may find yourself suddenly banished from his bath or shower, wondering why he was embarrassed or even angry. You will suddenly have a new message about his penis and how he feels about it.

Even if you have brothers, your father is the beginning of your education in the facts of male sexuality, because his feelings, his attitudes—and his body—simply carry more authority.

So does his voice. It is probably louder, deeper, more definite than your mother's, certainly more so than any older sister's or brother's.

My father's voice was deep, definite, authoritative. I must have recognized early on that his voice had the last word—that he had the power to silence my mother's voice, to make it trail away into indefiniteness under his challenge.

My father could at any time instantly silence my brothers, as well as myself. From downstairs would come his deep, ringing command to *Pipe Down!* when things got out of hand on a rainy afternoon. His voice never contained the slightest trace of nervousness or hesitation, never rose to a high pitch of hysteria as my mother's did when she was upset or angry. It would be unthinkable to challenge my father's voice. It *was* authority.

So was his size. Even though he was not a tall man—five feet nine inches, just average—he was, as I have said, the biggest person in my family. My mother was tall for a woman, five feet six, but it was natural for him to be taller. And his body was powerful in its weight and solidity. He had thick, strong bones, perhaps inherited from German peasant ancestors.

Size, of course, is an attribute of power among men. To say "He towered over everyone in the room" suggests dominance. Small men must fight harder for deference; often, they overcompensate and become cocky, strutting Napoleons determined to conquer the world.

To be a female, a daughter, and to look at your mother and father, to know that when you grow up you will, like her, still be shorter than most men, is to start with knowledge of a physical difference that speaks volumes about the balance of power between the sexes. Do we learn to speak softly for fear of Daddy's wrath? My father liked to say, *"Please—sweet and dulcet tones,"* when I got carried away with excitement over an idea or an argument, as I still do. But I also still think it is the mark of a lady to speak in a soft, contained voice and to possess a slim, straight, fine-boned body. To be neither too loud nor too tall.

Alas, in body, as in voice, I take after my father more than my mother. I, too, have broad shoulders and thick peasant bones. At five feet eight inches I am, for a woman, tall. If he were alive today I would tower over him in heels; he would, of course, have shrunk with age.

For a woman to be tall is still, despite the fact that six-foot women are an asset in basketball, felt in many quarters to be unseemly. Boys worry about being too short; girls about being too tall. In adolescence, we wear flats and slump. As women, we search for the man who is taller than we are. The odds are it feels right to both of us; when I find a man who is big enough to pick me up, I feel wonderfully feminine.

Even though my size means I seldom fear harassment by men on the street, I still slump. It is not appropriate for a daughter to be as tall as her father—or, by extension, any man. This is an elevation sons might aspire to; but when I was an adolescent, to reach my father's height in heels always felt strange, if sneakily powerful—and it didn't change the way he recognized me. It may have made him step back from me even more than he might have if I had been small. Large women are threatening to cockproud men, and my father was not, perhaps, really as tall as he would have liked to be.

To possess an inappropriate power is, for a daughter, a hard thing to handle. I became large, awkward, burdened with a height that was useless. I wanted to shrink away from my flesh. My body was wrong for its purpose, which was to stand daintily and gracefully beside a man, to make him, by its contrast, appear tall and strong.

Such a body, for a girl, puts the future in doubt. As my feet grew, and my shoulders broadened, it felt inescapable. There was no place for me to grow up to, no future for me with all this heavy flesh, that was neither man's nor woman's. Even after hips and breasts had changed my shape, it was a long time before I learned to live comfortably with my size.

This comparing of bodies, of shapes and sizes, is the beginning of learning who we are in the world. Our first passionate attachment is with our mother. With her, we start out with sameness (just as our brothers do), the symbiotic bliss of the first few months of life, when we don't, literally, know that there is a "me" or a "her." We blend into her. (If a father were our full-time caretaker from birth we would, presumably, have the same feeling about him—an interesting proposition that has not, as far as I know, been much pursued.)

The things that make our mother physically different from our father make her more like an infant: softer skin, soft, cushiony breasts, softer voice. Then, too, when our mothers cared for us, held us, diapered us, their touch, the curve of their arms and hands, resonated with their knowledge of their own bodies, of their own identities as women.

Our father, as we came to be aware of him, was the real Other Person—he was Out There. He came and went frequently, he was less likely to be responsive to our emotional needs, to understand our different cries, for instance, and what they meant, just as, later, he was less likely to be aware of our cues for more complicated needs for understanding and communication.

What lured us to him was, from the first, his difference. Scarcity made him exciting—but so did the way he was likely to handle us. While he may, in fact, have molded us, as tiny infants, into his shoulder or the crook of his arm as sensitively as our mother—some fathers are better at this than mothers—he was also, as soon as we were big enough to deal with it, more likely to roughhouse with us. Even fathers I spoke to who spent equal time with their wives as co-caretakers of their daughters, had done so from birth, saw this difference between themselves and their wives by the time their daughters were two, three, or four.

So from the beginning Daddy was there, but he was the Other, he was different. Mothers are sameness; they are ourselves. This is comforting, and we go on needing it. But at some deep level of our unconsciousness, they also represent a time when we were *not*—when we merged with someone else. As we grow into toddlers, navigating around on our own feet, moving physically into the world, Daddy becomes important because he is Out There. Because he is not our mother, because he represents all kinds of unpredictability and excitement, because *he goes away from Mother to work*—for all these reasons he represents, to us as well as to boys, independence. His is the world of the autonomous person, the separate self of competence and achievement.

So a father's first role in our lives, the first in which he is really different from our mother, is to help us realize we can move away from Mother and go it alone, to trust ourselves and our independence. We identify him with our independent selves—and we identify with him in our independence.

And then we fall in love with him: delicious, all-consuming oedipal love. And because this love comes on top of our first identification of him with our new, exploring, independent selves, we are in a sense imprinted with an association between independence and loving Daddy that lays the foundation for his enormous influence on our later capacity for the two things that give meaning to life: love and work.

Much of this process is exactly the same for a tiny boy: the early fusion with the mother, the sense of sameness and intense attachment that drives the child outward, toward a different kind of person. But when we arrive at Daddy, our paths diverge. The little boy soon learns that this powerful, exciting person is his own future. What we as girls must learn is how to cope with the fact that we are not, no matter how much we identify with him, going to grow up to become Daddy.

"The boy," writes Simone de Beauvoir, *"thinks of his father's superiority with a feeling of rivalry; but the girl has to accept it with impotent admiration"* (italics mine).

Here is where a daughter's future becomes problematical. Unable to identify with the most powerful person in her universe (and it is arguable that, for all the reasons described above, a little girl will see even a relatively passive or nondominating father as more powerful than her mother), she is thrown back on other strategies. She must develop an alliance with him to help her separate from her mother. He becomes a boundary for her. She will, usually, identify also with her mother's methods of attracting him. *Since she cannot become him, she must love him*—and rely, in turn, on his love for her to give her the sense of self-importance the boy can give himself by identifying with his father, realizing his own future as a dominant male.

Here was the beginning of my need for my father to single me out, to "deify" me, to tell me who I was.

Here, too, are all the ways in which he still tells me who I am.

Take the roughhousing. It is hard for me to separate memories of my father from those of my brothers. With them, it was tickle-and-tumble from an early age. With him, I think, things were more restrained. I suspect tickling, though, and certainly some horsing around at bedtime, me falling out of my shirt while he held the sleeves up, or turning somersaults on the bed. And certainly I must have been hoisted occasionally on his shoulders, because I can remember my sense of both excitement and dread at the elevation, the intimate contact with his neck (bristles at the edge of his haircut, a mole, sun-reddened father-flesh), and the sudden dark gulf to the ground.

There were other games, of which he was very much in control. If he chose to hold me upside down by my heels and swing me around, it was a dare: I should like it. I wanted him to think well of me.

So, early on, I felt dread as well as excitement. Of his power, of the terrible gravity of his judgment, of the relentlessness with which he pursued his own vision of everything and everyone, including me.

Recently, I sat by a swimming pool where a father was holding his eight-month-old daughter. "I don't want her to be afraid of the water," he announced. So he sat on the edge, with his feet dangling in the pool, and, holding her away from him, he dunked her—head and all. Just for an instant, but she came up sputtering and grabbing for his legs, which he wouldn't let her reach. He held her tight, yet away from him. He was in control. His image of her, of the way he expected her to be, was blinding him to her real needs: first, not to be dunked; and second, having been dunked, to be able to grab onto him for safety.

A young father of a three-year-old daughter told me he had expected her, at two and a half, to learn to stop sucking her thumb. He was thinking about orthodontia in the future. He was not a tyrant, he was an equal-time Daddy, had been since her birth, taking on a good half of all her care. But he expected this of her and she wasn't ready. So there began months of tears, of subterfuge, of her learning to lie. She wouldn't do it in front of him, only in the privacy of her room. "Did you do it?" "Yes." Tears. She was learning that Daddy's expectations are difficult.

Finally, at a meeting with other parents of the day-care center their daughter attends, he talked about the problem.

"She isn't ready," they said. "What harm will it really do?"

He tells me that the relief he saw in her when he told her she no longer had to struggle to live up to this too-difficult goal was a revelation. So, too, was the release of energy, of openness in their relationship. She can trust him again, and he her.

The books say Daddy is the one who is *supposed* to expect us to grow up. But if he expects too much, if he is blind to our reality, what we learn, instead, is our own inadequacy.

Some experiences I no longer even remember, I think, may have given me my distrust of roller coasters, my penchant for getting sick on top of the ferris wheel—and my dread of risk, of the unknown, of trying something new, which is as great as the excitement such possibility also arouses.

Daddy. His vision controlled my life for more years than I want to admit—still controls me in ways I regret. I have had, all of my life, difficulties with both love and work.

My search for my father is a journey in search of myself. Of the self I am because I identified with him, because he loved me in certain ways but could not deal with my sexual maturity, because he saw too much of my mother in me and not enough of me—and because, although he expected every bit as much from me, academically, as he did from my brothers, he refused to see that I might take myself seriously, that I needed his respect just as much as I needed his love. And even his love became so hedged about with crippling conditions that, in the end, I have had to choose between his vision of me and my own, over and over again.

When a father's vision of you and his love are the same thing, when your own vision of yourself as an independent person is tied up with his love for you, when so much power of body, of money, of worldly achievement is invested in this man who has, from the beginning, told you who you are as a woman and as a person in the world, how do you untangle the knot he has tied?

CHAPTER TWO

Don't Worry, Everything's Under Control:
Daddies in the World and in the Family

E ven before he came home from the war, my father seemed to me to be omniscient. When I heard Bing Crosby on the radio singing *Santa Claus Is Comin' to Town,* telling us we'd better watch out because Santa Claus could see every move we made, waking or sleeping, and was watching all the time to see whether we were bad or good, I was terrified. I had heard about coal in the stockings of bad little girls. What had he seen—Santa Claus, my father, up there in the sky with God?

I would wake at dawn Christmas morning and sneak downstairs to examine the piles of presents, each with its own sign in Gothic script: John, Richard, Chris . . . a moment of panic. Where was mine? If he had *really* seen me, seen the times I hid from my mother, or fought with my brothers, there would be no presents at all for me.

On the other hand, I still had hope. He might discover the special, inside, me. I might find some Christmas that the only pile of presents in the room had my name on it, in glittering letters, ten feet high: SIGNE'S DADDY THINKS SHE IS THE BEST DAUGHTER, THE MOST SPECIAL CHILD IN THE FAMILY! IN THE NEIGHBORHOOD! IN THE UNIVERSE!

All my life I have envied daughters who got the equivalent of that sign—the Princesses whose fathers are putty in their hands. As it was, my father kept me sweating to earn his approval. He defined what was good and what was bad, what was masculine and what was feminine, what was socially acceptable and what was not. He had the power to judge us all, my brothers and my mother included.

It's true he was a tyrant. Oh, I know they aren't supposed to exist anymore—they went out with the nineteenth century, when the stern Victorian patriarch turned into the sweet, sappy Daddy of *Father Knows Best.* But my father, born just four years into the twentieth century, never realized he was out of date.

I've always identified with Louisa May Alcott. There she was, in 1835, a child in the nursery, and her father was *watching* her. Bronson

Alcott kept detailed journals on the development of his first two daughters, Anna and Louisa. He would set up little temptations for them and then see how they reacted, like leaving an apple out in plain sight and telling them it belonged to him, so of course they shouldn't eat it, should they? But they did, and then there was a terrific scene of confession and repentance. Bronson Alcott believed in guilt.

Anna was a Good Girl. "Give up your want to Father's," lectured Bronson (lectures were a great preoccupation with the old-fashioned father), "and then you will begin to love me more. And the more you do so, the more you will go on to love me, till, by and by, you will love me well enough to give up your want always."

It sends shivers down my spine. Succumb to Daddy. Give up your puny will, your tiny, selfish desires, and become Daddy's slave. A slave of love—what a glorious temptation!

Louisa, though, was a little more difficult. She needed to be, because eventually she would grow up to write *Little Women*, get rich on royalties, and support the whole family, including her father and docile Anna. But it was an uphill struggle, a constant battle with her father. "Louisa required authoritative measures in a few instances," he wrote; "her deep-seated obstinacy of temper is far from being conquered. *She is by no means docile*" (italics mine).

Louisa May Alcott has been dead for ninety-four years, but her father's injunction is alive and well in the memories of living women. Louisa May Alcott's rebelliousness, and her struggle to be "good"— meaning to please her father—is still a dilemma for daughters today, which may be one reason *Little Women* continues to sell briskly. I always knew I was Jo, the heroine whose model was clearly the author. Jo was full of moods and temper and had an uncontrollable desire for freedom. Yet secretly I wished I could be sweet, timid, domestic Meg, the one of whom, even as a child, I knew my father would really approve, as Bronson Alcott had approved of Louisa's docile sister Anna, the model for Meg.

To be a Good Girl meant making hateful compromises with my own developing sense of being; but more than anything I wanted my father's love, and the price of his love was obedience. So I was thrown into my first conflict over the question of how to deal with male power, male authority.

My first and most enduring lesson in power was that my father simply was not accountable to me. He did not have to respond when I spoke to him, to be there when I needed him, or take into account, at any time, my needs or my limitations.

As a girlchild I was, of course, accountable to him. I studied his needs and learned, from my mother, that anticipating and serving them was the right way to relate to him. The only way, in fact. It was understood that first as a child and second as a female I would not be able to bend him to acknowledge me unless he chose to. Even our inevitable moments of flirtation were always, it seemed, originated by him. My role was to wait and try to gauge his mood. This was all part of his idea of the proper relationship between the sexes; my mother, alas, acquiesced in it.

My father had one responsibility: to be successful enough in his work to support us all in the style he and my mother demanded. Beyond that, he really seemed to have no responsibilities. He was not one person in a relationship with me (or with my mother, for that matter), he was Captain of the Ship, Leader of the Troops, the Boss, the Master. He was remote, taboo: a priest who worshipped on the altar of work. Other people in the family had to be home in time for dinner—dinner was ready for my father when he got home. He could not, by definition, be late for dinner.

Even now I am appalled by my audacity in conjuring up my father, in grappling with the difference between his image and my experience, in trying to find his reality. He was like Svengali, George du Maurier's fictional character who had the power to make an artist's model with a tiny voice into a singing star simply by imposing his will on hers until she became exactly what he willed her to be.

On the other hand, I gave my father a lot of power. I wanted him to be able to see my secret need—how else would he know that he had to come home and rescue me? It was a great comfort to think, "He's out there somewhere, and he's looking at me! He's looking for me. When he finds me, I'll become everything I want to be. I'll be more powerful than my brothers, more attractive than my mother. My Father, my Prince, will make me his Princess, transform me magically from anonymous girlchild to co-ruler of the world."

When I got to be eleven or twelve or thirteen, I endowed certain movie and rock stars with the same power. Confused about my identity, I was once again looking for someone who would give it to me, who would discover the secret, the special, the *unique* me and raise me up to the stage or screen with him.

"Oh God, if he sees me I'll *die,*" we would shriek, waiting at the stage door for a glimpse of the hero.

But my father was Svengali in reverse. He had me convinced from an early age that I ought not to try my own wings. Become a writer? Nonsense; he didn't even want me to leave home.

It's really not too long ago that I began to grow up, away from my father's vision, and find out that there is a great deal more to me than he wanted to allow. It took me years to arrive at a sustained belief that I will not disappear when I am out of his sight. He created for me an image; my job was to become the person he wanted to see.

The hardest work of my life has been to find other images for myself.

Not that the images weren't always there; it's just that without his approval it was nearly impossible to believe in myself in any version other than his.

And if I become someone he cannot see, or refuses to recognize, can I look back and see him, reduce him to word or image?

Can I possibly match his valuation of himself, standing in the photograph on the deck of the wonderful wooden, white-painted, teak-decked 1930s motorboat, in his Al Capone snap-brim fedora and pin-striped, wide-lapelled navy blue suit with vest? Can I live up to the satisfied smile on his face, to the self-consciousness with which he measures his pose, the careful ease of the hand in the side pocket of the coat, thumb casually draped over the edge, while the other hand cups a cigarette held a few inches from the smile that itself misses smugness by a fraction of an inch?

He is a man who knows he is getting away with something, and what he is getting away with is his pose. The pose is the measure of his power to impose himself on me.

Daddy has a power derived from our earliest terrors. In Judaism, the name of God is never spoken. In Judaism and in Islam, God's image cannot be painted or sculpted.

In Islam, women are eternally captive to fathers and husbands. Only in the West, where God's name came to be spoken and written, where His image could be drawn and painted and secularized into the face of the father, the fierce old man with the long gray beard—only here, so recently, do women begin to speak with a voice we may call our own. How do we see this man, the father? How do we measure him, who has always measured us?

Daddy is the original namer of names: his power goes all the way back to the Bible, the Old Testament, the Pentateuch, in which God gave Adam the power to name everything in the Garden. And so he named me: "woman," and "Eve"—Eve, who was his wife but also (bone of his bone, flesh of his flesh) his daughter. The perfect helpmeet. And temptress.

Daddy. Creator of the image of the world. The one who described, and sculpted, and painted, and characterized women as he wished to see us. He has grudgingly given way to women's power to write; more grudgingly, he has even admitted that women can create a vision of the world in paint or bronze or clay, although on the whole he still maintains that our vision is far inferior to his. He still dislikes us, the daughters, to show him nude as he has shown us for thousands of years. As if, by exposing the penis, we are breaking the old taboo and revealing the face of God.

Daddy on the Outside

Daddy showed us what power was like whenever we went out into the world. If Mother drove us on our daily rounds of school and swimming practice, ballet and friends' houses, Daddy drove when we took a trip, or went out to dinner or to the movies. Whenever Daddy was in the car, he drove and Mother sat in the passenger's seat. Sometimes, as a special treat, a daughter got to sit in the front seat between them.

In the city, it was my father who decided what restaurant we would go to and who hailed cabs, initiating us into the lore of Checker cabs, with the jump seats on which the men sat as an act of chivalry but which always looked like more fun to me.

The people who controlled entrance to the restaurant—the hostess or maitre d'—looked to my father, ignoring my mother. She was herded with the rest of us ahead of my father to our seats, where the waiter also looked to my father, who gave all our orders. At home, Mother gave us our food; out in the world, it came through Daddy. He read the thick, red-covered wine list and ordered the wine, and we watched while a little was poured for him to taste. If he wanted, we knew, he could send it back, as he would often send back his meat if it were not perfectly cooked. At home, we ate what was set before us. And then, of course, at the end he paid the bill, decided the tip, retrieved my mother's coat and mine from the cloakroom, and held them for us to put on.

He loved these rituals of mastery, of dominance. He loved best a restaurant in which he was well known, in which a history of good tips and slight man-of-the-world flirtation with the hostess or man-to-man understanding with the maitre d' guaranteed him special deference, where he could claim his "usual table" and the waiter automatically brought him his favorite liqueur.

In his man-of-the-world pose he was generous, a good tipper. I, being daily exposed to his stinginess at home, did not realize that, out at a restaurant, we must all fall in with his act. I remember my confusion once, when he was taking us all out to the Rainbow Room for my grandmother's birthday. I, having been grudgingly allowed to look at the menu, said in a loud, clear, shocked voice, "Seventy-five cents for tomato juice! That's terrible!" My father frowned, the menu was snatched from my hand. I was disgraced. This was not the same Daddy who, at home, aimed to teach me the value of a dollar.

Thus I learned that it is a daughter's duty to support her father in his acts of mythification, and that, above all, at such times it is dangerous to speak the truth.

What he was saying with all this was: "Look, the world belongs to me.

In it, I create my own image. My path in it is smooth, and I have the power to smooth yours. Without me, your life in the world is much more difficult."

Which was true. Headwaiters did not defer to my mother as they did to my father. In fact, when I went out with my mother, we went to a tea room, where there were none of the rituals of power that surrounded dinner in a restaurant with my father. The rituals were *designed* to keep the world well oiled for Daddy, to impress the women and remind us that we lacked the same power. In these Daddy restaurants, of course, the expense was greater—in a tea room, there was altogether an air of scrimping, of things nice but not opulent. When there was real money to be spent, Daddy was in charge.

Very recently, women have acquired the right to exercise some of those rituals of power. Now we, too, can be shown to a table by the headwaiter, and order the wine, and pay for the dinner. But on the whole if a man is along, he will be the one deferred to, who will assume the Daddy roles. And we will, on the whole, love it, because it reminds us of the delicious sense of specialness, of being taken care of, of having power go before us to pave the way, so that we have only to sit back and enjoy it.

Such is the seduction of power. All we have to do is support Daddy in his myths, be his loyal cheerleaders, and there is no limit to what he can do for us.

For the rest of our lives we will be aware that, too often, Daddy and his heirs, the other men in our lives, make the difference between comfort and discomfort, between scrimping along on our own, getting seated behind the kitchen door, and sitting in style at a good table.

We are beginning to learn how to earn the money that is the first prerequisite of power in the world, and how to assume the air of authority that calls forth deference from headwaiters and even hostesses (who, as women, naturally do not like deferring to other women). A whole generation of young women, now in college or law school or business school, thinks it has a natural right to these things, does not realize how recently they were acquired and how easily they can be swept away. Many of these women plan to put their careers on ice for several years to raise their children, which is very nice for the children, who will no doubt thrive. But it will be interesting to see what happens to the new mothers' sense of authority-in-the-world once they are economically dependent on their husbands and stay at home most of the day with small children.

Divorced women, on the other hand, have experienced the speed with which their standard of living drops once they are on their own; they have had to learn, painfully, how to assert an authority they once could leave up to their husbands. Their daughters have watched life become more difficult for their mothers, and so for themselves; they may resent the father for withdrawing his aid, resent the mother for her failure to provide as generously as Daddy could. The lessons are being learned— will the daughters of divorce seize the power the feminists of my generation fought for, insist on their own authority in the world? Or will they retreat, reconstruct the family of their dreams, insist on putting a Daddy out there between themselves and the vicissitudes of the world?

This is what fathers have, traditionally, been supposed to do. They front for the women and children, dealing not only with headwaiters but with moving men, lawyers, doctors, school principals (when things got really serious), college admissions directors, the IRS, as one authority to another, the head of the family to the representatives of the state—who are also Daddies, as are senators, representatives, state assemblymen, mayors, governors, and the president of the school board. Women are creeping in here and there—a governor here, a representative there— but by and large it is still a world of Daddies, doing business with each other.

In addition, since he earned the money, until very recently Daddy would take care of mortgages, bank loans, overdrafts, creditors of all kinds. If a contract was made, it was made in his name (of course, the whole family went under his name, but he personally usually made the contract). If we shopped with credit cards, they were issued to him. He paid the bills for school and college; he decreed we must get a job or must not work at all.

If he fronted for the family out there in the world, Inside the family Daddy fronted for the state. In giving him the power to make contracts for the family, the responsibility for its credit rating, including all its debts (the ad in the newspaper goes: "I, Herman T. Jones, am no longer responsible for my wife's debts"), in giving him the power to name the whole family, the state was saying that Daddy was its representative inside the family. He would see that the family kept the state's laws, paid its share of taxes into the state coffers, attended state-accredited schools.

As the sociologist Leonard Benson put it, "Family members must adapt to environmental demands, and it helps if their behavior is based upon a reasonably accurate understanding of the alternatives available . . . there is no substitute for the advice and guidance of older men in this regard."

Daddy was the original Older Man, the Man of the World. Even when he came Inside the family, he remained Daddy on the Outside.

How he got there is a story recently thought to be as long as evolution itself. But it may in fact be only as long as human history.

Fathers: A Brief History

The word "father" can imply a whole range of behaviors, from total lack of involvement with infants and the young to a level of nurturing identified in our culture only with mothers. Animals may be fathers, too; most people know that male birds, for instance, share the building of the nest and the feeding of the young with their mates. Human beings are mammals, and very few mammals do much, if any, fathering. But we belong to a particular order of the mammal line, the primates, and among the other members of our particular primate superfamily—the chimpanzees who are our closest cousins, gorillas, orangutans, gibbons, and siamangs—are found a wide range of fathering behaviors.

The bottom line of fathering, of course, is to impregnate a female and so beget a child. That is the minimum amount of investment that qualifies any male animal as a father. Beyond this there are indirect investments like leading and protecting a whole troop or tribe without distinguishing one's own child from the others. Then there is the modern human father's traditional role of providing food and shelter as well as protection for a particular child or several children acknowledged as his own. And, finally, there is real nurturing: feeding, playing with, grooming, soothing, and teaching that infant or child.

Among human beings the leading and protecting have been, on the whole, Outside work, while nurturing has been Inside, between mother and child and, in modern Western families at least, between wife and husband. The provision of shelter has been sometimes men's work, sometimes women's, and both have usually helped provide food. Only in the postindustrial West has the provision of both food and shelter been considered to be the sole responsibility of Daddy.

But, worldwide and throughout human history, the Inside has been, irreducibly, the mother-child unit, and, by extension, the home and family, the place in which our early childhood is spent and in which our earliest emotional experiences and development are shaped. The Outside is the world beyond home and family: the world of work and politics and institutionalized religion, traditionally the province of men.

The popular anthropological theories of the 1960s and 1970s explained this tradition by speculating that male hunting and warfare provided the spur for the evolution of apes into *Homo sapiens*. Climate changes led omnivorous protohominids to rely more and more on meat, and to kill big game they needed weapons. To develop weapons they had to think, so evolution selected for bigger brains. To hunt, they had to cooperate, so evolution selected for male bonding.

Females, who had no part in any of this activity, apparently developed intelligence only through genetic inheritance from their fathers. Females were concerned only with infant care and the family, so evolution selected for sexiness (to attract those wandering hunters), reproduction, staying close to home, and bonding with infants, children, and men.

The "hunting hypothesis" caught on, and book after book assured us that men were selected by evolution for aggression, dominance, and performing work in groups with other men. Not only were they not designed to be tender and nurturing or to bond with infants and children, but any attempt to change the natural order of things could wreak havoc with the grand evolutionary design, built into our genes and sanctified by millions of years of development.

The modern hunt might be for success in the corporate world, and the meat the modern hunter brought home for his family a paycheck, but men still functioned best in their all-male group, the corporate team, where they spent most of their time bonding with other males as men had been doing for millions of years.

Women, we were told, should not change, unless it was to become better mothers. Increasing numbers of child-care experts—most of them male—were providing advice about how to do this.

The theory very neatly buttressed the status quo, traditional sex roles and the ideal suburban family, all of which, in the sixties and seventies, were being questioned by the hippie and youth movements and by feminism. (The book that rocked the suburban ideal to its foundations, Betty Friedan's *The Feminine Mystique,* was published in 1963.)

But if women shouldn't change, men, it seemed, *couldn't* change. Fathers, as men, were a given of evolution, and to expect any change in their behavior was to invite chaos. No properly dominant, aggressive male could nurture his infants.

The two traits, nurturing and aggression, were widely considered to be incompatible. The same individual could not possibly exhibit both, and males were incontrovertibly more aggressive than females. This was even one of the handful of innate differences between males and females discovered by Eleanor Maccoby and Carol Nagy Jacklin in their monumental 1974 survey of the existing research in the field, *The Psychology of Sex Differences.* So society, it seemed, was right in assigning nurturing to women and aggressive behavior like competitiveness and ambition to men.

The writers and anthropologists who advocated the hunting hypothesis selected evidence from existing primate reseach to support their ideas. From observations of baboons in their natural habitat came the view of the primate male as aggressive, dominant, controlling, and possessive toward females, who were physically much smaller and uniformly submissive to their male superiors. Females were occupied solely with infant care, except when, in heat, they became the property of a dominant male. A true Inside/Outside distinction seemed to exist.

Baboons, who live in troops, spend most of their time in all-male groups, rather as humans do. So male bonding seemed to be derived not only from a human hunting past but from our distant primate relations as well. And among baboons, as everywhere in nature, the all-male group is a dominance hierarchy. The two—all-male group and male dominance hierarchy—seem to be synonymous.

It was easy to see that human all-male groups are no exception to the rule of hierarchy. From the corporation to the Senate, the Pentagon to the Vatican, human all-male (or even predominantly male) groups are structured as dominance hierarchies, in which there is one most-dominant male. We may call him the boss, the leader, the general, the Pope, the President, the Senate Majority Leader—he is still the dominant male.

The males in human male dominance hierarchies have always assumed that, as members of the hierarchy, they are superior to all females. It is not hard to find parallels for this in primate life; while female chimpanzees, for instance, form their own dominance hierarchies, even the dominant females will generally defer to all adult males.

Yet one rule of evolution is that, even though males dominate females, it is females who select males to mate with. This rule is called, logically enough, "sexual selection," and it has a companion rule that says males compete for dominance in their groups in order that the most dominant—meaning the most successful—will be chosen by a desirable female. This means that the best genes in the group will be passed on to future generations, as insurance that the group will survive. Among chimpanzees, for instance, a female in heat usually mates with nearly every male in the troop; but the dominant male generally gets the first chance, which means that he has the best likelihood of inseminating her.

So male dominance is, at bottom, part of the basic reproductive strategy of group-living animals—as are the size, strength, and weapons (antlers, fangs, superior political savvy) with which males assert their dominance over other males.

It isn't hard to see sexual selection at work among humans, too. We expect boys to learn to compete, to use every weapon they have to get as far as they can in life. And while men expect to dominate women, it is also true that the most successful men are usually the most attractive to women. They can have their pick of the most desirable women around, while less successful men must settle more nearly for what they can get.

So the hunting hypothesis seemed to explain contemporary society very well, including both male dominance and the whole rigid Inside/Outside dichotomy we have evolved.

The only trouble with the theory was that it ignored the fact that one of the identifying characteristics of primates is our adaptability. We live all over the world, in and out of trees, on deserts, mountains, and islands, in tropical jungles and big cities. We have a remarkable ability to change our behavior to suit the requirements of different environments, which is what adaptability means. It is, of course, our supreme adaptability—of which our superior intelligence is one aspect—that has made our own particular primate species, *Homo sapiens,* ruler of the earth. But our cousins, the apes, are also large, tailless, smart, and adaptable. And even monkeys, smaller, less intelligent, and in full possession of tails, share this quality of adaptability to changing environments.

Take the rhesus macaque, for instance. The research psychologist Dr. William Redican describes him as "aggressive and inflexible." In his natural habitat he is not much of a father. Toward infants, he may simply be indifferent; if one interrupts him at his meal, he may attack it.

But put him in a different situation and he becomes a new male, almost a Daddy. This was first discovered in captive colonies, when mothers were either removed or incapacitated. Left alone with the infants, males began to nurture; they played, groomed, carried. When Redican carried out long-term laboratory studies of male-infant pairs and compared his results with studies of mother-infant pairs, he found that males groomed infants as much as mothers, played with them more intensely, and protected them more actively (males attacked an intruder). They held the infants close against their chests less often than mothers; but on the other hand, as time went on, they became increasingly attached to their small charges.

Similar behavior was observed in a wild baboon troop when a mother couldn't nurture as usual. In fact, troop-living primate males, for all their male dominance hierarchies, may do a great deal of what Redican calls "male parental care." He points out that those very same dominant baboons, for instance, are normally very protective of infants—and the most dominant males are the most protective of all. At three months, infants may climb onto their backs and sit on their shoulders. As the infants develop, adult males will break up their squabbles or rescue them from the terrorizing of older juveniles. Both baboon and gorilla males have even been known to adopt orphan infants and nurture them as mothers would.

So the evidence from the primate world does not support the idea that aggressive, dominant males can't adapt to nurturing. Redican shows that some primates, particularly New World monkeys, even live in monogamous pairs with their offspring, who might range in age from infancy to adulthood, just as in a human family. Males who live in families like this are not much bigger than the females, and there doesn't seem to be much male dominance. Both parents, rather, focus on infant care.

When Jane van Lawick-Goodall took the novel step of going out into the jungle to see how chimpanzees live in their natural habitat, she found, among other things, that while chimpanzee males are bigger than females and do spend much time in their dominance hierarchies, they are only occasionally possessive toward females. Independent chimp females forage for their own food, build their own nests, and may exercise considerable choice over mating arrangements.

Mary Maxwell West and Melvin J. Konner of Harvard University have pointed out that virtually our entire human and protohuman history was characterized by "warm-climate gathering and hunting," in which much of a group's food—the same nuts, roots, fruits, and vegetables eaten by other omnivorous primates—was gathered by women, while as little as 20 percent came from male hunting expeditions.

Today's gatherer-hunters, point out West and Konner, don't have rigid Inside/Outside distinctions. Neither men nor women work very hard, and couples spend a lot of time with their children. Fathers, while they don't do many of what we think of as child-care "chores" like feeding, nevertheless do a lot of holding, fondling, and talking with infants and children. If this is how evolving man lived, how did we come by our rigid modern gender roles? The work of West-Konner and Redican suggests some answers.

West and Konner observe that, in nonindustrial cultures where men are preoccupied with warfare, and especially if they are polygamous (have many wives, as in harems), fathers don't participate in child care but are as distant as the typical "workaholic" Western executive.

In such cultures, the men are often herders. War becomes an obsession because they add to their herds by raiding the flocks and herds of neighboring tribes—when they often carry off women, as well. The Bedouin, before oil wealth brought them off the desert and into the office, were typical of such tribes. So were the ancient tribesmen who swept down into Greece and started the culture that gave us the philosophy, myths, plays—and a whole set of attitudes about men and women—that underlie so much of our own culture. The other strand of our Judeo-Christian heritage started with warlike, male-dominant Hebrew tribes, who were also herdsmen and whose culture produced, of course, the Old Testament. So our particular cultural origins were in fierce, warlike, extremely male-dominant herding tribes, not the peaceful gatherer-hunters.

More recently, our European roots are in the equally fierce, warlike tribes of Scandinavia and northern Europe, who crossed oceans and continents in the vast patterns of raid and migration that marked the period between the fall of the classical world and the Middle Ages. Modern Western civilization is the product of cultural patterns that, looked at in terms of millions of years of evolution, were atypical.

The observations of West and Konner seem to suggest that human beings are as capable of adaptation to different patterns of nurturing as are baboons and monkeys. And Peggy Papp of the Ackerman Institute for Family Therapy in New York City pointed out to me that an effective way to change the behavior of one parent in a human couple is for the other to alter his or her behavior. This is, it seems, a standard principle of family therapy theory and practice.

It is, of course, what mothers have already begun to do. Our image of the ideal father has been changing slowly for a long time, from that of the Outside man, the protector and defender of wife and child, the provider of food, shelter, and material goods, to that of Daddy, a man equally at home in the nursery and in the office, a man who leaves the Outside behind when he comes Inside to be a second—equally important—source of nurturing and human interaction for the infant and small child.

In the last ten years, women have left home in increasing numbers to go to work, so there is now more pressure than ever before on fathers to contribute more than the bedtime story and weekend romp of the traditional nuclear family pattern. Full-time fathers, while still rare, have become the subject of great interest and attention; equal-time fathers have become, in some circles at least, the new heroes of our culture myths.

But all this is, in terms of human history, quite new. Our heritage, right down to our own mothers, has more typically been Daddy on the Outside and:

Mother on the Inside

Mothers in American culture became very much of the family. There was a time, in European society, when a "woman of the world" might be admired for her sophistication, her knowledge of the world and all it contained, her ability to deal with men. But in America, the "worldly" woman has always had a lingering taint about her, a whiff of sin, a suggestion of promiscuity. This is perhaps a legacy from our Puritan ancestors, whose notion of the perfect woman was the homebody, the "goodwife," an image that persisted in the small towns of Protestant America.

Even when Mommy worked, she seldom claimed knowledge of the world. She would usually defer to Daddy on major decisions. A new house, a new car, a move to a different city, college for daughters or only sons—fathers generally claimed the last word in these matters. Mommy seldom made enough money to claim an equal share in the decision, and even if she did, the odds were she was busy propping up Daddy as head of the family, and so made no *direct* claims at all. As we shall see, she was more likely to be indirect.

Mommy's power in the family was emotional, a mandate she received from society at large. Freud, for example, decreed that women and the family represented instincts, to which feelings are closely allied—both of them primitive and, from a man's point of view, suspect. And Talcott Parsons declared that women are "expressive" while men are "instrumental." What this means is that Daddy is supposed to be the executive, the decision maker, the doer, the representative of the state—while Mommy *feels* things. He fixes the toaster and mows the lawn; she is sensitive to his needs and has his cold beer ready when he finishes his chores. She also keeps the emotional conduits open so that Daddy and the children, who hardly ever see each other, still think they are relating. If Daddy is go-between for family and world, Mommy is go-between for kids and Daddy. That was one reason why mothers used to spend so much time interpreting fathers to children (especially daughters), and vice versa.

This notion was a very convenient one. It enabled men to assign the messy parts of life—emotions and the body, which, like emotions and instincts, are closely related—to women. From the instant little boys hear, "Boys don't cry, only girls cry," the lines are drawn. While men indubitably do have feelings, they find it more convenient to deny them, to "put them in their pocket," as one young father expressed it to me, so they can get on with the job.

There is no denying that feelings can interfere with performance. If you are out there keeping your eye on the environment, scratching out a living, ready to lay down the reality principle to the family, you have to keep your feelings under wraps.

And there is no denying that women by and large are more closely connected to their feelings, live more inside them, than men do. Still, younger women today are trying to resolve the "action versus emotion" dichotomy, and many social science professionals have always recognized that, in reality, Mommy performed a number of instrumental tasks while taking care of home and family. The difficulty lies in our lingering association of Inside/Outside with female/male.

The handing over of all emotional life and power to women, so that Daddy is free to be, unconflicted, the active man, has had some disastrous consequences. The biggest one for women is that, having given all the emotional power to Mother, men have blamed her ever since, in portrayals from Philip Wylie's "Mom" to Mrs. Portnoy. The tyrannical mother castrates her sons and colludes with her daughter to make a fool out of Daddy, poor Daddy, who comes home so tired from work that all he wants to do is settle down in front of the TV.

This is the Sons' Myth, the myth of the dominating mother. It has some truth in it. Mothers have been dominant—at least in the sense of being inescapably *there*—in their children's lives because Daddy was never home. And when he was home, he usually left the business of relationships in the family completely up to Mother. Relationships, after all, depend on recognizing your own feelings, being responsive to other people's feelings, being involved, in short, in the whole flow of feelings between and among people. Daddy has always felt uncomfortable with all this, especially at home, where he is surrounded by women and children, those people with whom, for the sake of his masculinity, he must not identify.

So he retreats to the TV or the newspaper in his den or basement workshop, where he can *do* something—whether vicariously, through the football game on TV, or in reality, at his workbench or desk. He wants facts or figures, something definite in the newspaper, rather than this messy ebb and flow of emotional life that always threatens to get out of control.

This is the famous passive or withdrawn American father. He is the classic American Daddy, and it may be that withdrawal is his classic method of maintaining dominance.

There is a wonderful scene in the movie *The Great Santini* in which the father, Bull Meechum, Marine officer, is reading his paper in the kitchen while his wife fixes dinner. Naturally, she isn't saying anything to him.

He is disturbed by the children, who come in and want him to pay attention to them. He soon gets rid of the two boys, but his daughter is more persistent. He goes out on the porch, sits down, and holds up the paper so it hides him. She follows him out, sits at his feet, and, to see whether he will react, tells him a story about herself and a boy that gets wilder and wilder.

He hides behind his newspaper, a wall between him and his daughter. A shield to deflect all those annoying, female feelings, *demands*. He doesn't hear a word she is really saying—just the demand behind her words.

Finally, he yells at his wife to make his daughter stop bothering him.

There may be a good reason why so many fathers feel uncomfortable with women's emotions, and with their own. It has to do with the fact that their own fathers were out working most of the time, were retreating behind the newspaper at home, and generally felt uncomfortable with *their* feelings (as their fathers had done before them, and so on).

When little boys have to give up the first great love of their lives, Mommy, they have to find some way of dealing with all the complex feelings that surround this love—the tenderness, the warmth, and the wish for closeness, as well as the anger, disappointment, and loneliness that go along with losing her.

Their fathers give them all too little help in handling these emotions. By being absent so much, by leaving little boys so much in the hands of the mothers from whom the boys have to separate in order to become masculine, fathers have made it harder than it need be for the boys to separate.

What boys are told, usually, is to bury the tenderness, the warmth, the expressiveness—and to work out the anger and disappointment through sports and other forms of competition. And the harder the process of separation from Mother is (particularly if a father, through work or divorce or death, is absent), the more a boy's feelings may seem suspect to him, proof of an inner femininity he is eager to deny.

A warm, close father can help a boy integrate his feelings and discover that an inner life is not antithetical to masculinity. A distant or rejecting father can set up a dilemma: if Father is absent, Mother is all too present. She seems dominant, if only because she is so much more present in her son's life than her husband is. Her son's feelings for her are very strong, almost overwhelming—and they threaten him because they are associated with a woman and with femininity.

So what happens most of the time is that boys deny whole areas of complex feelings, saying, unconsciously, "All that belongs to Mother. It's her fault I'm having so much trouble."

Such boys find their comfort in a retreat from Mother—and from feelings—into activity, where the rules are set down clearly and life seems simpler. To them masculinity is, in part, about control, and it seems very clear compared to the complex feelings women evoke. Such feelings also seem to belong to a time before a boy felt securely masculine, so that the threat of a woman's dominance contains the threat of loss of masculinity, of a regression back to the time when a boy was an infant, part of Mother and not yet a self.

Emotional passivity is, then, an assertion of masculinity. The boy grown to manhood is heterosexual, but he remains most at ease among other men. He leaves the emotional life of the family up to his wife.

The American Daddy

Back in the 1830s, Alexis de Tocqueville, a French visitor to America, commented on the fact that the energies of American men seemed entirely absorbed by business. They had no time for the bourgeois or upper-class drawing rooms of European and British tradition, in which adult men and women conversed or played cards together. The American businessman was already a workaholic.

A little earlier, Frances Trollope, an English observer (she was Anthony Trollope's mother and became a celebrated writer in her own right), found that, from the Middle West to the East, American men and women seemed to live almost entirely sex-segregated lives. "With the exception of dancing," she wrote, "which is almost wholly confined to the unmarried of both sexes, all the enjoyments of the men are found in the absence of women. They dine, they play cards, they have musical meetings, they have suppers, all in large parties, and all without women."

Nineteenth-century American novels also reflected a world without women. From *The Last of the Mohicans* to *Moby Dick* to *Huckleberry Finn,* the archetypal worlds of our fiction were those in which men confronted the Outside world together.

Mrs. Trollope and de Tocqueville came from traditions in which there had for centuries been places—from the courts of royalty to aristocratic ballrooms and hunts to intellectual salons and middle-class drawing rooms—where the sexes could meet on a more or less equal footing. Women were always present in the courts of royalty, and their roles were as often political as social. By the sixteenth century in England, dancing and the arts of manners and witty conversation were as important to the education of a gentleman as horsemanship and swordsmanship.

Not surprisingly, when the English middle class evolved, it enthusiastically adopted the aristocratic virtues. Late-eighteenth-century upscale bourgeois drawing rooms were beautifully skewered by Jane Austen, but for all the silliness of her families, the fact remains that in their drawing rooms, men and women—even men and women of different classes— lived their social lives in each other's company. Thus, in *Pride and Prejudice*, the aristocratic Darcy and the bourgeois Elizabeth Bennet go head-to-head for several hundred pages of conversation.

In America, drawing rooms never made much headway. We took our manners from below, rather than from above. We aimed to do away with aristocrats and kings, so frontier chic was a powerful element from the start. Men may have valued women, but not the gentlemanly arts of getting along with us. Their models were the rough-and-ready bluntness (and the violence) of the frontiersman, the working-class man, the man absorbed in his work. So the American businessman was born—and for all his middle-class morality, his self-image has always included aspects of the freebooter, the pirate, the frontier scout, and the cowboy.

De Tocqueville, a man and a Catholic, was astonished by one aspect of American social life: the extraordinary freedom he thought was given to unmarried girls, daughters. He found them to be well educated, free to travel, and, thanks to the largesse of their adoring Daddies, extremely well dressed.

Mrs. Trollope and another visitor from England, the journalist Harriet Martineau, found a less rosy picture. True, the unmarried did dance. But daughters as well as wives were swallowed up by "the sordid offices of household drudgery," and when Mrs. Trollope tried to organize a picnic, she was told by a "young lady" that "it is considered very indelicate for ladies and gentlemen to sit down together on the grass." Martineau found that daughters were given a superficial education designed "to fill up time"; and while they were freer to travel than their European counterparts, they were so indulged by a kind of exaggerated chivalry that they became like "spoiled children," demanding "the best of everything."

In truth, businessmen Daddies and husbands then, as now, found it easiest to indulge both wives and daughters, to give them clothes and carriages and trips. "Indulgence," wrote Martineau, was "a substitute for justice." So the American Princess was born, long before the now famous Jewish Princess evolved from the original Protestant prototype. Fathers and husbands worked long hours to provide their families with material goods; but they couldn't include them in their lives, or bend their own habits to fit in with their wives and daughters.

Nearly a hundred years later, on the eve of World War I, the American novelist Edith Wharton wrote in *The Custom of the Country* of the differences between European women, who were included by their men and so returned their interest and attention, and American women, who suffered from male indifference. "Where," a character asks, "does the real life of most American men lie? In some woman's drawing-room or in their offices? The answer's obvious, isn't it?"

Forty-five years after Wharton's novel was published, when I was an adolescent in suburban Pennsylvania, I found my own workaholic father—and all the others on our block—to be exactly the same kind of man. It was his comings and goings we noticed, far more than his presence. And at parties the men and women still split into sex-segregated groups, just as they had in Trollope's day. And, of course, the masculine rituals of Super-Bowl Sunday and Tuesday night poker games are alive and well in the 1980s.

The ethic of frontier chic with which the country started still hangs on. Male role models—the cowboy, the gunfighter, the soldier, the cop—are all Outside men, defined by their work, by their violence, by their silence, by their control.

So American Daddies grow up with these themes. Masculinity implies dominance and control; control over feelings, dominance over women. To dominate your feelings is to control them, and to dominate women is also to control them. Feelings are feminine—women display them, men don't. A boy becomes a man when he ceases to be dominated by a woman, his mother, and asserts his own masculine authority.

Of course, men aren't always, or even very often, successful at dominating or controlling women, but the aim is still there. It is harder than it used to be to fulfill that aim because Daddy has lost many of the buttresses of religion and law that used to prop up his authority as Outside man. In a secular age it is more and more difficult for him to claim the authority of God as his right, except perhaps in the most orthodox of Jewish or Catholic families. Now that married women can make contracts and apply for credit under their own name—can even keep their maiden name or use whatever name they choose—now that so many mothers work and so many fathers don't live with their children (or, if they do, they sometimes take on the role of mother as well as father), Daddy doesn't have automatic authority.

No wonder men guard so jealously their prerogatives of executive capacity, of power-in-the-world, of earning more money than even a career wife. And no wonder control over feelings becomes equated with control over women—the ones who show their feelings, and who stir up the complex feelings in a man that make him feel vulnerable.

When he feels vulnerable, the easiest thing to do is to retreat. So Daddy hides behind his newspaper, works late, sulks. And his daughter may find herself feeling rejected because Daddy withdraws when she makes a demand on him, as Bull Meechum did. Or she may enjoy the knowledge that she can make him feel uncomfortable, and so fall into the ancient role of Eve, the "Bad" woman, who so upset the neat order of Eden.

The power to stir a father's hidden emotional life is an immense one. When the balance tips too far, when Daddy is too passive, a daughter begins to feel she is completely responsible for the relationship and for his emotions. If Daddy is unhappy, it's her fault. If he has trouble relating to her, that's her fault, too. She's not lovable enough, or good enough, or pretty enough.

In this situation, Daddy's wife is probably also caught up in the trap of responsibility, so she, too, gives cues to her daughter. And by giving his womenfolk this responsibility, Daddy gives them, as well, all the power of the emotions he fears. The passive-but-dominant male sets up both his wife and his daughter to fill the ancient role of the castrating bitch, and the Sons' Myth is perpetuated into the next generation.

Oddly enough, though, what the daughter of such a father learns first is control.

Sunday Drives

My father sulked. He ruled us by the sheer, sullen force of his personality—by the withholding of approval, by tight-lipped silence. His black, glowering rages were never expressed openly, but they ensured that I continued to be afraid of him long past the point at which other daughters reached a comfortable accommodation with their fathers.

What I feared, I see only since I have grown up, was the implied force of the violence behind the rage that he kept at all time barely in check. The rage was there behind the sudden cold mask his face became when I had jolted him with some direct emotional appeal. I could *feel* his withdrawal from me—and the mask would clamp down (literally, I could see his jaw muscles tighten with the effort). I could feel also his surge of anger—stopped, too, by the clenched teeth.

He had learned, somewhere along the way, that men never express anger at a woman. This is still part of the training of a gentleman, and its intent is a good one, to protect women from the full force of male physical violence. But, in fact, the male who is uncomfortable with the feelings evoked in him by a female, the male who can't express his feelings, is more likely to resort to physical violence when he feels things are getting out of control. Violence becomes the correlate of withdrawal—of passivity.

Like most men, my father had learned to channel his anger and aggression Outside, into self-assertion, ambition, and competition. He felt comfortable in that old primate male dominance hierarchy; at home alone with a female, even a daughter, he felt less secure. Perhaps he feared he might easily go out of control.

My sense of my father was of a man always removing himself from the pain of an emotional encounter. Under less stress, he would simply shift his body away—by the classic father gesture of pushing his chair back slightly from the dinner table and crossing one calf over the other knee. This was usually the signal for a Pronouncement, one of those sayings Daddies deliver to their children as a substitute for personal response.

Pronouncements have been raised to a fine art by Daddies, who use them to deflect a messy personal encounter while keeping everything under control. "I can't decide what to do about X," I might say, deeply perplexed. "Most people," he might say—he was very fond of starting with "Most people," implying that he, and by extension all of us, his wife and children, were not most people, were distinctly superior to the mob—"Most people are afraid to make their own decisions in life. They just want to do what other people do."

This didn't make me feel superior. It made me feel what I always felt around my father, inadequate. I was supposed to be superior, and what that meant was that I was not supposed to need to ask anyone else's advice, least of all his. In fact, I ought really, if I were a truly superior person, as superior as he himself, simply to *know* what to do. Feeling doubts and hesitation or confusion was a sign of my general messiness, an inherently female failure to keep my feelings under control.

"Louisa," wrote Martha Saxton in her biography of Louisa May Alcott, *Louisa May,* "was completely unsure of herself with her father and could never make sense out of what appeared to be his superhuman self-control. Since he defined quiescence and withdrawal as good, and exertion, expression, and aggression as bad, Louisa could only conclude that he was saintly and she, like her mother, was damned."

Not all fathers are as rigid, as obsessed with control, as my father or Bronson Alcott were. Yet the ideal still permeates the culture. In *Ordinary People,* men finally were shown, in book and movie both, as people learning to express their feelings. But cops and G-men and football players still do their stuff every night on TV.

Even the antiwar hippie movements of the sixties, with their attraction to Eastern religions and drugs, were in the end obsessed with control. Drugs are a means of distancing the self from the complications of feeling; many of the disciplines of Eastern religions are designed to exert total control over the transient emotions that sway our lives. The whole idea of being "laid back" is exactly the same as the "quiescence and withdrawal" that Bronson Alcott prized. And both the Oriental religions and the communes that survived the sixties are, on the whole, supremely male-dominant.

To a greater or lesser extent, most daughters have grown up with this legacy from their fathers and mothers: dominance and control are related, and are masculine virtues. Feelings, and the flow of relationships, are related, and are the particular province of femininity.

Yet Daddy is often moody, even irrational, although he would never admit it. It's not easy to exert so much control. Those feelings he keeps bottled up are always threatening to emerge.

One of the few places where my father allowed himself to release his aggression directly was on the road. Like many fathers, he had a favorite ritual: to put his whole family in the car and drive somewhere. It didn't matter where—what mattered was that he was behind the wheel. My mother drove, of course; indeed, she was our main chauffeur. But on those family outings, it would have been unthinkable for her to drive. At the wheel he was Father, the master at the helm of his ship.

He did not release his aggression by fast driving, as many men do; he believed in safety and control on the roads. What he did was to keep up a steady stream of imprecations against the bitches and bastards driving the other cars. They were all, obviously, lousy drivers, Sunday drivers, amateurs. (The fact that we, too, were out for a Sunday drive made no difference. In my father's view, he took everything he did so seriously, and was so superior at it, that he was by definition a professional.)

No, what angered him about the bitches and bastards in the other cars was that they occupied road space. They got in his way—and this infuriated him.

The other people who got in his way were his children. A seething mass of humanity on the back seat, we represented a greater threat even than the other cars. With the chaotic energy of childhood, we represented mutiny, potential anarchy.

For us, these drives were torture. He was constantly threatening to pull over and make one or the other or all of us get out and walk. Our continual needs for toilet stops threw him into paroxysms of barely concealed rage. He would stop with a jerk that threw us all forward, get out with elaborate care, jerk the seat forward, and stand glowering while we slunk off into the bushes. I was usually too scared to pee.

My great disgrace on these drives was car-sickness. It terrified me because it was such a complete and humiliating loss of control. It represented everything my father demonstrated every day that he was most against, most in danger of—and which he had spent a lifetime resisting. Loss of control, whether of emotions or of stomach, was the unforgivable sin.

Of course, babies and children continually lose control—and the more control that is demanded of us, the more frightened we become of our lapses, until we grow up to be miniature replicas of this being who towered over us, his face an iron mask behind which the most violent loss of control continually threatened.

I would feel the first signs of dizziness and nausea soon after we got into the car, especially if it was hot. I would wait, miserably, trying to breathe as little as possible because the combined odors of gasoline, stuffy upholstery, hot rubber, and asphalt would do me in.

Inevitably and regularly, though, I was sick. The big question was whether I could time it perfectly. If I announced that I felt sick and asked to stop the car, I was instantly in disgrace. If I got out and stood by the road and was *not* sick, I had held the whole family up for no good reason at all. Perhaps it was a "trick," just another devious, childish way to gain attention, yet another evidence of my general untrustworthiness.

If, on the other hand, I waited too long and was sick *in the car,* I had ruined everything. The car, everyone's Sunday afternoon—and, nearly, my father's control. He would grip the wheel, his knuckles white with tension, while his face reddened. He would yell more loudly at the bitches and bastards.

Where was my mother during all this? She sat meekly beside him on the front seat, saying little. She would pass back a handkerchief. I don't remember whether we would immediately turn around and drive home, or whether we would look for a gas station (this was long before super-highways with regular rest stops and comfort stations).

My best solution, seldom achieved, was to be sick out the window while the car kept going. My father did not have to be interrupted, there was no mess on the inside, and I was relieved. The car could easily be hosed down when we got home.

That was my father. You could not get around him. There was no question of appealing to his reason. In a situation like this, he didn't have any.

It never occurred to anyone to leave me home, bring a bucket, or provide regular stops for me to get out and breathe and settle my stomach. If we were going for a drive, we did it his way: we all went, and we didn't stop until the drive was over. Anything less was simply proof of our inadequacy, or worse, of our incorrigible determination to sabotage his Sunday, his control.

*   *   *

It is a peculiar feeling to know that, as a daughter, a female, a girlchild, your chief effect on your father seems to be to threaten him with loss of control. If I hadn't been so afraid of him, it might have been a great game to watch him expand and expand but never quite explode.

But there is something very frightening about an overcontrolled person. He maintains dominance easily, since there is the force of so much emotion behind his control. Women respect him, since his control says, over and over again, "I am superior to you—I keep my cool."

That all this control made him pompous and rigid was something I couldn't see until I had gotten well away from the family, and discovered some men who had, or at least expressed, feelings.

Daddies in some cultures are allowed to express feelings. There are Eastern European traditions in which men laugh and cry with gusto, as they also drink, dance, and rage. Some Italians are certainly emotionally more volatile than WASPs, and the French man traditionally may embrace another man when saying hello or goodbye.

The WASP tradition, the one that organized and first predominated in America, is the most emotionally impoverished of the lot. Yet there are variations in individual temperament; many Italians do not express feelings easily, for instance. And men from peasant cultures all over the world—whether Eastern European, Chinese, French, Italian, or whatever—come from traditions of endurance and stoicism that do not always allow emotional expressiveness.

But when they came to America, Daddies from all the other traditions ran straight up against the great American Daddy traditions of silence and withdrawal.

Not every father is like mine. I have seen relaxed and genial fathers, joking with their wives even while driving. But in my mind, one enduring image of a father is a man who feels continually threatened by the child in the back seat.

Part Two

CHAPTER THREE

Save Me the Waltz:
Fathers, Daughters, and Sexuality

The Raven-Haired Daughter
Callie Opal

*C*allie Opal has fine white skin and long, shining black hair, and she sits very straight on the velvet couch in her small one-bedroom apartment. She keeps her hands loosely folded in her lap, looking perfectly relaxed yet ready for action at any second. Her Southern drawl is undercut by a precision nearly prim in her speech as well as by the firm angles of jaw and cheekbone. Each word is measured, weighed: so much and no more. You know that whatever she says is exactly what she means.

At twenty-seven, she has accomplished something no one in her family has ever done—transplanted herself body and soul out of the South, where her family's roots go back two hundred years or more and where everyone, including her older, married sister and her little brother, lives within fifty miles of Cherokee Corners.

She began making plans to move out as soon as she discovered the library and began to read about places that were not Cherokee Corners.

But she started out, too, as Daddy's Girl.

When she was small, they were buddies. "I was the second girl, and he had given up having a boy, so he decided, well, I'll make do with what I have." She laughs, full-throated, with the perspective of a twenty-seven-year-old but also with the nervous sharpness of a woman who found out early that being Daddy's pet carried a double edge to it.

Part of it was purely wonderful: "I went everywhere with him. Every Saturday we would get up before the rest of the family and have coffee—I remember when I was three years old, drinking coffee with my Daddy. Then all day Saturday we did whatever he had to do. We went to the barbershop, to the fish market, to junk shops to look for pieces of cars, to the fillin' station. Whatever he did, I was taggin' along behind him."

D.W. himself is a large, taciturn man with a sun-reddened neck and big, work-scarred hands. His paunch sits comfortably on the belt of his chino pants.

"She was a funny little thing," he says. "Oh yes, I took her hunting and fishing with me until her brother was born. Her sister was never interested in that kind of thing, but she seemed to like it. When he was big enough, though, he was just naturally the one to come with me."

Callie was older, by then, and says she had other interests, and didn't mind being replaced by her brother. But some of it must have been a loss.

She had sat in Daddy's lap to drive the pickup truck, and he took her hunting and fishing, taught her to stalk a deer and kill clean. She wasn't afraid of blood or the knife, and she knew just where the meat they ate came from.

But the fun of hunting wasn't really the act itself, since she never did too much actual shooting. It was being with Daddy—the glamour of it, of being singled out, the excitement of this special relationship that was beyond anything her sister had, who was just an ordinary girl. Callie loved being a tomboy. She would walk for miles and miles, sit under the trees for hours fishing, and the excitement of being outdoors and free would fuse with the excitement of being with him.

The same went for cars. Callie's father spent hours tinkering, but the mechanical stuff itself never interested her too much. She just liked to hang around the garage, pass him the wrench or whatever, spend those companionable hours.

But it was forcibly brought home to her that she was a girl, and that different standards of conduct applied, "because when he works on things he hits his fingers and gets mad and talks *very* ugly, as my mother would say, so she would come and get me and tell him, 'If you talk like this she can't stay around you.' "

When Callie quotes her mother, her voice changes, rises, takes on a slightly hysterical pitch, and she suddenly talks very fast. Then she becomes deliberate again.

Her father, too, drew a clear line between Callie as *his* daughter—the child with whom he identified and to whom he could pass on his fatherly knowledge of the world—and Callie as his *daughter,* a girlchild, very different from himself, who must learn early that she would not grow up to be like him and so was not entitled to the privileges a boy might have had.

He wouldn't get her a BB gun. "I never liked dolls," she says. "I wanted boy-type toys, a pellet gun or a knife, but it was always, 'No, go play with your dolls.' It was like they were telling me, 'You're not *supposed* to have a pellet gun'—it was always that I got shoved over."

But he had brought her this far, given her so much freedom to tramp the hills and share his adventures; he must have known on some level what it would mean to deprive her of the gun, the final, ritual seat of approval and inclusion.

I know how Callie felt. My father didn't hunt, but he taught us all to shoot, target practice with rifles in the back yard. I was a good shot—got my triangles clean inside the center circle. But it was my brother who was given the beautiful Daisy BB gun, with pump action and genuine leather thong hanging from the butt.

Not to be given the gun meant an arbitrary limit was placed on your identity. It meant that you could not be trusted to shoot a gun, that you simply were not competent, could not from the beginning expect to be as competent as Daddy, the man who owned the guns. You were defined as *girl*—set apart. "No," says her father, "we didn't think she ought to have a gun. It didn't seem right."

Of course, the denial of the gun created tremendous envy, maybe more for me, with three older brothers, than Callie. An old-fashioned psychoanalyst might say wanting the gun in the first place was penis-envy. But it is more probable that being denied the gun creates the festering envy that leads tomboys to identify, stubbornly, with their fathers and brothers and with men in general, to want to be the men who have the right to own the gun.

Of course, to be given the gun could mean simply that you were a girl who shot a gun, so the gun would be defused, would become merely a tool, an object, rather than the fetish, the masculine-identity symbol it undeniably is in America. But then, if girls routinely could have guns, men would no longer value these weapons. And it is undeniable that for Callie, as for myself, the real value of the gun lay in its intimate association with the males we adored. Would we have cared as much for guns if girls had used them as routinely as dolls?

The knot of frustration is what is important here—the moment of being turned away from activity that meant identifying with Daddy, and the stubborn, inward turning back. And the price of that turning back.

Undeniably, it was Callie's father who started her traveling, moving her out of the house with him as soon as she could sit up and drink coffee, rather than making her stay home with her mother and sew.

Callie's mother was always a housewife. "She really didn't have the education to do too much, and my father never thought she had the sense to do anything" (here the Southern lilt runs suddenly high and shrill) "except be a great wife and mother—now that was okay! But he was very protective toward her. She did a little dressmaking at home, but he didn't much like it."

Daddy is a good ole boy. He traveled quite a bit in his youth, working as a master electrician on building sites all over the country, but he came back to Cherokee Corners because "there's no place like the South—no place like home." He doesn't much like foreigners, which includes everyone outside the South and especially Northerners and more especially cityfolk.

He believes in protecting his women, especially against the devious tactics of foreigners, who can be out for only one thing—the ruination of a gullible woman.

"Women, you see," says Callie, "have not got a lot of common sense. Oh, we can learn, all right—we have college degrees, more than one apiece. He's all for that."

Yet Daddy always draws the line. "No matter how much learning from the books you have," he says, "it doesn't mean you have the sense to get in out of a shower of rain."

When it gets down to the nitty-gritty, to real life, only men can manage.

Even so, it was something for a man who'd worked with his hands his entire life, a good ole boy who believed that a woman should marry a man and depend on him—it was something for him to push his daughters to go to college, to be able to earn a living if they had to. They should have that much independence.

Then, too, Callie points out, "He doesn't think I should go home and depend on *him.*"

And there was always the possibility, since a woman is gullible, that one of his daughters would get stuck in some miserable, unhappy marriage for lack of the skill to support herself. He was fond of his daughters; he wouldn't wish that on them.

So despite the fact that there was no money, they all went to college, with scholarships and jobs. Callie, in fact, has been more or less financially independent since she was five, when she started out clipping coupons. The neighborhood grocer, who grew up with her father, redeemed them for cash, and then redeemed all the empty Coke bottles she could find or scrounge. Later, she went on to babysitting and then—inevitably—at sixteen, to Woolworth's, where her mother had worked in her own adolescence.

Money, in fact, was the occasion of Callie's first open defiance of her father, at fifteen. She was short, for once, and asked for the loan of a dollar to buy something: "He started giving me a lecture on money—and here I'd always pretty much earned my own. It made me mad. I told him he could keep his dollar, and I would never ask him for another penny as long as I lived. And I never did. That was the first time he got any inkling that if you go against a certain belief or principle of mine, I don't take it lightly." She was as stubborn as he was.

So she was ready and able to take care of herself, and her father was giving her powerful support by encouraging her to go to college, even though he never dreamed she really would leave the South. But she got another jolt in adolescence when she found out what her father really meant when he called women gullible.

Actually, she had been hearing it for years. Her Aunt Sara was widowed young when Callie's father's brother died.

"I remember her coming to the house when I was little. I really liked her, but it was obvious he didn't care for her too much. One day I said to him, 'Daddy, Aunt Sara is such a nice lady, why doesn't she get married again?' And he said, 'Nobody's going to buy a cow when you can get the milk for free.' "

Callie puzzled over that one for a long time. And then a little later her older sister had an abortion. She had been dating the boy all through high school, and finally they had an accident. Nobody would have found out except there were complications and Callie's aunt, with whom the sister was staying, had to take her to the hospital. The aunt, of course, immediately told Callie's father, and there were a lot of hard words about Callie's sister. Because the next thing that happened was the boy suddenly married someone else he had knocked up at college. So D.W. went around saying the boy was no good, and his daughter had messed up her life, and just let herself be used. He went right on saying it when, still in college, she began going out with an older man, until she married him. "He hasn't said much at all since then. He couldn't believe he wasn't right, so that's that."

Callie, who pieced all this together from things she overheard, puzzled over the cow and the sister until her mid-teens, when she figured it out: "If you are going to let someone sleep with you, then they are not going to marry you, because their only reason to marry you would be to sleep with you."

Whereupon, Callie decided she was never going to get married.

All of this was made very clear when her father started in on the perils of men: "You know, be careful, be careful, be careful. You could tell from his attitude that he accepted the fact that you were going to go out on dates, but he never felt good about it."

Because of course what the boys wanted was to go to bed with his daughter, who being a female would be easily seduced by the first fast-talking bimbo who came along. And once she let one of them get to her, that would be the end—no one would want her anymore.

It's not that he saw his daughters as whores; they weren't temptresses, leading a man on. But he does think that "a man will always try to talk a woman into something. Any man worth his salt will keep on at it until she's bound to give in—that's just the way things are. Men are more persistent."

Thinking this about men, though, and thinking of the weaknesses of women, made it very hard for him to face the fact that his daughters were growing up and dating. It was too painful. He couldn't face his feelings, so he withdrew instead, in a typical American Daddy's ploy.

"He would completely ignore the fact that I was going out on a date," Callie remembers. "If he found out about it, he would make sure to be gone when the boy arrived. And he would not want to know anything about it, so he never waited up for me or asked me anything the next day. He just tried to block it out of his mind completely."

Callie thought this was funny, and called him her "disappearing father." When he did meet one of her boyfriends, he was perfectly pleasant, and they always liked him. He was, after all, a good ole boy just like their fathers.

But somewhere D.W. was keeping track, because he did notice if Callie had two different dates on the same weekend, "Because if I were popular enough to do that there must obviously be some reason why."

This was a blow; to find out that all the things Daddy had said about her aunt and her sister applied to her, too—the favorite daughter, the hunting companion, almost a son.

It led Callie, as it so often does, into an alliance with her mother. "My mother, I found out, is a very interesting person. On the outside she seems to be very quiet and nice and ladylike and lets my father make all the decisions. But she has a mind of her own. And she doesn't believe all this garbage of my father's, all his negative feelings toward men. She always said he was so suspicious. So if something came up that I wanted to do, then we would work it out so that I could do it by not telling my father the whole story."

So if Callie wanted to go to the beach with a "mixed group"—meaning two different sexes—"I'd tell my mother and she would say, well, we won't tell your father who you're going with. We'll let him think you're going with Mr. and Mrs. Jones for chaperones. What he doesn't know won't hurt him."

What Callie pieced together from family stories was that her father's absolute distrust of boys, even, or especially, the sons of other good ole boys, came from very good evidence—himself. He had been what they call a "real hell-raiser," meaning that after he got engaged to Callie's mother, he left her living at home with her mother for several years, "while he went and raised hell, knowing that when he got tired of doing everything he wanted to do, he had my mother to come back home to and marry. So of course he sees every other man as being like he was, just wanting what they can get, but wanting to marry a good girl."

And the good ole boy and the good ole girl call each other "Mother" and "Daddy" and live a very quiet life—never go out, never entertain, live "like a brother and sister. I never saw them touching each other, or sitting next to each other. I'm sure they had sex, but you could never tell." They have the kind of relationship of which you say, as Callie does, "They love each other, I never had any doubt about that. They never fight."

So Daddy sows his wild oats and comes home and ties Mother up in

this "boring, platonic relationship," and Callie can't see the point in repeating it.

In fact, she coolly confesses, sitting on the couch, with her long black
hair shining, "I've always wanted to be a boy. I want to be a father—I
never wanted to be a mother. I don't like babies. My father tells me men
will take advantage of me. *I* want to be the one who does the taking!"

Nevertheless, she is tremendously attractive to men: for one thing, she
is beautiful and under thirty, and for another she had too many years as
Daddy's pet not to be fond of men, underneath it all.

Yet her father's attitude took.

"He just managed," she says, "to completely warp my relationships
with men in terms of sex. I'm very, very suspicious when I first meet a
man; he has to prove to me over a long period of time that he is sincere.
And even then I still in the back of my mind have thoughts that nag me
about how maybe he's using me, and I have a lot of problems with how I
feel about sex. I always wonder, even if it's a long relationship, if he likes
me or if I'm just a body at the time."

She used to have nightmares after sex; in them, her father came into
the room where she was sleeping with someone and looked at her with
great disapproval. In fact, she had to leave home and travel several hundred miles north before she could first sleep with a man.

Like many women who have been passionately attached to their fathers, once she got to sex she found she had no problem having an orgasm. Her problem is that she can't make any connection at all between
sex and love.

"There is no way," Callie says, "I can feel love and give love through
sex."

She finds that too often when she really only wants to be held and
hugged and kissed, when she wants affection, her signals mean seduction
to the man and she winds up in bed. It's too bad, this kind of confusion: it
leads Callie to wish, often, that "sex would just go away. It complicates
things."

Which is startlingly close to the way her mother feels: "She would
rather ignore the whole thing, too. Sex was when you were married—it
was like your duty as a wife to have *babies,* you know, and this was the
way you had your babies. I don't think she ever thought of a woman
going out and screwing around for fun."

Of course not. That's what men do. Good women, the women they
marry, stay home and wait for them.

And when a man like D.W. looks up and sees, not *his* daughter—
hunting companion, almost-son—but his *daughter,* a female, he thinks
about how she has to be a Good Girl and affection is the last thing on his
mind. When she was little, Callie was always welcome on his lap, but she

can't remember a single kiss or a hug. Intimacy was based on companionship. They would be together for hours, hunting, but never a conversation, certainly not a heart-to-heart. Daughters like Callie don't confide in fathers like D.W., who would feel as uncomfortable with emotional intimacy as he would with the notion of incest. That's all secret stuff, far below the surface.

But Callie had been emotionally seduced by him from the beginning, with all those private cups of coffee in the kitchen, and the private expeditions. Seduced and identifying with the seducer, her father, the traveler, the sower of wild oats.

When she announced she was heading north to work in a hospital—she is a nurse-specialist in the intensive-care unit—he could not bear it.

"He would walk around the house and scream, 'You can't do this! You don't know what you're doing. The people up there are different. You won't understand them, you don't know how their minds work. They're foreigners; you're not going to fit in. They'll take advantage of you, they'll use you, they'll try to sell you the Empire State Building!' "

She had already checked out Northerners in college and nursing school, and found out she liked them, liked their directness and the apparent lack of possessiveness of their men. Northern women didn't seem to have to play as many games as Southern women did, didn't have to pretend they were virgins when they weren't, for instance.

There was no question of her giving in and staying in the South; she was as stubborn as her father. And more. As a daughter, she had long ago learned how to manipulate him—that power that is compensation for the possessiveness of fathers toward daughters, for their (the fathers') refusal to take their daughters seriously.

She had two ways to do it. One was "just to be very nice to him, the way he liked for me to be." Smile for Daddy. "And cut up with him. I would joke a lot with him, and tease him, much more than my sister did. I could get away with it. He wanted me to take things seriously, and I would let him know I didn't."

The other way was to get mad at him. "He could not stand for me to be mad at him. If you wanted to get anything out of my father, all you would do is get mad at him, and not speak to him for a while, and he couldn't stand it. He always thought twice about clamping down on me, because he knew I was very strong-headed. If I really wanted to do something, I was going to do it. He would mumble a lot of things and tell my mother she was ruining me and spoiling me, but he wouldn't stop it."

That's what happened when he found out about the beach parties, and that's what happened when Callie went north.

First she teased him, then she stopped speaking to him, and then she left—and he kissed her goodbye at the airport.

Now she lives alone, and she has plenty of lovers. But there are some funny things about her lovers. Not only has she fled as far from home—psychologically, at least—as possible, but she is also dating men as far removed from her father's type as possible. If he thinks Northerners are foreigners, Callie goes one step farther and looks for real foreigners: European-born doctors, German businessmen traveling for their firms who make regular circuits around the East. She demands that her men be, above all, sophisticated. If she does go out with an American, he's an executive in a three-piece suit.

"I like men who don't even care about doing all the things my father thinks men are made for. I'm better at carpentry or fixing a lamp than the men I date—they were all city kids. When I find a down-home, earthy type, I run the other way. I always see him thirty years from now, sitting in a rocking chair with his feet propped up, not wanting to go anywhere, not having any real zest for living. . . ."

On the other hand, maybe she really hasn't gotten all that far away from D.W. For one thing, she prefers older men; they are more secure, she feels, less threatened by a strong-minded woman like herself. These older, sophisticated men remind her of the fathers of the Northern students she envied in college, who would come in big cars to take their daughters out for dinner. Her father, if he came at all, came in a pickup truck.

For another thing, despite the fact that she can only stand to go home two or three times a year, she has reached a conclusion about D.W.: "We had good vibes, my Daddy and me. Even though I can look at some things and say, 'My father is the one who caused me to feel this way,' none of it ever really affected the way I felt about him, because I always loved him dearly. I never really held his faults against him. I never really rebelled against him. I just learned that he is a certain way, and I can't change him. I have to accept him. He's going to have to learn to live by my rules a little bit, and I will try not to rock the boat. When I was very young we sort of made a balance which we hold to this day."

It's hard to stay mad at Daddy. And when Callie talks about running away from down-home types like her Daddy she admits that sometimes she catches herself liking one and sees him a couple of times. "But in the long run I'll drop him. I have this thing about being too down-home and too earthy and turning out like my father. I have a great fear of getting caught up and having to marry someone who is just like him."

A favorite daughter stays enthralled in spite of herself. It's the sort of thing that's very hard to give up. What German businessman in his three-piece suit will ever be able to match the glamour of Callie's childhood father, or offer her the certainty of such a love?

"I had a special place in his heart," she says, "and I knew it. I was his raven-haired daughter."

Vice Is Nice,
But Incest Is Best
Blaise

She is tiny, with close-cropped red hair, fine white skin and a sprinkling of freckles across the bridge of her nose. Her father was a California divorce lawyer; Blaise spent her childhood in upper-middle-class comfort.

As an only child, she was her father's special pride. He took her horseback riding every Sunday; in the summers they sailed. At ten, she was winning races. Their incestuous relationship was already two years old.

Blaise doesn't remember exactly when it started, just that at a certain point it became a regular nighttime ritual. She would go to bed, and wait until her mother had tucked her in and gone to bed herself. Then her father would come into her room and sit on the edge of her bed.

"I would sit on his lap, often straddling him, and fondle his penis, and sometimes kiss it, and induce an erection," Blaise tells me, her tone eerily clinical.

He was gentle and encouraging. While she fondled him he would talk to her, grown-up talk about life and love. He never ejaculated.

She thought of herself as doing him a favor.

When she was ten or eleven, he taught her to bring him off, but he never tried to enter her—seldom, in fact, ever so much as touched her sex, although he would take down her panties. By eleven or so, she remembers, she felt "an inchoate desire for him to go down on me or something, without ever understanding what that was." He would tease her, touch her briefly until she was aroused, without satisfying her. She was meant to service *him,* so he kept her on edge.

When she was fourteen, he died, suddenly, of a heart attack. It was over, but it continued to shape her life.

If a little girl dreams of capturing Daddy for her very own, of growing up to marry him and have his child, the early adolescent adds the equipment for real seduction to the old oedipal dream that returns, briefly, at the very moment when what a girl really needs is for her father to let her go, with his blessing. She *knows* she wants this, but she still has dreams about him, and sometimes a disconcerting sense of her own newly intense sexuality when she sees him in Sunday morning pajamas, or freshly after-shaved and shining in a three-piece suit on his way out to dinner with her mother.

Usually, both she and her father simply deny their sexual awareness of each other. It makes them too uncomfortable. The tension between them gets expressed, often, through bickering and criticism; daughters may think their fathers don't dress well enough, while fathers think their daughters wear too much makeup.

But for Blaise, it was different. By adolescence she had become, if all unconsciously, habitually seductive. It was what her father had trained her for: Smile for Daddy. Even the riding and sailing had always been part of his continuous seduction of her, so that everything in her life became sexualized, and sex became the focus of her life.

He had made her feel special. He had, as all Daddies do, that power. And Blaise felt, "I was such a nothing in all the ways that children want to be something. I was not popular, I didn't have boyfriends. I was never one of the gang. I was eccentric, and I had a bitchy edge. I was the sort of child adults would put in charge of other kids, but I was never popularly regarded as student leader."

After her father died, all Blaise wanted was "to be just normal, and be in with everybody else." In a city high school, where there were so many cliques and clubs there was something for practically anyone to join, she didn't join the art club or even the sailing club.

Her seductiveness didn't help in high school because she was, otherwise, too full of spiky defenses, too shy, too intense. And she wanted too much to be ordinary.

This is a characteristic of people with secrets. The knowledge you carry that you have been part of something peculiar isolates you from your peers; you feel, in fact, as if you have no peers. What you want is to be exactly like everybody else. The point is never to single yourself out, because then you remember what happened. And besides, maybe by this time you have lost the power to give yourself the distinction of specialness—it has become so connected with Daddy that you aren't sure it exists without him.

Blaise's father had trained her into a compliant, controllable woman, who automatically, and completely unconsciously, arranged herself into a pose of invitation for the nearest man. She could never say no.

Yet, paradoxically, one of the lasting effects of her father's seduction and of her precocious apprenticeship in being sexually aroused only to service someone else was that Blaise lost the vital connection with her own body.

"I never could find my clitoris for myself. I never sort of knew where it was, and I didn't learn to masturbate until I was nineteen. I never experimented, because I had no association with my own body. Sex came from being with a man. It still does, pretty much."

It was a man, her third or fourth lover, who showed her her clitoris, and, using his hand, brought her to her first orgasm. That's how she still comes, mostly, although she can occasionally manage it herself in masturbation. With a man inside her, she hardly ever feels much, although she always pretends to be excited. She has become the perfect woman for a certain kind of man: obliging, compliant. Push the right button, and she has no will of her own. Daddy takes over.

So, all through adolescence, "I was scared of my own . . . the only thing I can call it is compassion. My own *tractability,* which is a problem I've always had with men, since I will do almost anything, even the most degrading things for myself, before I'll reject a man. This is really the most horrible thing for me. It's so hard for me to say No. I was always afraid boys would insist on having sex."

Smile for Daddy. Give him what he wants, what he needs. To be feminine means to be nurturing, right? Caring, responsive to other people's needs, especially to a man's need for sex. "If a man needs me, boy he's got me. What *I* want is irrelevant."

But there is always this fear of being taken advantage of, of being *degraded* in this act of giving your all to service a man.

"They can take," says Blaise in a very calm, small voice, "anything they want from me, because they need me. And, if they choose, they can leave nothing. That's how I can tell whether a man is a good man or not—whether he will, unbidden, leave me something of myself."

As I hear this, I feel a tightening in my own stomach. How often have I had the same feeling? It's the oldest piece of folk wisdom known—that for a man, love is part of his life, while for a woman, it is her whole life.

If you can't say No to a man's demands, you can't stand up for yourself. Your self. You give up your self to him, and you're lost in the terrible isolation, the alienation from self that has always been the lot of the woman condemned as promiscuous by the same men who dreamed of that selfless woman.

It's an irresistible fantasy, one that runs so deep in the culture it is taken for granted. "She gave herself to him completely. She was his forever." It is in every Gothic novel.

And how many women have not had the same fantasy? The desire to be swept away, to lose our will to a superior force? To be nullified. Carried to extremes, this fantasy becomes the ultimate fusion of eroticism and aggression that creates sadism and masochism, *The Story of O.*

"She wants it," thinks the man. "She wants it anyway. *It's not my responsibility. It's hers.*"

Father-daughter incest, say the anthropologists Lionel Tiger and

Robin Fox, "is understandable enough. . . . Fathers dominate daughters, and only the most insensitive father could deny that one claim his daughters make on his time and concern is a wily feminine one."

"Insensitive" here does not mean "insensitive to a daughter's real needs," but "insensitive to flirtation and other seductive cues a daughter may give." Tiger and Fox are saying that every father notices his daughter is a female, an Eve, who is both "wily" and "feminine." If she is "wily," she must be at once knowledgeable and responsible. The authors are implying that really daughters seduce fathers, and no father could be blamed for giving in. It's all her fault. He can't possibly be responsible for his actions.

But a father is responsible, *must be* responsible. He has so much power. And she needs so much to feel that he loves her.

To believe, as some writers do today, that incest is not harmful to daughters is to believe that women don't need ever to develop a sense of themselves as people who can stand alone, without depending on a man for their sense of identity.

It also plays into the second oldest male excuse in the world—that any female creature, of whatever age, who behaves in a way that any man (even her own father) could interpret as flirtatious is asking for it. (The oldest excuse is that he can't control his *own* sexuality, and shouldn't have to.)

This is also the excuse for rape, the one that Susan Brownmiller exorcised in *Against Our Will.* Incest involves a more subtle form of coercion, usually, than rape, but it always involves coercion.

"I guess I was afraid," says Blaise, "that he would rape me. Although I didn't think of it in such violent terms, it would be a kind of rape. And then when I was thirteen, and said I didn't want him coming into my room anymore, he played on my compassion. He needed me, how could I desert him?"

Incest is the conning of the weak by the strong, of the child by the parent who is supposed to be the protector and nurturer. It is also the ultimate objectification of a daughter, who is deprived of any identity other than that of sexual object.

Men who can't deal with grown women, who feel uncomfortable with adult sexuality, do dominate their daughters, and this makes them feel strong, masculine.

But for a daughter, such domination can all too easily translate into lifelong dependency on men.

"I have fantasies," says Blaise, "of being kept by a man—of becoming a mistress. Because then it's very clear what is expected and what is given in return, and I like that. It seems to me men are always expecting more than they give. I feel bound to male need."

One current rationalization for incest is that the incest taboo makes fathers afraid to touch their daughters, to be tender with them, and that this does great harm to the daughters.

Here, of course, is the crux of the whole thing. Daughters need to flirt with fathers. They need to have their sexuality affirmed by Daddy. This means, practically speaking, that at some point Daddy has to admit to himself that his daughter is a sexually attractive young woman. But the way he shows her that he approves of her sexuality—and of all that implies in terms of her growing up and leaving him—is to approve of her and let her go.

Incest is a way of hanging on to a daughter.

Ultimately, the point of the incest taboo may be not that incest is immoral but that it prevents a child from learning how to be an independent person. Daddy *must* be a safe male. That is part of his job.

The sad fact is that men have not cared very much whether daughters grow up to be independent persons or not; on the whole, they would rather we didn't. So, as the quote from Tiger and Fox shows, the incest taboo that is so crucial for us may be of less significance to them.

Blaise married a man she met in college, whom she didn't love. "He was," she says, "like my father should have been. He had no interest in sex." Nevertheless, when he asked her, she couldn't say No. "My response was pure terror. I thought, now look what I've done! I've gotten him all in love with me and he's asked me to marry him and now I'm going to have to."

It lasted for five years. There were no children; everyone thought they were an ideal couple. She thought she liked a life without passion, but when she had to beg him to satisfy her she just felt degraded. When the marriage ended, she thought it was her fault. She *should* have been happy with him.

Luckily, she was good at earning a living—all that special attention from her father had made it second nature to her. She knew that most work is just a form of seduction, so she got into customer relations. That part worked fine. Her problem wasn't work, just love.

Except that she didn't want to be a customer-relations representative. She always thought that she had it in her, somewhere, to be an artist, if she could rechannel the energy that had always been trapped in sex. So a couple of years after her divorce, she moved to the country to paint.

As she sits in the kitchen of the isolated West Coast farmhouse where she lives, at the moment, in seclusion, she looks so calm, so unflappable, that it is hard to connect this present person with the past she is describing. She has the cultivated detachment produced by the WASP woman's refusal to give way to feeling, by her determination to maintain at all times a controlled and, if possible, even slightly humorous point of view about anything, even disaster. The humor is always self-deprecating, because the WASP woman's method of control is to maintain maximum assertion of responsibility and minimal contact with feelings: if you did it yourself, you've got it halfway licked.

The responsibility is chilling.

First of all, her father told her she was responsible for the whole thing, from the start. She was a seductive little girl, he was only a man. What could he do?

This sort of thing makes a daughter feel, naturally, terrible—not only guilty but Bad. Yet her "badness" is really only perfectly normal sexuality; it's her view of herself that's warped. How is Blaise supposed to deal with what she calls "My own evil tendency toward eroticism—and its manifestation in sexual activity"?

That's how she talks. A big, abstract word like "manifestation" keeps the feelings under wraps.

She has beautiful hands—even in the country, her nails are clean, newly trimmed. It's chilly in the early spring; she wears Levi's (not designer jeans) and a bulky sweater. Another WASP characteristic: impeccable appearance always combined with practical efficiency. The fingernails are not an end in themselves but an aspect, part of having everything under control.

Except, of course, that it isn't.

There is the possibility of maintaining a detached attitude toward her father: "I wasn't responsible for what happened, and yet he was also very troubled. I can't say he was evil—he was not an evil man. He loved me, and he was weak. And he had not worked out his problems to the extent where he could play out his needs on a woman who was more appropriate. I was his vulnerable, available child to do that on. I don't think that makes him evil. I think he was weak, and perhaps despicable."

But the rage she feels still must be boiling underneath? No, she claims, she hasn't felt much anger. She feels mostly pity.

And then, of course, all children feel they are responsible for what happens to them, because if the *adult* were responsible, the burden would be too much for any child to bear. This father, the money-earner, the household ruler—if *he* is unstable, what protection does a child have?

And you can't get angry at him, because his rage in return would bring down the universe.

So you practice detachment. You Smile for Daddy. And you service men.

If all children chronically overestimate their responsibility for the weird things adults do, little girls commonly exaggerate that overestimation to the point where the responsibility overwhelms them completely.

Psychoanalysts call this "identifying with the aggressor," which is an elegant and abstract way of saying you *become* the other person. Daddy takes over.

Identifying with the aggressor is what made it possible for witches, for instance, to accuse themselves and decide they deserved to be burnt. It happens to men, brainwashed by North Koreans or North Vietnamese or their Marine drill sergeants. It happened to Patty Hearst in her closet. Daughter of a powerful man who seems to have been a rather passive Daddy, she succumbed to a more aggressive powerful Daddy in Cinque, the revolutionary, and took over his vision, the identity he prepared for her. It happened to the girls in Charles Manson's "Family," who gladly murdered for him.

It is much easier for little girls to lose themselves in this service relationship to an aggressor than it is for little boys, and the reason is simple. Boys aren't generally asked to serve. They are asked to imitate Daddy because someday they will become him.

The difference is crucial.

If a little boy sees himself through Daddy's eyes, he knows that someday he will be a man like Daddy, will have a similar vision of the world. When a little girl is asked to Smile for Daddy, she waits for *his* response. She has become, at the beginning of her life, what Simone de Beauvoir calls the Other—the Second Sex, defined by men, with no distinct vision of its own with which to see the world.

He's Not Sexy, He's My Father

Abby and Calvin Bartlett

*C*alvin Bartlett is having a very good time with his daughter, Abby, "Fourteen going on twenty-eight" and ripening into adolescence, first stop on the fast train into adult sexuality.

"I find her adolescence delicious, delightful, and problematic," he says. "It is definitely a whole new phase of fathering, and so far, each new phase has been better than the one before."

Calvin is as different from D. W. Opal as it is possible to imagine. He is the sophisticated father Callie would love to have had, the one she is trying to catch up on by having affairs with Europeans. And, unlike Blaise's father, with whom he shares at least the nominal status of upper-middle-class urban-cultivated WASP male, Calvin is an integrated man, a grownup who knows the difference between a grown woman and a girl—however sexy the girl might be.

He is a tall man, with hair going just a bit gray at the temples, urbane and rather more elegant than one expects a college professor to be; he wears shining black dress shoes instead of suede boots, and his tweed jacket is both well cut and new. As we talk, he chain-smokes, and we are interrupted frequently by his secretary with papers for him to sign, or with a phone call he really ought to take. He seems to be an accessible man.

He is also a dominant male.

But his wife, Joan, is a feminist who teaches in the Women's Studies Department of a college just outside the southern city where the Bartletts live in a renovated townhouse, part of a thriving urban redevelopment program. They chose the city after years in the suburbs, where Joan was a full-time mother and housewife. Now the children (Abby's brother Dan is seventeen; the oldest boy, nineteen, is away at college) are pressed into service for daily chores, and Calvin's dominance is being reshaped to accommodate the visions of independent women.

Sort of.

For instance: Calvin is extremely busy, with classes and administration of a large university art department, as well as a guest museum curatorship. His life is full of meetings, programs, symposia, openings, program planning, student conferences. He doesn't always get home in time for dinner, but like any father, "He always expects the food to be on the table when he comes home," says Abby. "My brother and I have to make dinner because my Mom works. It's a little hard sometimes, and I get a bit aggravated, because they're not home that much. Sometimes he comes home too late, and we'll already have eaten, and he'll be a little mad. He thinks we should wait, but we can't; we're hungry."

Abby is very pretty. She is still slightly pudgy, squared off with baby fat, but the corners are melting and her face is emerging soft and womanly, with her father's determined mouth and her mother's thick, wavy brown hair. She is a horseback rider of show-ring caliber, and her father goes to see her compete whenever he can.

When I ask Calvin about how he feels, watching Abby in the ring, his answer is a nice mix of that double vision fathers have of daughters. Abby is very definitely *his* daughter, but she is also his *daughter*.

"It's extraordinary," he says, "to see this little creature up on that enormous beast, in such total and absolute control." Compared to six-feet-two Calvin, Abby at five feet literally is tiny. But what a sexy image, a daughter on a horse!

Calvin, unlike D. W. Opal, has looked his sexuality straight in the face and accepts it. Which means that, also unlike D.W., Calvin accepts his daughter's sexuality, too.

But more: Calvin Bartlett is actually able to acknowledge to himself the fact that his daughter's body inspires sexual fantasies. This is a rare father. Rarer yet, he can tell me this, quite calmly.

"She is," he says, "an attractive young lady in a physical sense. It's fascinating. There are times when I can have physical thoughts about her. I know it's nothing more than a fantasy, but I'll find myself thinking, 'Yes, that's a very good-looking young girl.' I'm sure she knows it, absolutely, and cherishes it, and plays with it."

Does she, I ask, flirt with him?

"Sure," he says, without hesitation. "In her own way, absolutely. I don't think it's conscious, but sure. She comes down with the hairdo of the day, or the clothes of the day, and she wants to be damn sure it's been noticed."

Does he notice?

Calvin's "Yes" comes in a tone that says, "How could you doubt?" He thought it was "delicious" when Abby began experimenting with makeup. "A month or so ago we took Dan and Abby to the theatre and I couldn't believe I was sitting next to this young lady in stockings and high heels. It was a very special sort of pride, and I guess I was also thinking, 'Wow—that's a very nice pair of legs.' She was still all of her youthful, ebullient self, but at the same time she was all dolled up, like a little lady."

Abby, coming into awareness of her sexuality in a relationship with this dominant and extremely attractive male, is a good deal more guarded in her own assessment of the situation. "Flirting" is not a word she would use to describe any of her behavior with her father. In fact, she interprets the term "little lady" quite differently.

"I am his little lady—I think in his eyes I'm not fully grown yet. I'm his little girl."

That's a safe spot for a daughter who, while she hasn't yet had her first period, is still beginning to be disturbingly aware of the sexual currents between herself and her father. For her, the need is to minimize or deny them altogether. It is all still too new, too overwhelming.

The father is the one who really needs to be aware of what is going on. For two reasons: one, so he can deal with his response to his daughter's sexuality; and two, so he can give her the seal of approval that will enable her to feel her sexuality is okay, part of herself, not just something to be turned on or off, or faked, in response to a male initiative, but a good thing on its own terms.

This means he has got to let her flirt with him, test out her attractiveness on him, without responding in kind.

Neither D. W. Opal nor Blaise's father could do these things. Blaise's father had given up on adult male sexuality a long time ago, when he came to Blaise for child-sex, so safe. When she hit adolescence, he could not let her go to grow up and away from him.

D.W. hung on in his own way, too. He had to deny Callie's sexuality to protect himself from the conflicts his inevitable attraction to her stirred up.

But the choice doesn't have to be between incest and disapproval. A father like Calvin Bartlett can occupy a middle ground. He can respond to his adolescent daughter just enough to tell her he approves of her developing femininity and finds her attractive. At the same time, his self-control tells her he is a "safe" male; she need not fear that he will be provoked into too strong a response. This will, of course, encourage her to direct her efforts to attract a male elsewhere, as she should. It will also help her gain confidence both in herself and in a man's potential for self-control.

This middle path, which the psychoanalyst Marjorie Leonard calls "desexualized affection," is very difficult for fathers like Callie's and Blaise's, men who have never really learned to be comfortable with themselves, never integrated bodies and minds, reality and fantasy.

In fact, the real key to a father's turning off may be that he has never learned the difference between fantasy and action.

Then, too, he has probably been brought up to believe that he is not responsible for his own sexuality. After all, he can't control the times when he gets an erection, can he? And the thought that possibly he might start feeling a physical response while sitting next to his daughter panics him.

So, he turns off, and his daughter pays the price. Cut off from his own sexuality, afraid to experience it, he cuts her off from hers, too—thereby making it very hard for her to learn any confidence in her own sexuality. And because sexual self-confidence is related to other forms of self-confidence and assertion, he may be preventing her from developing confidence in her ability to achieve successfully, too. In short, he will pass along to her his own problems with love and work.

Even Calvin, who clearly *does* know that a fantasy is not the same thing as an action, is not entirely comfortable with his awareness of Abby's attractiveness. When I ask him, he hesitates before he says, slowly, "Y-e-e-s—in the main. I think there are times when one spins a fantasy a little bit further than any kind of action would ever follow. . . . The other night I came home and she was bouncing around in shorty pajamas, and I took a look at her and I don't know what was in my eye but she said, 'Daddy! These are pajamas, not *panties!'* There must have been something in the look."

To know the difference between fantasy and act, to be able to admit the fantasy and yet control the act, is to be grown up. It also means a father is able to grant a daughter her own sexual identity. Abby feels very secure in her father's physical affection, and in his respect for her need for new boundaries now that she is older.

"Daddy was always physically affectionate," she says. "I still sometimes sit on his lap—like at the dinner table, after we've all eaten, and he wants me to scratch his back.

"But it's changed because I've grown up. There's not as much playfulness. I can't get on his back for piggyback, I'm a little too big. And he respects me as growing up and maturing."

Abby sees her father as basically shy, and her brothers as just like him. She and her father agree that she, like her mother, is an extrovert. For her father, Abby has been something of an education, perhaps, in closeness.

"She's never lacked for contact," he says. "Hugging and holding are a natural way of life for her."

With his sons, though, he was more reserved. He told me that he and they have grown much more demonstrative as the boys have grown older. "We've gone from stiff handshakes to big teddybear hugs."

Is it possible that the freedom to be physically affectionate with his outgoing, impulsive daughter has carried over into physical affection with his sons, enabling Calvin Bartlett to overcome the ancient strictures against American males touching each other except in sports or war?

It's a nice idea.

Calvin is very sensitive to the possibility of a need for greater reserve with his daughter as she develops. He says, "We still kiss and embrace, the way we always have—I don't know whether either of us, later, will resist a lip kiss, or an embrace."

He will watch and see, and be sensitive to his daughter's needs.

Yet he remains the dominant male, and his daughter has a lively awareness of the realities of the power structure in her family. When it comes to domestic money matters like allowances for the kids, for instance, Calvin diplomatically describes the process in which his two younger children negotiate for a raise: "I guess ultimately I have the final word, but I manage to work it out so we all agree."

But Abby says flatly, "He controls the money."

She also has a subtle appreciation of the relationship of money and power. "My Mom," she says, "has a separate savings and checking account with her money. If one of them had to lose their job it would be my Mom, because she gets paid less."

She sees that "their jobs are equally important to themselves," but thinks that "he has more power. He always showed more power in dealing with us. My Mom was always there to go shopping, and she's still around more, even with working. In that way, dominance would go to my Mom, because my father is not around as much. But my respect for my Mom is more love than respect for power, because when my father comes home he's more forceful. If you don't do something you should do, for instance, my Mom will get up and do it herself. But if my father says, 'Would you do this?' and you say, 'No,' he'll say, 'Yes you will.' "

Where does feminism come into this picture? Calvin and Abby have slightly different views:

"I'm not sure," says Calvin, "how aware of feminism Abby is. Yes, in theory, of course—we've discussed the ERA and so on. But as to what it really means, I don't know. She hasn't experienced anything of the marketplace—the prejudices, the lack of a network."

"When I was little," says Abby, "my father wanted a wife in the kitchen. My mother didn't work. He would sit around and watch the baseball games and drink beer, and wouldn't take care of us. My Mom had to. That's just the way it was in the sixties."

Calvin has now been educated into feminism: "I'm very positive about what is happening to women today. Joan is involved with her classes, and in the family there is a strong atmosphere of my support for her work. I think that kind of support from men is going to be stronger in Abby's generation."

But Abby, the daughter, sees also the secret, inside part of her father's relationship to women—and so to feminism—and she suspects it's not all that simple:

"My father has always been aware, and he's always helped my Mom, and he likes her to work because it brings in more money. But sometimes I think he's chauvinist because of the things he says, and one thing I don't respect him for is his playfulness about it. Like I'll talk about Genuine Risk, the filly, losing the Kentucky Derby, and he'll say, 'Oh, that's just natural for a woman, she belongs in the house.' I know he's only kidding, but sometimes I think it may be what he feels inside. I mean I would love to go out and work and have my husband stay home and do all the housework."

Along with Calvin's dominance comes the traditional male prerogative of teasing: the teasing that is often, with fathers as with older brothers, a mode of intrusion, an intrusion that is in effect a gentle remainder of dominance, a hint of control.

For instance, Abby tells me, "I talk on the phone a lot and sometimes he'll answer the phone and say, 'Hello, Abby Bartlett's residence.' Or he might get on the phone while I'm talking and say, 'You have three minutes left.'"

It's all in fun, of course; but still, as Abby points out, "That intrudes on what I want to say and on my life, because if I have to cut the call short people will think I don't care about them."

Abby sees Calvin as the enforcer of the rules in the family, even though her mother may actually make them, and Calvin agrees, seeing himself as stricter than his wife, although if there is "anything major, we work it out together." What he cares more about is "moment-to-moment behavior"; "Don't eat with your fingers," or "Stop that."

Yet when it comes to a large matter like Abby's freedom, Calvin is infinitely more sensitive than Callie's father was. The protection that a dominant male traditionally extends to the females in his care does not, here, extend automatically to the kind of "repression for her own good" offered by fathers like D.W.

Here is the problematic part of fathering an adolescent girl. What do you do, for instance, about her need to feel some freedom to travel around a city that, like any other city, has its dangers?

"I'm torn," he says. "Yes, absolutely I'm concerned when she's out, and we set limits—when she comes back, how she should travel. That's life in the city. But I don't want to structure it so tightly that she isn't free. So far she hasn't had any negative experiences, and I have only talked to her a little about possible dangers. Once she saw a flasher, and she was a little upset, but she was with a bunch of girls, so they all made light of it. Her mother talked to her later, about having the same kind of experience.

"We have tried to foster confidence in her ability to move around, by both cab and public transportation. Again, where that's going to be when she's more physically mature, in two or three years, I don't know."

In the best of circumstances, male protectiveness is translated into tenderness, caring, cherishing, and concern for a daughter's experience. In short, a concern for her integration of mind, body, and emotions.

Abby is moving into relationships with boys with a light heart: "My father knows I go out with boys; I've been going out since sixth grade. We go out pretty much in groups of boys and girls. You might have a date, but the two of you would be together in the group. We don't say 'going out,' that's a form of going steady. My parents don't understand that. We don't use 'steady' anymore. I guess steady is when you're older.

"He'll pick up boys' names, so if I say I talked on the phone, he'll say, 'Who was it, Tom, Bob, John?' He's very aware of that. But he doesn't say, 'I want to meet Bob.' I see lots of people, and when they meet him, he just says 'Hi.' He won't take them aside and tell them all about my life, or anything.

"He's aware that if he embarrasses me, I'll tell him."

Intimidation is not an aspect of Calvin's dominance. On the other hand, confidences of an intimate kind are not part of Abby's relationship with him.

Is it the sheer or simple sexual difference that makes a daughter reluctant to confide in a father? Or is it the addition of the distance that power gives the authority figure, while a mother is more about "love than respect for power," in Abby's words?

"I have not," says Calvin, "really discussed sexuality with her. She and Joan have talked—you know, Mom-daughter. She's had a couple of good biology and sex-education courses in school. And talk is fairly free at home; there are no real constraints. God knows" (here a nervous cough, the male ill at ease on alien turf) "what goes on between her and her girlfriends."

Abby remembers: "When I was little, about fourth grade, I was friends with a boy. We would go over to each other's houses and stuff. And even today my father will still remark about that boy. It's harassing, because sometimes it's a pain, but it's funny, too. He'll always remember. Like in the car the other day he said, 'How is your boyfriend?' It's neat, it's funny, it's a good relationship—but I'd rather confide in my Mom, because my father will always remark on that boy in the fourth grade."

Even the gentlest of male intrusiveness can be a barrier to the impulse to confide.

Abby's method is to tell her mother, with full knowledge that her father will thereby find out. "He'll know," she says, "when I start menstruating. I'll probably tell my Mom, and she'll tell him, and he'll make a remark, like, 'Oh, you're a lady now.' It'll be a little embarrassing, but I'll understand."

The male, the father, is, after all, eternally outside these mysteries.

And what of the greater mystery of sex itself, the still future sex life of a daughter, the sex life she will have and he won't share, that will be a sign of her growth up and away and out from his house, his protection, his responsibility?

Calvin is refreshingly honest about his visceral reaction, which is definitely the reaction of the male-in-charge: "The thought of anybody putting a hand on her, molesting her—even the thought of that first physical experience with someone else—I've often said, 'I'll kill him!' "

And then he laughs, and remembers he is also a civilized father, able to deal with the realities of life, concerned with his daughter as a person, not just, in the ancient atavistic way, as male property: "I don't think I really will kill anyone, but I just hope it's a very happy experience for her, as it should be."

What, I ask, if she were to have a first affair as early as high school, no remote possibility these days? Again, Calvin is honest about the ambivalence involved in a feminist-educated, liberal male's response to the new sexual freedom when it might apply to his own daughter.

"I'd probably," he says, "have a mixed reaction. Intellectually, I'd say, 'Fine. You know how to take care of yourself, and as long as you do— and as long as it isn't emotionally injurious—fine. Enjoy it. That's what the body's all about.'

"How far that gets translated into the reality that this is my own daughter, I really don't know. I would hope I would be able to make that translation."

But in fact Abby has no plans to test her father in this way. "I would have sex," she says, "when I'm older, when I'm around eighteen."

How does she think her father will react?

"I think he would understand, and he would respect me. He wouldn't say, 'Get out of my house.' He would just want to make sure I really liked—loved—the boy."

Would she be likely to tell him?

"I think I would talk with my Mom. I would rather have her tell him."

The distance is necessary for a daughter, who needs to grow up and away from a father whose presence cannot fail to be overwhelming. He was the first man in her life, the first male to whom she felt sexually drawn—the male, in fact, with whom she developed her whole sense of heterosexual being. This male and no other was the first set of sexual stimuli to which she responded. Coded into her body-memory are his signs: the color and texture of his hair, his eyes, his skin. The style of his clothes. His height. The precise gesture of his hands when she goes to him to be hugged. The feel of his hands against her back. The length and width of his fingers, the size of his palms, the tightness of his grip when he lifts her up.

Whom she marries, whom she lives with, whom she casually sleeps with—each of these men will be measured, in some deep internal place of which even she may not be aware, against these signals.

Daddy was, for her, the original sexy male, whatever his charm or lack of it to the outside eye, the eye that was educated on some other shape or style of Daddy.

But now she is older and her adoration for her father presents her with some conflicts. She knows she needs to grow beyond Daddy, to a man of her own. She feels a strong identification with her mother, and a new closeness based on the female sexual mysteries her father cannot share. She *likes* her mother.

And here is this intrusive, powerful male, a father, and he loves her. Sometimes it's too much. It can be a blessing, at this age, that a father does work, is away from home so much.

"Now that I'm older," says Abby, "I like my privacy, and I don't mind him being away as much. Life would be a lot harder if he were around, because he would always be demanding things, 'Get me this, get me that.'"

The pride that Calvin feels when he finds himself out in the evening with this blossoming daughter carries more of a burden for Abby, because the intensity of her emotion, her side of the relationship, is not yet much diffused by relationships with other men, other contexts. So she has mixed feelings about his evident pleasure in her.

"Sometimes when he takes me out, he'll say, 'This is my daughter,' and I can see that he's happy that I am who I am, that I'm not an ugly child. That's cruel to say. I mean, I can see sometimes that he's happy that I'm maturing, that I have a bright smile—"

"That you're attractive?" I sum it up.

"Well, yes."

"Does that make you feel good?" I ask.

"Sometimes," says Abby. "And sometimes I wish he'd just leave me alone. He'll say, 'This is my beautiful daughter, Abby.' It embarrasses me, because I'm just a normal person, although in his eyes I'm a very special person. I wish he'd keep that a little more private, let people see for themselves."

As for Calvin's sexiness—Abby isn't ready for that at all.

Daughters have to deny that their fathers are sexy because Daddy has too much power. If the passionate attachment of childhood continues beyond adolescence, it becomes very hard for a daughter to grow up emotionally and find her own boundaries. It is similar to a daughter's earlier need to deny an attachment to Mother, who was, in infancy, an overwhelming physical and emotional presence and power in her daughter's life. Then, the daughter had to move out and away from Mother to Daddy, who carried the promise of freedom. Now, in adolescence, the daughter has to move out and away from her father.

"My Mom," says Abby, "thinks my father is sexy, but I'm not too sure. He has a lot of friends, but I don't think they see him as sexy, just as a man, a teacher, a friend—a nice man.

"Sometimes he's sexy to my mother when I'm around, but he's not to me—he's my father. I couldn't see my father as being sexy."

Save Me the Waltz:

Fathers, Daughters, and Sexuality

A friend of mine recently went to a wedding. At the reception, after the bride and groom had danced together for the first time in their married lives, the father of the bride took his daughter in his arms and swung her onto the floor. Slowly, gravely, they moved in a spiral, the circle of the waltz looping into the circle of the dance floor, swoop and glide, stately and elaborate.

It is a ritual performed thousands of times a year. The father has just given his daughter away to another man.

Even so, reports my friend, as they danced, "all the sexual energy in the room flowed between the father and daughter. There was a sense of hopelessness—and a great beauty."

If the mystique of perfect love is at the heart of the father-daughter relationship, behind the mystique lies sex.

In the long dance between fathers and daughters, sex—and the avoidance of sex—provides the energy, the cadence, and the pace.

The First Steps of the Dance

From the moment he knows what his daughter's sex is, Daddy reacts to her as a sexed being, a female. In her infancy, he flirts with her, tells her how gorgeous she is, what big blue eyes she has. He feels her to be infinitely more in need of his protection than her brother.

He begins to create his ideal little woman.

Fathers can have what feels like a disturbingly erotic response to their infant daughters—a response they may hide behind a whole repertory of attitudes and feelings.

First, as tiny babies, active toddlers, little girls surely are above all innocent. No shadow of sexuality can have crossed our minds, disturbed our small bodies.

Because if we are innocent, then so too, in his love for us, is he. At the dawn of his own early history, he found out that his devoted love for his mother, his own first passionate attachment, was forbidden. Loving us he is, at last, absolved of oedipal guilt, like Oedipus himself, who, exiled after discovering that he had married his mother and murdered his father (the first, at least, still commonly the wish of three-year-old boys), found peace with his devoted daughter, Antigone.

Yet the currents of sexuality run deep, and there are many degrees of sexual awareness. Just as a mother is likely to be quite aware of the sexuality of her infant son, so a father will be aware of the sexuality of his daughter.

This awareness makes him tender, seductive, but not too seductive. He woos us, he flirts with us, but he doesn't go too far, doesn't fall toward sex. He doesn't *want* that—only the delight, the emotional bond, the warmth, the cuddling, the laughter.

When small, we are the beneficiaries of this sublimated delight. It makes our fathers see us as very special, makes them adore us. And behind the sublimation, usually enough eroticism comes through so that we are, as we must be, "seduced" into femininity, into heterosexuality.

We may be aroused by him at a very early age. According to Dr. John Munder Ross, clinical associate professor of psychiatry at Downstate Medical Center and a noted psychoanalytic theorist in New York City who has participated in several studies of father-child interaction and has written extensively on fathers and fathering, daughters are noticeably excited by fathers by the time they are a year old. If a man walks into an observational center where there are infants of both sexes, says Dr. Ross, "the boys will be very interested in him but the girls will be turned on, and start exhibiting and flirting."

As a daughter gets older, at two and a half or three, she will love to lean against her father or sit in his lap, molding her body to his, feeling the sensual closeness all along her own length. She will engage him face to face, and he her, both of them using eye contact, both of them flirting.

A daughter's heterosexual eroticism, points out Dr. Lora Heims Tessman, a clinical psychologist at M.I.T. and in the private practice of psychotherapy with adults and children in Massachusetts, grows out of the pleasure she takes in the relationship with her father. If she is lucky, then, she begins her first heterosexual fantasies in the context of pleasure and excitement. And part of her pleasure may involve fantasies of perfect mutuality, of "the erotic coming together of differences."

Lucky Daddy. He can capitalize on whatever discontent a little girl feels with her mother, whatever *lack* she felt in that original symbiosis, that may not have been as blissful as she wished. Now comes Daddy, with new possibilities for fitting together. And if he is loving, if he shows enough warmth and approval of his daughter's excitement, she will slip easily into heterosexual femininity.

Lucky daughter. A loving father can flesh out her world of love.

Of course, a daughter's first love object was her mother, and she doesn't really reject her when she turns to Daddy. At two or so, she still has erotic feelings for her mother, and they don't disappear completely; instead, they may form the basis for future warm, close relationships with other women. When she discovers her new feelings toward Daddy—or rather, when her long-established excitement becomes erotic—what she does, in Dr. Tessman's words, is to "add the father to her repertoire" to make a triangle, the oedipal triangle.

And as her response to him becomes, from about two-and-a-half to three-and-a-half, increasingly erotic (by three or four some girls experience distinct "inner genital" sensations), as she expresses her "active loving exuberance," Daddy's loving approval tells her, unconsciously, that her sexuality is a good thing. This early relationship with him will form the foundation for her ability, as an adult, to combine sex with intimacy: to form, in short, a long-lasting pleasure bond with a man. And the small girl's fantasies of having Daddy's baby are a rehearsal for adult life, just as a small boy's fantasies of marrying Mother are.

So a girl's love is active from the beginning. Yet there is that other, quieter element as well. And our urge to mold ourselves to Daddy was certainly one factor that led Freud and his early followers to define women as passive in every part of their lives.

Psychoanalysis was following a cultural prescription, and a favorite male fantasy (the more passive she is, the more active, read masculine, *he* is). By the 1950's we were being told that a real woman, a proper woman, was always passive.

The absurdity of this pronouncement, made as it was to girls who were growing up to drive cars and go to college, even if they didn't yet expect actually to use their educations, was part of what underlay both feminism and the great backlash against psychoanalysis.

But it is time to see that one reason the prescription was so effective for so long is that it exploits a small piece of reality. We are very vulnerable to assuming a passive position next to Daddy. He is the one who will take care of us, defend us against Mommy and other enemies, pay for our designer jeans, make sure we get into the right schools and meet the right kinds of men.

We are vulnerable partly because, biologically, we want to attract, to receive, to draw a man to us and, ultimately, inside us. To a little girl, a father's penis looks powerful, and perhaps a little scary; it's also attached to the man who represents independence and excitement. It's not hard to see how, with a little push from a mean Daddy, we could fall into masochistic fantasies. Nor is it hard to see why so many of us get hooked on power and want to have sex with powerful men, whether rock stars or Presidents.

With the arrival of feminism we have begun to see ourselves as active, rather than passive, in our sexuality. To draw a man in is active; "to be penetrated," the clinical term, is passive, and sounds rather brutal. But the potential for that fatal passivity is always there. It is all too easy for Daddy to capitalize on it—as, for instance, Blaise's father did, when he taught her to respond to his needs, to serve him. And if Mother thinks that she, too, has to serve Daddy, then a daughter may fall right into the pattern of passive dependency on men.

The Dark Side of Daddy's Love

A father's first, gut reaction to a new baby is physical, narcissistic, self-identifying. Why else do all men, Dr. Ross believes, want, deep down, to have sons? A son is an extension of the male self, a form of immortality.

A daughter can create a problem of identification right away on the deepest level: the physical, biological level that is the bedrock of gender identity. It all depends, says Dr. Ross, "on his own history and his ability to accept and integrate feminine identifications into his overall sexual identity."

And this is the basis for the conflict a father has, and passes on to his daughters: the conflict between his response to *his* daughter, the person with whom he can identify, and his *daughter,* the female, who may seem alien or even defective but who is in any event different, the Other. She represents no part of a man's own identity; rather, she represents polar opposites, the whole collection of feminine gender characteristics he was taught to avoid in order to become a man.

It may be that feelings like these will cause him, in reaction, to see his daughter as all the more fragile and beautiful and, possibly, ethereal—a little being who is set apart from the general female failings of messiness and incompleteness.

If he is a fairly controlling sort of man, he will not want to have anything to do with some aspects of her body. When diapering involved her feces, if he was a traditional father he would often call for her mother. This happened also, of course, if the baby was a boy, and for both son and daughter such fatherly disgust may have translated later on into unconscious disgust for other uncontrollable outpourings—feelings, for instance, and menstrual blood.

A daughter may feel this disgust about herself, because she absorbs the masculine equation of "female" with "lack of control." And if, as a baby and toddler, she experiences a controlling father's disapproval of her erotic excitement, she may, points out Dr. Tessman, associate her internal excitement with "badness," with a "feeling of intolerable excitement." She may fear that her "inner feelings are out of control," and come to fear her own sexuality. Later in life, all of this can make it difficult for her to let go of her self-control sufficiently to experience the release of orgasm.

Such a father will value his masculinity as a form of control over his feelings, over his body, and over women. All these will threaten him.

A father who is not quite as well adjusted as Calvin Bartlett—who has not integrated his femininity into his whole self-image, who has not learned the difference between sexual fantasy and sexual act, and who fears the apparently uncontrollable nature of his own sexuality—such a father is going to suffer from sexual overload in relation to his daughter. He is going to have to fend off this overload, as D. W. Opal did, with various strategies.

One strategy, unfortunately, according to Dr. Ross, is to "avoid or disparage" her at the "critical point" when she is developing her "feminine sexual identity and basically male object choice." To reject her, in other words, when she most needs his approval and warmth.

The evidence suggests that a father's warmth and love are very important for heterosexual development. In studies, homosexual women have described their fathers variously as cold, rejecting, belittling, and frightening. Fathers have also been described as "possessive and infantilizing," which suggests that a too-intense father relationship can be as destructive as an unloving one.

Recent evidence also shows that infants may have a genetically determined predisposition toward heterosexuality or homosexuality. Nature plays a part as well as nurture, but parents are still a powerful influence. And mothers are no longer considered to be solely or even mainly responsible for how their children develop.

"In general," writes Dr. Henry Biller, Professor of Psychology at the University of Rhode Island and author of many books and articles on fathering, "available research has suggested that inadequate fathering is more of a factor in the development of female homosexuality than inadequate mothering is."

It makes sense that Daddy has a role. Our first intimate physical relationship is usually, after all, with a woman, whether our mother or a nurse. If Daddy is rotten, we don't have much incentive to move away from that first intimacy into a new and different kind. With such a Daddy, any little girl could find it safer, more comforting, and more pleasurable to maintain her erotic attachment to her mother and, subsequently, to other women. She would simply fail to add Daddy to her repertoire.

Not incidentally, the kind of fathering that produces securely masculine sons is also warm, involved, and nurturing. Most men worry about the kind of masculine "image" they will provide for their sons, as if their job consisted solely in providing a role model for their sons to imitate. This is a convenient notion, of course, because it fits in comfortably with the traditional idea of Daddy's noninvolvement with his children. Daddy is busy working—and he *should* be, because that is the appropriate masculine image he expects his son to emulate.

But sons need an incentive to turn away from Mother, too, something to replace that warm physical intimacy they had with her.

Like Calvin Bartlett, too many fathers are inhibited in showing warmth to their sons. In extreme cases, fathers reject their sons altogether, and this may be a more powerful incitement to homosexuality than the overpowering mother, who has been blamed so often for destroying her sons' masculinity. Sons who blame their mothers might begin to ask instead: Where was Daddy?

The father who can't cope with his response to his daughter might also do what many men do with women, relate to her only as a sex object.

As Dr. Ross puts it, he will "eroticize" the relationship: "Fathers exhibit themselves to little girls all the time—they pee, they take showers with them—they are uninterested in them except in terms of a sexualized kind of relationship. That is one thing you do see."

How does this relieve a father's anxiety? If he is anxious about sexuality, this constant erotic focus is his way of acting out (and so, temporarily, relieving) his anxiety. It can also be a way of keeping a distance between himself and his daughter: by emphasizing *only* the sexual aspects of her—and his—personality, he avoids dealing with troublesome emotional questions like why he feels he can only relate to a female in this way. (Similarly, pornography and sex shows create a distance between men and adult women.)

Such a father's eroticizing stops short of actual incest; but Daddy's exhibitionism is highly seductive, and because of his size and the size of his genitals, more than a little overpowering. A daughter who is exposed to it may grow up prone to eroticize all her relationships with men. But where a man who relates to women only as sex objects can still function quite well in the male world of work, a woman will have problems—she will be seductive where it's not appropriate, for instance. Or she may not even perceive her power to arouse men sexually as real power; she may feel frightened and overwhelmed by it. Such a fear could also lead her to avoid heterosexual love.

On the other hand, it may be that many fathers who start out this way do at a certain point (usually about the time a daughter falls in love with them) begin to feel the need for reticence. They become aware, as one father put it, of just how much they are "turning on" their daughter, and they retreat, stop taking showers with her or parading around naked in front of her. The only trouble with this is that they may be retreating because their daughter's newly emerging sexuality frightens them; so they may also withdraw the affection and approval she needs.

Still, retreat is preferable to incest.

It is a very interesting fact about incest that most of it begins, not when a girl has reached puberty and become sexy, but rather when she is between eight and twelve, before puberty.

In *Sexually Victimized Children,* David Finklehor sees two peak periods when girls seem to be especially vulnerable: at eight, and again between ten and twelve. Pre-adolescent girls, while sexy to a certain kind of man (like Humbert Humbert in Vladimir Nabokov's novel *Lolita*) and certainly themselves curious about sex, are too naive and inexperienced to be able to avoid or fend off the advances of an older male, particularly since he is likely to be someone the girl is already close to: a brother, a father, an uncle.

Finklehor's sample was not large—530 women college students who went to a variety of New England colleges, were mostly white, and had family backgrounds ranging from working-class to upper middle-class, in a wide range of ethnic-religious mixes. But he tests out his information against that of other studies, so his conclusions are provocative.

Nearly one fifth of these women had been sexually victimized before they were eighteen—*over half of those by adult men when they themselves were under twelve.* (By contrast, less than a tenth of the 266 college men in the study reported any sexual victimization up to age eighteen.)

Other estimates of sexual abuse of girls show that *as many as a quarter of all girls in America are victimized by someone—most often by adult men when the girls themselves are pre-adolescent. And most of these men are relatives or friends of the family.* (Eighty-three percent of the boys' experiences, by contrast, had been with acquaintances or strangers.)

How many of these girls were victimized by their fathers? Finklehor found that a little over 1 percent of the 530 women had experienced incest with fathers or stepfathers.

One percent sounds like a very small number, but Finklehor puts it into an interesting perspective: ". . . it means that approximately three quarters of a million women eighteen and over in the general population have had such an experience, and that another 16,000 cases are added each year from among the group of girls aged five to seventeen."

In addition, the women in Finklehor's sample cited incest with brothers as the most frequent—39 percent of all the incest reported. If a brother is a great deal older than a sister, he has much of the authority of a father; in Finklehor's sample, *almost half of these brothers were adolescent or adult, while the girls were most often nine or ten.*

Finally, *not one* of Finklehor's college men reported incest with his mother. Truly, "For girls . . . the family would appear to be a more sexually dangerous area."

Indeed, as scholars have begun to point out, the facts refute Freud's theory that the sexual hysterics who made up most of his patients in early-twentieth-century Vienna were simply having sexual fantasies or delusions when they reported to him that they had been sexually abused by their fathers.

What makes thousands of fathers a year decide to release their sexual urges upon their pre-adolescent daughters' bodies?

It appears that male dominance is a big factor.

Normally, a father copes with his sexual overload by stressing his daughter's innocence, her nonsexuality. This creates a good defense against incest because it brings out a father's desire to protect his innocent little daughter from predatory males, including himself. It also allows him to keep up a mild flirtation, safely within bounds, enough to let his daughter know her sexuality is okay.

The protection bond is the traditional, socially approved father-daughter bond. It is the way a father has been expected to "nurture," by providing for his daughter so she can live safely and comfortably (today, by earning money) rather than by being directly responsive to her emotional needs. (That is the mother's job.)

By undertaking, so to speak, to protect his daughter's innocence, a father forges a bond that is difficult for him to break. Why? Because, as the anthropologists Robin Fox and Lionel Tiger argue persuasively, one kind of bond tends to drive out another. The same thing happens when a couple has children and then finds it difficult to keep up an exciting sex life. They have created a parenting bond that tends to drive out their original sexual bond.

A father who commits incest is refusing the protection-of-innocence bond to which his small daughter is entitled and is perceiving her, instead, as a sexually available female in his possession.

Male dominance is also the reason that mother-son incest is so rare. The dominance of males over females is a more powerful factor than the incest taboo, which is relatively weak where fathers and daughters are concerned. It also takes precedence over the mother's age dominance relative to her son.

And the fact that Daddy is on the Outside, leading his daughter away from Mother, means that somewhere deep in the unconscious of both men and women, his incest is less a sin than hers. A mother's incest with a son will keep the son tied to her; a father is only doing what some other male will eventually do. And if a daughter is not supposed to become independent it doesn't, as I pointed out in the story of Blaise, matter anyway.

And then, after all, she is a *sexy* little beast.

"She made me do it," says the incestuous father, or the seducer, or even the rapist. "What could I do? I'm only a man. I couldn't help myself."

Here it is: projection. Throughout history, men have projected their own sexuality onto girls and women.

Women are responsible for man's sexuality. Men are not.

We have all grown up with this doctrine; After all, it is the first story in the Bible following the creation of the world. Eve, the temptress, the archetypal woman, seduces Adam out of his state of grace and innocence into sex. Without her, he would be happy! Jews and Christians share the story, Muslims share the attitude—it is why Muslim women are veiled from head to foot.

And, of course, if men are not responsible for their sexuality, any provocation at all can set them off. They can't help themselves.

So incest is her fault. Or, worse still, it doesn't exist at all. She is simply the victim of her own incestuous fantasies, as Freud decided his hysterical female patients were.

Stop the Music! My Waltz at Adolescence

I am going to a friend's daughter's Bas Mitzvah ceremony—a Jewish girl's coming-of-age celebration. She is thirteen, and, I think, this will be a good time to observe fathers and daughters together, at the moment when their relationship is changing forever, when he is about to lose his treasured, innocent little girl, and she is moving away from Daddy to other males—first to boys, then to men.

But these girls are so cool, so calm, so crisp in their long eyelet dresses, just a touch of mascara, a faint blush of lipstick. Their fathers are jovial, confident, grown up, proud of their daughters.

These daughters, I think, can't be feeling, inside, the feelings I remember at adolescence. They are too cool. I remember nausea, a sense of stifling heat, of suffocation. For the first time in my life, my sheer physical existence *burdened* me: the size of me, the heat of my body. My terror of sweat, of body odor.

The first time I menstruated, I was thirteen. I knew what it was, but I didn't want to admit it. I came in from playing outside on a summer's evening, dressed like a child in shorts and a T-shirt, and there on my underpants were the brown stains. I told my stepmother, she brought me the pad and the belt, I put them on—the ancient female ritual, passing along the lore and equipment of female sexuality from mother to daughter.

But I knew that what passed between us didn't really matter. I was surrounded by men and somehow they would find out. They always did.

I didn't have long to wait. At dinner that night my father made his announcement to my brothers: "Signe is a young lady, now. You're going to have to remember to treat her differently. You can't roughhouse with her the way you used to." Putting his mark on me.

Silence. I felt my body swelling—huge, bloated, obvious—to fill the space of that silence at the dinner table. There was never a word from my father to me. But he knew. They *all* knew. It was as though my insides, bloody, sweaty, dirty, disgusting, had been laid out on the table for them all to look at.

What did it mean? They would treat me differently. I could no longer disappear into games of make-believe, never again wrestle affectionately, unselfconsciously with a brother. Always I would be brought up short: *What do I look like? What does he see? What if he touches my breast?*

They became critical. My father told me every day, "If you could just see yourself as others see you," meaning I certainly didn't come up to the mark. "Ladies don't chew gum." "Don't cross your legs—do you want someone to see up your skirt?"

The atmosphere of hostility, of repressed sexuality, was palpable. My father's attitude toward me was one of reproach.

I had sexual-anxiety dreams, falling, falling backward into black space. I would sleep endlessly, hoping to miss Sunday breakfast, to miss everything. My father would come in to wake me up—sit on my bed, lean over me intimately. I am paralyzed. His hand caresses the back of my neck. I feel his breath on me. I can't move.

Yet I flirt with him. I pass his bedroom door, ajar as he settles in for a nap. I say something amusing, he smiles, I am dizzy with happiness. He noticed me, he approves of me, he likes me!

He fascinates me—literally. I am a moth circling around a flame. I desperately want him to compliment me, but he is all critical, forever noticing blackheads or baggy stockings. He warns me not to start shaving my legs. I will regret it, he says, because I will never be able to stop. He is right. But still, I sit on the edge of the tub to shave them while he is brushing his teeth.

We have a pact, my father and I, based on his deep need to see me as innocent despite his formal announcement of my arrival at puberty.

My father protected himself by projecting onto me his own version of the virgin/whore split. This is the classic device used by little boys to deal with their sexual overload in relation to their own mothers: the good, nonsexual mother becomes the model for the good women men like D. W. Opal marry when they grow up; the "bad," sexual mother becomes the prototype of the girls they sleep with. Alas for daughters, this double image is not only the most primitive but the most tenacious and deeply rooted picture of women that most men have. To some extent, it colors nearly every man's fantasies.

D. W.'s version emphasized the weakness and vulnerability of women; my father's focused on the woman as seductress, the whore.

If I close my eyes, I can hear him. He liked to tell a story at the dinner table. A woman is asked by a man if she would sleep with him for a million dollars. Of course, she says. What about ten thousand? She might consider it. Ten dollars? Of course not, what does he think she is—a whore?

We've already established what you are, the man says. Now we're just trying to establish the price.

A cruel story. It was a form of entrapment. Like too many fathers, mine equated love with money. Since his usual method was to withhold both, to offer me ten thousand dollars would be like saying he loved me *that much*. This would be a nearly irresistible lure for me. But, if I accepted, he would lose all his respect for me. I would be a whore for accepting his offer of what looked to both of us like love.

He would tell the story standing up at the head of the table as he liked to do, whether to carve the roast or take a stretch over coffee and liqueur. He would wave the carving knife or a fine Havana cigar as he spoke, and by the time I was twelve or fourteen he seemed to be looking at me with peculiar significance when he came to the punch line. Looking back, I think he was—although neither of us realized it consciously.

I didn't know that by telling his story, my father was condemning not only his attraction to me but his own sexuality. Child of a Victorian culture, he must have learned very early the fear and guilt he was displacing onto me. But the message I got was that my sexuality was a dangerous burden. If I allowed myself to accept the offer of a man's love, I would always be liable to wind up as the outcast, the whore. So, like Callie Opal, I grew up with an irreconcilable conflict between sex and love, sex and intimacy.

* * *

Fathers and daughters both suffer from their sexual overload; and if men project their own sexual confusion onto women, even onto their own daughters, women, as daughters and as girlfriends, lovers, and wives, all too often accept the responsibility. Many of us never do realize that the sexual problems of men are their own, that we have no more caused them than we can cure them. (We sometimes dream of that, too.)

Fathers have a difficult job. They have to accept their daughters' sexuality; even accept, however unconsciously, the fact that their daughters are sexy. Yet they have to resist their own attraction. Daddy is supposed to be a grownup, a protector. And in order to fill this role, it is natural for him to insist on innocence.

If he isn't too threatened by his own feminine side and can, like Calvin Bartlett, learn the difference between fantasy and act, he, too, can acknowledge his fantasies without either coming on to his daughter or turning off in what amounts to rejection. Yet he must, as a minimum, accept responsibility for his own sexuality and for approving of his daughter's.

Younger fathers, whose childhoods were less repressive and who have grown up in a generally freer time, are more likely to be able to handle their response to their daughters' sexuality than the fathers of Callie's or my generation were. More of them will be like Calvin Bartlett, and perceive their daughters as people who are sexual beings.

But this kind of flexibility and awareness is, alas, both recent and, as yet, rare.

Part Three

The Softball Player

Fran Nobile

*W*hen she was in the seventh grade, Fran Nobile wanted to play shortstop on the girls' softball team just started by the wealthy Boston suburb where her internist father had a group practice. He said No.

"I sobbed," she reports, "for a whole year. The next year I was allowed to play. And of course after that I went on to play softball all the more—I still play, on my radio-station team."

"It bothered me," says her father, "that the boys wouldn't have had enough places to play, because there weren't a lot of fields to play in and here there were six million little girls running around. My thought was that softball really isn't the best exercise for them—it isn't going to lead someplace, it isn't going to make them stronger in whatever they do, it isn't going to help them be leaders or anything else. They have to do other things, play tennis or golf, or ski. In my mind, softball and baseball and basketball are boys' games. I know there are girls' professional softball teams now, but to me it's a way that men have of expressing themselves. It's something that men should do, not girls."

Fran is twenty-seven, grown up and married now, but she has never forgotten that summer when he wouldn't let her play softball.

The way she sees her life, she has been engaged in a continuous struggle for identity in the face of her father's persistent definition of her and his clear vision of how she should live her life as a girl and woman. The struggle has been clarified and focused by what Fran perceives as her father's obvious favoritism toward her three younger brothers—especially the oldest boy, Tom, just one year younger than Fran and, until well into high school, smaller, shyer, lighter, and less well coordinated than she. (He is now six feet tall and an accomplished golfer and skier.)

This doesn't mean Fran lost out on her father's love. She has always had that, always known she had it, in full measure—the more so, perhaps, since she is both the oldest child and the only girl.

What it does mean is that she has always been intensely aware that while her father undoubtedly loves her, he has always valued her brothers' achievements more, taken them more seriously *because he identified with them as fellow males,* who would grow up to be men like himself, Daddies and breadwinners—men on the Outside. By coaching their baseball teams, taking them fishing, he wasn't, as he would see it, showing any favoritism; he was simply helping his sons along into masculinity, initiating them into its rites and rituals, being a good father.

The irony is that he has been a very good father indeed, to both his sons and his daughter. Through his particular kind of passionate attachment to his daughter, he has molded her into a strong, self-confident woman, a woman who is absolutely sure of her heterosexual femininity. She knows she is attractive to men, she knows how to love men and be loved by them, and furthermore, she *likes* men. She feels comfortable with them, and she enjoys being with them.

This has, after all, been considered one of a father's main jobs: to mold, train, or accustom his daughter to be a woman who will get along well with men, whose femininity will fit well with her father's—and later, her husband's—masculinity.

So the father puts his stamp on his daughter. And so, inevitably, he will have some problems identifying with his daughter in quite the same way he identifies with his sons. How could he not, when his main task and inclination is to polarize her into femininity?

So when Dr. Nobile looked at Francesca, his *daughter,* he saw a female who, no matter what else she did, would someday grow up to be a wife and mother. To her father, this is axiomatic. Like many fathers, he simply takes it for granted that this is the structure of the sexes in society. Women may work, certainly. But when all is said and done, men and women live in entirely different worlds, coming together essentially only through marriage and parenthood, in which each sex should—is destined to—play out its traditional, appropriate role.

A daughter, then, until she does get married and becomes a mother, is, in a sense, a plaything. An indulgence, a luxury.

"I wanted to be sure I had one daughter," says Dr. Nobile, "because we were all sons in my family." He certainly didn't worry when his daughter was born first: "I thought I would have just what I wanted to have, a daughter and then some sons. And I did."

Fran is very much like him. They are both charmers, self-confident people with high energy levels, who smile easily and often. Both impress a visitor immediately as being strong-willed, decisive, and dominant. They both have warm blue eyes and thick taffy-blond hair, and both are beautifully tanned. When she talks, Fran refers often to her father's energy and aliveness. How he loves parties and is extremely generous—with money, with time, with emotional support. He in turn refers often to her independence and assertiveness.

How can this be? Why hasn't Dr. Nobile taken care to bring Fran up in the model of a dependent future housewife?

Because he has identified with her very strongly as a feminine version of himself. And she, as daughters will, has picked up on that message and become very much like him, adapting his traits and integrating them into her own feminine identity.

Although not always easily, because there is always a catch. He was able to encourage her independence partly because he has always been certain that it wouldn't stand in the way of her ultimately falling into motherhood and retiring from active involvement with the world.

And even before Fran becomes a mother, she isn't, as he sees it, really part of his world, the real, Outside world of men, of Daddies, of work and achievement.

One survey of successful men found that while men in their thirties or younger took women seriously as competitors, older men did not. A middle-level bank executive was quoted as saying that, since it was unlikely that any of his women colleagues would make senior vice president, he "never considered them real threats. . . ."

Would such a man take his daughter's achievements seriously, as existing in the same world with his own?

George Gilder, in a 1981 *Playboy* interview, said that President Reagan "opposes the ERA but . . . felt he should give equal time to his daughter Maureen on the issue. So she uses radio time that he, Ronald Reagan, earned to attack his position. He wouldn't have done this on any other issue. It shows he isn't serious about it."

To such men, achievement counts, as does a statement or a political position, only when it is done or spoken or assumed by a man—and so is, by definition, an aspect or assertion of masculine identity.

I am talking to Fran in the apartment she shares with her lawyer husband. It is vividly decorated in reds on white and wood: white walls, one huge, mainly red, painting by a local abstract artist, red calico pillows on the white L-shaped couch. The immense, low wood table in the angle of the couch is filled with family photos in antique frames, with little ceramic vases and boxes, with a big bunch of dried grasses and flowers. The impression is of good taste and comfort, tending toward clutter.

I am finding out some of the reasons why Dr. Nobile doesn't take her achievements as seriously as he takes her brothers'. He can't; it isn't in him.

In addition to being a dominant male, he is an Italian Catholic, a combination that alone almost guarantees he will see motherhood as a woman's duty, destiny, and greatest contribution to the world. His roots are in the working class, as are his wife's. In fact, Fran's parents grew up together in the same Midwestern town, where their immigrant fathers worked in the meat-packing plant. They were childhood sweethearts, and when she became a secretary, it was to put him through medical school.

As soon as his practice was well established, she quit work. That was the ideal. She had gone back to work ten days after Fran was born, but it wasn't out of any independent self-image. Like so many mothers of daughters I interviewed, she had worked only as long as her husband needed her income to support his education or supplement his earnings.

Fran's father is, then, unabashedly a male chauvinist. She says he gets mad when she calls him this; later, he laughs when he tells me he is sure his daughter has pinned this label on him.

Yet Francesca is not just his *daughter;* she is also *his* daughter. And because he is the kind of man he is, he has invested a lot of himself in her. On this level, he takes her very seriously indeed—as a person who is, in a way, part of himself and so like him.

He has, for instance—and this is unusual for a Catholic father, especially one from the working class—given her, in many ways, a lot of freedom.

"My father," Fran says, "really respects well-thought-out actions. If he doesn't agree with something you do, he's not happy about it, but he's not going to hold it against you." One summer during college, for instance, she decided to waitress at a resort, which was fine except that her boyfriend was planning to room right across the street.

"My mother, who is a pretty rational human being, hung up on me when I told her. Then my father came up to school for Fathers' Weekend and asked me what I had decided to do. I said, 'I've thought it through, and I really want to do this, and if it's the worst thing I ever do—well, then, that's it.' And that was the end of the discussion. He never said another word."

"I just trusted her," he says later, in his office. "I knew she would do the right thing."

More than this, though, he really perceives Fran as a lot like himself: independent, decisive, quick to make friends, a leader. "I was president of the county medical society, editor of the state journal—that's the kind of thing she would do."

"Where," I ask, "do you think she got her independent views?"

He chuckles, delighted, and says, "From me."

"We had political discussions at the dinner table all the time," says Fran. "He always encouraged me to express my own views. He tried hard to make sure all our opinions were his, but when they weren't, I'm sure that underneath it all he's very happy that we can express ourselves."

So, whether or not her father ultimately takes her as seriously as his sons, he has encouraged Fran to develop a strong sense of herself as an autonomous person.

And yet, there is always the point at which his identification with her as a person stops, and his idea of her as a woman takes over—and with it, his indomitable will, his image of the way she should be, which is the way any woman should be, his daughter or not. He is confident that he has created her that way, and that whatever her protests, she will in the end be the kind of woman he wants her to be—and believes that she is, underneath it all.

"To me," says Dr. Nobile, "she was feminine from the very beginning. As a matter of fact, I resisted her being anything else but feminine," which, he says, is why he didn't want her to play softball that year. "Girls don't have to be leaders. I don't *want* her to be a leader in the business world—that to me is not what a woman is supposed to do. That's not the role women have."

What, then, did he want for his daughter? "I wanted her to do about what she did do—I wanted her to go to school, to decide in school on something that she wanted to do that would make her happy, and then get married and have kids and bring up a family." (She hasn't gotten to the part about having kids yet.)

He thinks the radio-station job (she is a public affairs producer and announcer) is a good thing, for now. He wouldn't have wanted her to become a nurse or a technician, not his daughter, not after he made it out of the working class securely into the upper middle; but neither would he have wanted her to go in for a high-powered career like medicine.

"If she had wanted to be a doctor, I *probably* would have encouraged her, although I don't think most women can devote the time they must to being a physician and still raise a family. To me, the individual who wants to be a physician is special—and will be all her life, hopefully. Otherwise she is going to be taking the space of some male who would better serve the public. It would bother me because I wouldn't want my daughter to be that special. I want her to have some kids, and live in the suburbs."

At the end of this speech he smiles sweetly, full of himself, very pleased and proud, completely confident in his prediction. Then he laughs and looks at me expectantly. He obviously thinks he will get a rise out of me, and enjoys the challenge in his words. "You can argue with me if you want. I've fought with her enough about it, so it's okay."

There is the man. He is charming and he is dominant. He knows exactly where women belong in his life. Sitting in front of his desk in the medical center—he, naturally, is behind it, still in his white smock—I find myself laughing a lot with him, wanting to please him because I would not want him to cease to be charming. I see that his will is very strong, that he has a clear view of the world, and it seems to me that he will be charming as long as I defer to that view. (At the end of the interview he guides me to his car with one hand on my elbow, opens and closes the door for me, and decides just where he will take me to get a cab to the airport. Passive, I bask in this ritual of caring, and of dominance.)

But he never wanted a sweet, passive daughter. He is pleased that she was a leader at college, among the other girls, her own kind. He took time off to watch her high-school tennis matches. He is proud of her. He *encouraged* her to argue, to stand up for her own point of view, to compete.

He and she remember the competitive part a little differently, though.

Take skiing. The way he remembers it, he encouraged her to compete with her brothers. "There was no way Francesca wasn't going to keep up—no way the boys were going to ski any better. She would say that, too: 'You're not going to ski any better than I am!' And she'd go out, colder than hell. I thought that was great!"

The way she remembers it, her father took the whole family out on the slopes when she was in fourth or fifth grade, and they learned the basics together. Then she looked up and her father and brother were gone—up the chair lift for the real thing, males together, leaving her behind on the baby slope. Even her mother was in on the plan. Fran was furious. She felt betrayed.

"I didn't get all the lessons, or the attention. I always had to fight. I had to stay out in the freezing cold and I could never say I was cold, because that meant you were a girl and you went in and got warm.

"He *allowed* me to compete, but he didn't encourage it. He would never actually come out and say, 'Girls do this, boys do that,' but I knew girls weren't supposed to do whatever—and if I wanted to, that was okay, but it wasn't going to be easy."

He made her a fighter, whether he intended to or not. But at the same time, he indulged her, in the way that many fathers do, to please himself and bend her to his will.

This story involves college and a silver Corvette. As with the skiing, father and daughter have a somewhat different view of what went on. One thing is clear, though. Each was manipulating the other, in the classic pattern or dance between fathers and daughters, a Princess-Daddy pavane, with Fran's own addition of a kick-up-your-heels solo.

When she finished high school, Fran, under the spell of the dying hippie movement, had "some vague idea about going off to New Mexico and living barefoot in a hut," or, failing that, at least going to a big, coed university with lots of action.

He intended her to go to a small women's college.

"He stayed up pacing the kitchen floor until two A.M., telling me I couldn't decide against college until I'd tried it. I thought, 'Okay, I see room here for bargaining,' so I said, 'I'm not going to Wells unless I can have a car.' He said I could have one if I paid for half of it."

Her rebellion was to pump gas out on Route 128. She wore red overalls and earned a lot of money, and best of all, "I thought he was going to kill me—*his* daughter was working in a gas station! He said, 'No daughter of *mine* is going to do that.' Then I got the silent treatment."

But he had her where he wanted her. When I asked him how he felt about the gas-station job, he gave a long, slow chuckle: "It was so far away from what she really was that it was a lark. So I thought, 'Okay, it's fun, she'll remember it for a long time, and she's not getting into any trouble.' Oh, I made a lot of noises about it, but I didn't really resist."

On the other hand, she did get her car, exactly the one she wanted, even though the money she'd earned didn't amount to half its price.

But he has the last word, so far: "It was *my* daughter. She could have asked for a lot more if she wanted it, but she only wanted that Corvette, so that's what she got."

Loving Daddy. What kind of girl has he raised? She became a feminist in college, and he wasn't prepared for that. She said she would never marry, but she has. She swears she will never stop work, that she and her husband will raise children in the city. He predicts they will move to the suburbs as soon as she has a child.

He says that if he had another daughter today, he would let her play softball. He also says it's much harder to raise a daughter than sons. The distinction is emotional: "In high school, she was a fighter, and she would get upset if she couldn't do this or that. With the boys, it was easier for me to say No. If they argued, it wouldn't make any difference—that's what they were going to do and that's the end of it. Which was true with Francesca, too. But it disturbed me more to see her upset than to see the boys upset. I don't know why—because she was a girl."

There it is. Always the point is reached at which a father's ability to identify with his daughter as an autonomous person stops and his view of her as a female, a woman, full of mysterious and unsettling female qualities like emotions, takes over. The twist in the vision—is she a person like himself, or is she female, the Other? How far can he identify himself with her without compromising his masculinity, or his view of her femininity?

Some fathers, as we shall see in the next bio, are quite consistent from the beginning. They polarize their daughters into an image of femininity, and that's that.

But when a father finds a lot in his daughter to identify with, he is also, very often, going to visit his ambivalence on her in the form of these mixed messages: "Be independent, but go to the college of my choice."

Or: "It's okay to compete now, because later you'll be out of the running."

Dr. Nobile was sufficiently unambivalent about seeing Fran as a version of himself, though, that he gave her a firm grounding in autonomy. So she, naturally, taking herself seriously—as daughters will—picked up on that and wants to go on with it.

But she had to deal with her internal conflicts, the result of all those mixed messages—and the not-so-mixed ones that said her brothers' achievements were more serious than her own, and that her father would do his best to help her brother Tom surpass her, even though she was the oldest and might therefore be naturally expected to surpass him. Of course it would have been disastrous for a boy's budding sense of masculinity to feel he couldn't outdo his sister.

So it wasn't surprising that she had a really awful sophomore slump in college, that halfway house between home and the world, where children are supposed to be preparing themselves for the next step Outward.

What was the next step? Fran had been socialized into autonomy, but she was also very much Daddy's Girl, imprinted with all the circuits for close involvement with a man. She knew her father didn't want her to take up a high-powered career, yet she had been encouraged to be a very different kind of person from her mother. When she looked at her father and her mother, she couldn't see that she was supposed to be quite like either one.

If you've been trained to be, unashamedly, a golddigger or a Princess, and you're temperamentally suited to the role, it's not hard to fall into a slot. It hasn't occurred to you that you could do anything for yourself— and even if it has, you don't believe it's necessary.

But if you have a father who takes real pride in you as *his* daughter, you're in a bind. He has identified enough with you to teach you to think for yourself, to have an idea of yourself as an independent person. And then you find out that, after all, you're still his *daughter,* and when it comes to that, you don't quite count in a man's world. Perhaps you begin to suspect that his pride in you is ultimately possessive, the traditional male appropriation of the female: "See, look what belongs to me!"

So you are conflicted.

Not surprisingly, Fran was full of rage. She dropped out of college and came home, and couldn't get along with anybody except her three-year-old brother.

Her father was kind and gentle, but he felt helpless.

Francesca remembers that "at night I would be hysterically sobbing and my father would come in and sit on the edge of the bed and say, 'I don't understand what's wrong,' and I would sob, 'I don't know either,' and then he would pace around. He never intruded. I knew he cared very much, that he was going to do anything he could to help me. And he never said a word about losing a whole semester's tuition."

"There was," he says, "no way I could talk to her—nothing I could do to get to her to find out what her problem was. She didn't know what it was. To this day, we don't know what it was."

He did, finally, talk her into finishing college.

Loving Daddy. Confused daughter. How was she going to grow up to become a woman in the face of his mixed messages? Her formless rebellions—the urge to run away for a year before going to the school to which she believes she didn't want to go but to which he still believes she really did; the dropping out for a semester into regression and sullen anger—all came to nothing in the face of his will.

So Fran found another solution. In her senior year, she married a man who, like her father, is dominant, aggressive, and athletic.

But he is her peer, not her father, and with him she started out on a much more equal footing. He does not, for instance, question her determination to remain a working wife—and working mother. He, too, wants to stay in the city, and they are planning to buy a co-op apartment.

She thinks Bob is more patient than her father, and a better listener. And she admires him because, she says, he is "the smartest person I ever met."

He also makes a lot of money, so she can continue to live in the style of a Princess, to which her father accustomed her: "It was a very generous atmosphere. If you wanted something, or needed something, then you got it, whether it was a trip to Mexico or a notebook. You just came out and asked for it." None of the children was allowed to work while they were in high school, probably because Dr. Nobile never forgot that he had to start his first job at eleven.

Yet, she says, although "technically, I suppose, I'm a Princess, I wouldn't describe myself that way." Why not? Because one definition of a Princess is "a really obnoxious person, manipulative, for instance, and devious."

As we saw with the Corvette, Fran definitely isn't above manipulation, but then, neither is her father. They were a match.

With her husband? "I expect Bob to love me whether I'm being a pig or not, but I don't take advantage of that. A lot of women don't think they have to give because, as daughters, they only took. I was given a lot, but there were definitely things expected of me. I was expected to be kind, to be a leader, and so forth."

She is certainly a Princess in her sense of entitlement—she expects a lot out of life, from her husband as well as from her father, and she gets it. Yet she doesn't believe that she has to get everything from a man. As she puts it, she learned as a child that you carry your own skis. She grew up privileged, but not spoiled. And because her father identified with her as a feminine version of himself, she grew up believing that she could be an autonomous person and he would still love her. Despite the mixed messages.

And she was encouraged to compete with those brothers.

Surveys and studies of successful women seem, so far, to be almost unanimous in their verdict that it helps to be the oldest, which Fran was, and *to have no brothers.*

The idea is that fathers will so favor brothers that a daughter will give up. But in fact competing with brothers—whether as the oldest or, like myself, as the youngest—can give a woman a terrific amount of tenacity, determination, and ambition. You're always pursuing a goal out there, which has to do with wanting your father to accept you.

If he gives you even a little encouragement, you're off and running.

Fran may be, as yet, too young to be classed as "successful." She is certainly well on her way.

The other crucial element in Fran's relationship with her father was the fact that "If you wanted him, he was always there." For the development of heterosexual femininity, this may be the single most important element in a father, this reliability, this trust. Without it, a daughter is unlikely to be able to trust men enough to form a lasting bond with one; or, at least, a lasting bond in which her position in the relationship is positive, not masochistic.

If you don't learn from your father—or from a father-surrogate—that you can demand a response and get one, you are very likely to go on trying to relate to men who aren't, in various ways, there for you.

So a Princess's sense of entitlement can be a very healthy thing, as long as she isn't expected to give up her autonomy for the sake of the relationship.

Here, Fran's father's message was mixed, as we have seen, but she is by this time too much of a fighter to quit. (One of the first things she did after she met her husband—whom she married after a six-week courtship—was to break her ankle playing hardball when his roommate taunted her that girls couldn't play it. Her father wasn't in the least surprised.)

Actually, Fran really wanted to be a boy, until "I found out I could do things just as well as boys could do them, and still succeed on other levels." In addition to becoming a good skier, she discovered, in college, talents for acting and writing—both of which engendered enormous pride in her father.

It was, she says, only at this point that she came to believe her father really liked her. Now, she says, "I know my father likes me a lot, and he likes to be with me. I know he thinks I'm intelligent, and have well-formed opinions. And I also think he thinks I'm funny. I have a good sense of whimsy. I do crazy things, and I give funny presents. I meet people who are bizarre and turn them into a whole adventure—I think that's the kind of thing he responds to. And I'm also fairly independent; I'll tell someone to just go shove it if I feel like it."

She still sees herself as different from her mother in many ways, although certainly her mother's long, close, successful relationship with her father has helped Fran to feel that marriage is a good thing.

But she sees very clearly that her father has encouraged her to develop traits he wouldn't want in her mother, the woman he lives with. Her mother, she says, has many of the same characteristics she has—intelligence and a sense of whimsy—"but I have them in larger quantities, and further removed from him. If my mother were as assertive as I am, he wouldn't find it as attractive."

A father can, after all, encourage his daughter's self-assertion, her competitiveness, in complete confidence that she will never grow up to compete with him.

But a wife is a different story.

Most men still want—as they have always wanted—their wives to focus most of their energies on them, the husbands. They want a wife to be a reliable support-and-nurturance system so that they can get on with their work lives. They don't want to come home and find another person in the house who expects to be assertive and competitive. And they tend to assume that women who might be assertive and competitive outside the home will continue to be assertive and competitive with them inside the home.

This is, on the whole, a fallacy. Assertiveness, which is not the same thing as competitiveness, is a good thing in any relationship. To compete with the person with whom you live can be very destructive, but women who compete at work aren't necessarily going to compete at home, any more than men are. In fact, it may be that either sex brings competition into a relationship when they feel frustrated, unfulfilled, and without options elsewhere in their lives. Unfortunately, though, many men feel competitive with women for their masculinity, so that any assertion by a wife or lover seems to them to be a challenge or even a threat.

It is therefore not uncommon for men to want one thing in a wife and something else in a daughter. Freud was rather like Dr. Nobile in this respect. Before his marriage, when his fiancée said she wanted to learn about his work, he told her she ought to have nothing to do with the competition of the Outside, the world of men. He wanted her to retire from all that and tuck herself away Inside his home, no doubt so that he could expect to have lunch on the table when he took a break from his practice. His wife complied. What choice did she have, in a completely male-dominated society? But Freud made his daughter, Anna, his intellectual heir. She became a pioneering psychoanalyst in her own right, nearly as well known as her father. Freud would never have married a woman like Anna (who, in fact, never married but remained her father's daughter).

"I don't think Francesca is like her mother," says Dr. Nobile. "Her mother is not aggressive, not competitive—and I don't think she's devious, either."

He loves indulging what he calls Fran's deviousness—as when she invites him into the city for dinner so she can get him to a department store to buy an anniversary present for his wife, since otherwise he won't take the time. But a man wouldn't want his wife, presumably, to play tricks like that.

"I think," says Fran, "he probably believes Bob has a tough time being married to a person like me. He thinks Bob is very lucky to be married to his daughter, but not so lucky to be married to a person who's stubborn and aggressive, as I am."

Bob doesn't seem to have any problem with this, perhaps because his image of masculinity doesn't depend so much on his wife's being his opposite. As a younger man, he may be better able to respond to subtler cues, such as the fact that his wife both enjoys her job and likes living with a man. Fran isn't interested in attacking Bob's masculinity because she doesn't feel limited by her femininity.

"I think of men as my equals," she says, "even if they don't think of me as theirs."

Indeed. Perhaps this is why she "never had any sense that men are the enemy." At the same time, "I have always had a lot of male friends, but I never felt my world was going to fall apart if I didn't have a boyfriend, or didn't get married."

She's never felt helpless—or worthless—if she wasn't connected to a man. She never had to play a role to win a man's approval. After all, she could argue with her father, compete with her brothers, and still receive their love.

She is pretty good at being a Good Girl, at getting what she wants without making a man angry—a specialty of the Princess. But she hasn't had to sacrifice herself to loyalty and devotion; again, because her father enjoyed and permitted her self-assertion and even some rebelliousness, like pumping gas.

And she understands her father very well.

"My father never had any sisters," she says, "so he didn't know what to do with girls. I think he thought girls only liked certain things, only did certain things. They should get married, and have babies, and stay home and take care of them.

"So while all the time he's bringing me up to think for myself, and be independent and have my own opinions, I'm sure he is confused about what he thinks of all the rest of the women and what he thinks of me. In a way, he made a special case for me because I was *his* daughter."

Smile for Daddy

Holly Flax

*E*ven a passive father can have a powerful effect on his daughter.

It started when Holly was small: "He would come home from work every day and say, 'How'd you get to be so pretty? How'd you get to be so nice?'

"There were no demonstrations of affection in our house—very little touching, or hugging, or kissing, or even telling someone you loved them. This ritual fed me. It made me feel special. It was his only way of saying, 'You're my little girl, and I love you.'

"So I was programmed to be pretty and nice, and to stay pretty and nice, particularly with a man, and I thought that would get me wherever I wanted to go.

"It got me what I thought I wanted, but it didn't make me a successful woman, or a successful partner in a relationship with a man. It got me married at twenty, when I dropped out of college.

"I wanted to get married and have my own home, make cookies and make babies, and get away from my parents. It didn't occur to me until much later that marriage wasn't the only alternative."

After staying pretty and nice for two husbands, Holly began four years ago to take care of herself, when she went to work first for a caterer, then as a pastry chef in a midwestern restaurant. Now, at thirty-four, she has opened her own small bakery and dessert-catering business.

But she still wakes up in the middle of the night with anxiety attacks. She doesn't feel comfortable with money, and she's only beginning to work out a relationship with a man in which she feels like a real person instead of a Hallmark card.

You'd never guess these things about her from her apartment, which is full of fresh flowers, chintz, antique trunks, cooking utensils, and cool, cool blue glass. She looks completely self-confident.

Her family was in some ways conventional: three children—Holly was the second, and the only girl. Her mother was at home; they lived in an exclusive suburb.

But they couldn't afford it. Holly's father earned a fairly good living at

General Motors, but it wasn't enough to support three children in the style Holly's parents wanted.

"My parents," she says, "made a conscious decision that, rather than live in a less prestigious suburb, they would scrimp and save and sacrifice and deny—you know, the Christian ethic, duty and sacrifice.

"This was a real burden for me because it was very hard for me to live there and not have clothes as good as the other girls'. I was very aware that we didn't eat the way my friends' families did—we ate things like Spam, which I can't stand today, and lots of eggs. It's no coincidence that I insist on having fresh flowers in my apartment, and that I'm in the food business. My mother made my graduation dress and my wedding dress, which is okay if you have a choice in the matter, but I didn't."

She never got angry about this, though. It was a classic WASP household; nobody ever got angry. "Nobody," says Holly, "ever walked into my house and said, 'Okay, sit down, I want to tell you something,' or, 'You really pissed me off this morning.' Everything was very cool, everything was on an even keel."

So it was a family that cared most of all about appearances—where they lived, how they acted (no feelings), how their daughter looked (pretty and nice).

Holly's father cared as much about these things as her mother, possibly even more. He "didn't want his wife to work, he wanted to be the breadwinner"; even though a second income might well have made a significant difference in the family's level of resources—might, in fact, have made their sham of upper-middle-class living into a reality.

Holly's father died eight years ago. Her mother went to work "after she realized that she'd have to become the breadwinner," and since her husband's death, by a combination of shrewd investment and newly discovered talent as a real estate broker, has parlayed a small amount of insurance money into a comfortable income and a condominium.

Yet for most of their marriage she deferred to her husband's wishes. It is also true that mothers in that kind of suburb did not, at that time, work, so Holly's mother may have felt that not working was an essential part of the image, even after her children were all in school. But although she didn't work, she did, in a fairly common pattern, take charge of her husband's paycheck. Holly's father would cash his check every week and her mother "was standing in the kitchen holding out her hand for it when he came home. She handled the budget, paid all the bills, and made decisions like whether we could afford a vacation. She gave my father an allowance."

In one way, this gave her a lot of power within the family, and Holly says she was certainly the dominant partner in the marriage.

Children, it has been discovered, generally become more like the parent who is more dominant. They identify with the one who is stronger and healthier. (From this point of view, it makes sense that Fran Nobile should identify with her dominant father.) Why, then, did Holly, seeing her mother as dominant, still take her cues from her father, and mold herself into the sweet, passive daughter he asked her to be?

Because she was taking her cues about how to behave as a heterosexually feminine person from her father, the most important male in her life. And her father, like most fathers, was molding her into the kind of woman who made him feel enhanced as a man. So he said Smile for Daddy, because when she did, he felt big and strong and competent. Even—or especially—since he felt under attack from the other important women in his life, his mother and his wife.

Holly's father's father died when he was very young, so in a way he had been abandoned by the man with whom he was supposed to identify. His mother, a strong character who is still hale at ninety, moved in with Holly's parents when they got married. Holly remembers her grandmother telling her father not to forget his umbrella, while her mother fumed.

Holly's mother must have let her husband know that she was disappointed in him. "My mother *wanted* to be an obedient wife," says Holly. "She wanted my father to make decisions; but he didn't. I knew my father was not standing up for his marriage. He wasn't putting his wife first, he was putting his mother first, and that made me feel bad for my mother."

A strong, competent woman who defers to her husband as the man on the Outside, and then finds he can't defend the Inside (which should be her territory) against the encroachment of a dominant female, his mother, is bound to be unhappy. Might she have been all the more insistent that they keep up their false front, as a way of getting back at him by making him feel like a failure?

Complex games are started when men insist on deference.

So you could look at Holly's father either as a man who had been overwhelmed by—and lost between—two strong women, or as a man who had succumbed to the delights of being fussed over and competed for by two women. Either way, he had plenty of reasons for wanting his daughter to be sweet, quiet, and passive, different from both his wife and his mother. A girl who would never remind him to take his umbrella.

Fran Nobile's father also wanted Fran to be different from his wife, but Dr. Nobile seems to feel confident of his male dominance. So he hasn't needed to mold his daughter into a nonthreatening femininity to compensate for his wife and mother. Instead, he has enjoyed encouraging in his daughter traits he certainly would not want in his wife—assertiveness, independence, competitiveness.

The fact that he is equally confident about expecting his daughter to revert, more or less, to a traditional wife as soon as she becomes a mother is a miscalculation many fathers have made, partly because they really can't believe that a daughter might actually identify with them while still growing up to be heterosexually feminine. Women, to such a man, are—as mothers—so completely in a different sphere from men that such an identification seems, simply, inconceivable.

Both Fran and Holly were taking their cues from their fathers, learning how to be the kind of women they wanted. At the same time, each was becoming very like her father. Fran became dominant and charming; Holly became passive and sweet.

Fathers have this power. As *the* dominant male in our lives, they first shape and validate our identities as heterosexual females relating to men. Mothers don't have this power simply because they are women. But then, of course, by deferring to her husband's wish that she not work, Holly's mother was giving Holly a pattern for conforming to what a man wanted.

There were other cues, too. Like Fran Nobile, Holly was strongly affected by the way her father treated her in contrast to her brothers; but Holly did not feel encouraged to compete with them.

"In my family," she says, "I was lucky to be a girl. My father was very macho with my brothers. I don't think he saw himself as a strong man, so with them he would be like a Marine drill sergeant. He made them do pushups. He wanted them to be very physical, and strong. He was particularly hard on my youngest brother—he called him a sissy when he didn't get chosen for some team. I was fourteen or fifteen, and I remember feeling, *I'm glad it's not me.*

"I saw very early that it was much easier to be a girl. I was allowed to be feminine and nice, I was allowed to be a little girl. I was relieved of all his expectation; I didn't have to deal with his goals for the piece of himself he saw in his male children. I felt a tremendous sense of relief when I wasn't asked to perform, when I knew he was simply pleased by my presence—by my external presence."

It was a heavy burden for her brothers. The one who was called a sissy became gay.

But the image Holly's father demanded from her carried a heavy burden, too. Because while she didn't have to do pushups, she was also excluded from the dinnertime political debates. "My father would challenge my brothers, force them to debate with him, but not me. So the message I got there was that men are powerful, men count. A little girl was supposed to stay pretty and nice and quiet and not get in the way. I belonged in the background."

Her mother, too, stayed in the background, deferring once again to her father. So Holly saw that the Outside world, the world of work and politics, was the exclusive domain of men, and that when these things were brought inside the house for discussion they were not shared with women. Even though her mother handled the budget, she was dependent on Holly's father to give her his paycheck. And Holly certainly knew that, while they lived in the exclusive suburb supposedly to give the children a good start in life, they lived near Detroit because that was where her father worked.

So there was no incentive for Holly to compete with her brothers, no prize to be won in the form of her father's attention and approval; she got that by *not* competing. She got that by being passive. (It is interesting that today, when she is no longer passive, she has chosen self-employment, where competition matters less than providing a product that is wanted.)

But the worst part of the passivity Holly's father demanded from her was that it was mirrored by an immense passivity of his own.

A father who is chiefly preoccupied with keeping up his masculine image and browbeating his sons may simply have very little of himself to invest in his daughter. If all he wants from her is a pleasing appearance, he is offering, as well as demanding, nothing at all.

So another big price for Holly in her father's almost complete lack of involvement with her was a real loss in her sense of self, a loss that always comes from the lack of such an important relationship. A loss of vitality.

"It was almost as if he didn't have a lot invested in me. He never got angry with me, there was just no emotional response at all. I remember in high school I would come home with average grades—and I'm intelligent. I just didn't work hard, I was into having fun.

"He wouldn't say, 'Look, you can get better grades than this.' He wouldn't say, 'Why don't you do your homework?' He wouldn't even get angry. He would sit me down and say, very calmly, 'I saw your report card, and you are not an average person. You can do better.' But he'd say it in such a *benign* way. He wasn't angry, he wasn't . . . anything.

"Sometimes I wished he would get angry, because it would have showed that he cared."

He obviously cared a lot about her brothers—cared destructively, competitively. They threatened his identity, and he attacked them or challenged them.

His daughter threatened his identity by being female, but his method with her was different. He wouldn't engage her; that was too dangerous for a man who felt done in by mother and wife.

He would simply keep her at arm's length.

Emotions are the connecting links between people. It is the emotional connection that makes people know each other, that makes intimacy possible. But this was a family that insisted on control of feelings at all times—a very WASP characteristic.

The continual withdrawal from feelings creates passivity, that masculine refusal to enter into a dynamic relationship. This refusal can be read by a daughter in a number of ways: as passivity, as rejection, as absence. It can generate an enormous amount of anger in her, but she may be afraid to show her anger because she knows that if she displays any feelings her father will withdraw even further—perhaps become actively rejecting.

Holly was lucky. She didn't read her father's withdrawal as rejection, so she didn't become extremely self-destructive. She did instead what studies have shown is common among daughters of distant or absent fathers, she idealized him.

"It was more important for me to please him," she says, "maybe because he was more idealized. I didn't have to deal realistically with him. I had to deal very realistically with my mother, every day, and I didn't like it. We would fight."

"Also I wanted to please him more than my mother because he was sweeter and more gentle. My mother only raised the hair on the back of my neck. If she said, 'Do this,' I only wanted to do the opposite."

Of course, in a household where no one is supposed to show any emotions, the inevitable stress between a mother and daughter is going to make a daughter worry about her own feelings. She is supposed to keep absolute control over her emotions, too, and Daddy is the one who looks as if he has that problem licked. You don't see *him* getting all upset because you didn't do your homework again; he doesn't even notice whether you've done your homework. So you attach yourself to him—and later to other men. You can idealize them, and through them, yourself, and keep all those messy emotions under control.

"Since my father," says Holly, "I've idealized men and I've liked it when they put me up on a pedestal. That's not realistic at all. You can only do that if you don't get too close and find out where the vulnerabilities are, the weak spots, the faults, the frailties."

But indeed that's the point—you don't want to get too close to anybody. A fault is a failure, a weak spot creates a mess, some feelings might leak out. Better to keep your distance.

The first tiny signs of rebellion against all this stifling niceness and passivity occurred when Holly decided to go to a Southern coed university. On one level, Holly was still living up to her father's image. This was a family, remember, in which appearances were all-important. Things had to look right. And Louisiana was the perfect place for a girl who was groomed to be pretty and nice to go to school—she fit right in with the Southern girls and, at twenty, married a Southern boy.

And yet, on another level: "I knew it would displease them. It didn't look right for a girl from our suburb to go to Louisiana to college instead of Vassar, or Wellesley. And getting married at twenty certainly didn't look right. Especially when I dropped out of school."

But such was her father's passivity that he wouldn't put his foot down in either case. "I don't remember much protest at all. Neither of these things made any sense to them, but all he would say was, 'Well, we don't really want you to do this, but if that's what you want to do, I'm sure you'll make the most of it.' "

Sounds like a lot of trust, a lot of maturity. But it came across to Holly as another example of his being simply *not there.*

Holly and her Southern gentleman soon drifted apart. It was practically inevitable since her marriage was less a commitment to a relationship with a particular man than a combined rebellion against and acting out of the "pretty and nice" role her father had programmed her for.

After her divorce, Holly went home for the summer to be with her father, who was ill, and give herself a chance to recoup. Her father's lack of reaction was true to form:

"Here I was home for the first time in two years. He never said, 'How are you, how are you feeling now that you're divorced, how are you feeling about your ex-husband?' Not even, 'What happened?' Nothing."

Not long after that her father died, and three months later Holly met a new man, Howard, a wealthy, urban man who had a wonderful father.

She fell in love with her father-in-law, a much livelier man than her own father, as much as with her husband.

And she finally got to play Princess.

"I got to be Howard's little girl. He took me under his wing. I got to run through a whole girlhood of piano lessons, beauty parlors, charge accounts—all the things I never had. It was wonderful. That's all he wanted from me. He would ask me what I had done with my day, and I would say first I went to the beauty parlor, then I had lunch with Susan, then I went to Saks."

And in the end, she was playing the same game with Howard she had played with her father: Smile for Daddy.

"I began to feel very kept. I was not in charge of my life, I was an acquisition in his empire, and I had to play the game by his rules."

Sugar daddies want a big piece of you—the piece that might otherwise be alive.

Nothing cataclysmic happened to Holly. She grew up, or grew alive, and realized she couldn't go on being pretty and nice forever, couldn't stand the deadness of the game.

She divorced her sugar daddy and went to work, and now she is on her own. She is terrified, but she feels good. The man she is involved with is another withdrawn WASP, but they are in group therapy and he's *trying.*

But she still feels sad when she thinks of her father.

"I'm upset that I never demanded more from him. I will never have a chance to say to him, *'Talk* to me.' I never asked him, 'Don't you want to tell me how you feel about dying?' or even, 'Please tell me how you really feel about me.' "

That terrifying emotional coldness or self-sufficiency of WASPs is, in the end, only a fear of feelings. Perhaps it is better to have a father who raged or sulked than one who never gave you anything at all.

"I do think my father liked me," says Holly, "and approved of me, yet he never verbalized it. He never said, 'Well, if you want my advice, I'll tell you what I think.'

"I worry about that vagueness. If I knew more clearly who he was, for me and for other people, I would have something more to hold on to and identify with. There would be pieces of me that I could say, 'Hey, I got that from him!' Maybe I could even think of him as a mentor, someone who is behind me. I would like to feel that. I would just like to feel I could describe him—I don't even feel like I could describe him.

"I have to *assume* he liked me."

Daughters Don't Have to Pay Any Dues
Steve, Alicia, and Patty Appleman

A licia and Patty Appleman, aged seventeen and sixteen, are smart, beautiful, and talented. Linda, their mother, has worked at least part time all their lives. When feminism came along, she took right to it; now she has her own full-time career as an academic administrator.

Steve Appleman worked his way through UCLA with high honors. In the classic oldest-son-of-immigrants, hope-of-the-family pattern, he married early and started a family right after college, working day and night to establish himself as a CPA. He and Linda have, from the beginning, let their daughters know that they have a choice: law school or medical school. In the fall, Alicia will go to UCLA herself.

So why are both daughters seriously considering that what they really might want is to find a couple of nice husbands (maybe a lawyer and a doctor) to support them?

They aren't typical Princesses, overindulged with money and things. In fact, until recently there never was all that much money in the family. Linda worked because she had to; Steve was not, for many years, the kind of success she would have liked him to be. They moved to this wealthy California suburb only two years ago. Before that, they lived in a less fashionable area and the girls shared a bedroom. Now there are four bedrooms.

"We have endeavored," Steve tells me, "to convey to the children a certain value of money, and a sense of what it takes to earn it. We've encouraged them from their early days to work for it in one way or another."

That's the way he talks: formal, objective, judicious.

He is a small, neatly made man, who carries himself with a certain detachment, as though his accountant's training had given him the tools to assess his own emotional conflicts and contradictions, divide them up, and put them neatly to one side.

He dresses neatly, too. It is a Saturday afternoon, and we are talking in his living room, with the rug in tones of blue and beige and the living-room suite—armless, austerely modular, but softly comfortable, in beige velvet. Steve is wearing tasseled Gucci loafers, razor-creased designer jeans, and a powder blue sweater. His crisply curling brown hair is cut short, and he sits quietly on the couch, considering carefully each word he speaks.

By the time Alicia and Patty were fourteen and thirteen, he says, they were earning their own money, by babysitting and holding painting and dance classes for toddlers. Alicia is the painter and Patty the dancer; they pooled their interests for the classes that developed out of their afternoon babysitting groups.

You would think that, with such parents, and such a background, Alicia and Patty would be heading for serious careers. But something has discouraged ambition.

They could almost be twins. Alicia is tall (taller than her father), tanned, with a fall of wavy black hair and makeup so polished it looks as though it has been applied by a professional. Not too much, just perfect She is wearing—naturally—designer jeans, and a boat-neck lavender cotton jersey that sets off her tan.

Patty, a junior at the same public high school, is also tall, also tanned, but more boyish. Her hair is cut short, her makeup is less carefully applied, and she herself is a shade plainer, the nose just the tiniest bit wrongly proportioned. But she is the one with the steady boyfriend.

The girls and I talk on the terrace, while Alicia plies me with fruit punch and cookies on a big wicker tray.

She would really like, she tells me, to be a set designer. She has already made the sets for a number of school productions, and she has an idea she is pretty good. But she feels she has been more or less slated for law school. "They're scared," she says, "that I would want to go into the theatre."

Patty is channeled toward medicine, although she, too, has other yearnings; she loves modern dance. But she is a Good Girl. "My parents," she complains, "never said, 'Study dance.' If I had taken more classes, I'd be ready to try out for a professional school. But from the time I was in first grade, I heard, 'Are you going to be a doctor or a lawyer?'"

Well, you can't blame Steve for that. Parents who spent long years securing their place in the upper middle class would not want to encourage their children to take the kind of economic risks inherent in careers like theatre and modern dance—not to mention the bohemian lifestyle.

If Patty and Alicia are going to choose theatre or dance, then, as opposed to law or medicine (the dichotomy sounds too pat to be true, but the conversation really did take place), they would have to have real ambition. They would have to take themselves seriously enough, *believe* in themselves enough, to defy—or, at least, disappoint—their parents.

Defy. The word sounds too harsh on this comfortable terrace. Defiance suggests challenge, resistance, rebellion—and intense feeling. None of these come up in our conversations. Alicia does plan to take some threatre courses at UCLA in addition to pre-law. But she worries about the liabilities of a theatre career: "I don't want to be the kind of person who goes to discos every night and can't pay the rent. I'm conflicted. I want to be a set designer, but if I went to law school, my life would be all set out for me; and in the theatre I wouldn't meet the same kind of people as I would if I were a lawyer."

Still, in college she plans "to make different contacts and see if I have enough trust in myself to go out and get a career."

Does she really not trust herself? Is she caught in the famous conflict between femininity and achievement?

She doesn't think so.

"I have no doubt," she says, "that I could make a lot of money if I became a lawyer." The way she sees it, with a shrewd awareness of the powers both of femininity and feminism, women have a lot of advantages over men. "Even though women aren't supposed to use a smile or a short skirt, I think many times a boss would rather see a pretty face in the morning than another guy. I think that can help us. And I think there is a great need for women doctors and lawyers, because women want to use them."

Money, in fact, is very important to both sisters, who want to live pretty comfortably when they get out of college. "My sister and I," says Patty, "would not like to live in a tenement."

No, indeed. "I want a big house," says Alicia. "I want a housekeeper. I don't want to do any housework; I hate it."

So why don't they go on to law school and medical school and earn lots of money so they can buy themselves nice condos or big houses?

There is the question of the drudgery involved; the sheer amount of work for goals they aren't sure they want anyhow. When they think about how much they *enjoy* theatre or dance, they can see that neither medicine nor law would offer as much pleasure. Patty thinks she might enjoy being a doctor, but she doesn't think she could "handle getting there." Her grades aren't, actually, all that terrific anyhow. And Alicia, who tried politics (which is close to law) for a couple of years, found that she didn't really like it; didn't like the constant wheeling and dealing, and the apparently endless hours of hard work.

So marriage is the logical solution. "If I could find a man to support me while I do what I want," says Alicia, "I would choose that."

"It's always nice," says Patty, "to have security."

This is a startling reversal from her mother's generation (and my own). Our parents told us to go to college to meet a good husband; we took up feminism partly in protest against their refusing, in this way, to take us seriously. We should be studying for our own careers, we said.

Would a boy in Alicia's class be talking the way she is?

"No," says Patty, "because he knows he doesn't have the choice. He's not going to meet a lawyer who's going to support him."

"I'd much rather," says Alicia, "have the choice."

And do the boys in her class expect to support girls like Alicia when they grow up? Well, a lot of them *say*, "My wife better know how to support herself," but, thinks Patty, "It's more of a joke."

Alicia says all her girlfriends claim they'll support themselves when they grow up, but that, too, is "more of a joke. Maybe one or two of them will. Because when you're growing up and your father supports you and your mother doesn't, it's very nice."

Patty, though, is either more of a pessimist or more of a realist, depending on your point of view. Her friends, she says, don't expect to have husbands to support them. Maybe that's because the parents of her closest friend are divorced, so "she's seen that the woman has to support herself."

So Patty is slightly less sanguine about marriage. In fact, she views both marriage and dance as, economically at least, equally risky: "I don't know how talented I am, so if I go into dance, I won't necessarily be able to support myself. And I know I have to support myself—I mean, maybe not, but most probably I do. Who knows when I'll get married, or to whom?"

Well, but what about Daddy's push toward a career? What about fatherly support and involvement, praise for achievement, encouragement of autonomy and independence? How come these daughters aren't goal-oriented?

For Steve is, according to both girls, a wonderful Daddy: he is really *there* for his daughters. "You can always," says Alicia, "count on him. He's steady, typically masculine; where our mother was always running around, doing what she wanted to do."

"She's less that way now," says Patty.

In fact, Steve has always been a tower of paternal support. When Patty skipped fifth grade and had problems relating to the sixth-grade girls, it was Steve who talked it over with her every night until she worked things out. When Alicia, at a teenage camp, was the subject of "a big to-do" over being caught out of her cabin after lights out, Steve took her side: "I think the communication was mostly with me, because I was available. I couldn't care less about that sort of thing, and I was very supportive." When Patty was accused of cheating on a test, she assured

Steve she hadn't, and he backed her up. He shows up at parent-teacher conferences whenever he's needed.

What's more, he has always been a mentor to both girls. He is, they agree, the smartest person they know—brilliant, in fact. "He knows everything," says Alicia. "He can fix the car, he knows English. You can always count on him."

"No matter what you need to know," says Patty. She tells me about a history report she couldn't organize: "Even though he was busy, he sat down for three hours and showed me how to organize it. He made a 75 report into a 95."

When Alicia took advanced math, Steve tutored her every night. He found out about a special design program for which she was eligible, and encouraged her to apply for it.

"He taught me to write," says Alicia with great enthusiasm. "Last fall I wrote an essay for a competition and he wrote another version. My Mom liked mine and after a while I did, too—and he admired me for choosing my own version!

"It was a monumental step, I thought, me being more independent. I had been feeling scared because ever since I was little he has helped me write my essays, but next year, when I'm in college, he won't be there."

Can it be that Steve has been *too* helpful, too much a mentor?

A man who actually writes the final versions of his daughters' themes (he does, they assure me, require them to write the first draft) is not encouraging his daughters to learn how to do things for themselves. He is not even encouraging them to think they are able to do things for themselves.

He is saying, Let Daddy Do It.

This is, perhaps, one of the commonest messages fathers give to daughters. And why not? Fathers are men, after all, and men have always loved the kick they get from showing women how things should be done. It makes them feel more masculine.

But it tells daughters that they probably can't do it as well as Daddy. Not only that—perhaps they *shouldn't even try,* because he gets so much pleasure from doing it for them. Maybe he needs that kick. Should a daughter take it away from him?

Steve believes that he has stressed "responsibility and independence of thought. If we've prepared them, they will be able to carry it on. They will be responsible for their own lives at some point, and we will be very little part of that, in terms of their own development, and progress, and success, and growth, and all that. My younger daughter has expressed an interest in medicine; if she wants to pursue it, that's fine. I have made an effort not to influence them. . . ."

There is an odd discrepancy between Steve's perception here, and his daughters'. They feel he has tried to influence them, although not in a way that feels quite *real* to them.

Steve and Linda both are workaholics. Their daughters tell me: "We grew up being told what we were going to be like. We didn't have a chance to decide for ourselves. We were always told, 'You're going to be honest, you're going to work hard,' because these are things my parents had to do, especially our father. So it's like, 'I worked hard at school, so you have to.'"

The "work hard" doctrine has recently been modified, though—at least by Steve.

"Our father has become less of a workaholic," says Alicia. "He recently told me that graduating with high honors, as he did, is not worth the price you have to pay. He said he wants us to have a good time."

"But," says Patty, "if she fails, he'll kill her!"

"It's a mixed message," says Alicia.

"I think," says Patty, "that we taught my father you're supposed to have a good time."

What does this mean? It means Alicia cuts school to go to the beach, and Steve makes a joke about it. "He'll come home on a rainy day and say, 'So, Alicia, did you go to the beach today?'"

It means Alicia complains that even when she does go to the beach, "I feel confused because I know deep down someone's telling me I should be working; so I don't think I get the fullest pleasure."

It means that when Patty wants to cut school one day, her father says she has to go to history class, and she does. But after that, she goes to the nurse's office. "They call my father, and I speak to him and say, 'Daddy, I'm sick, I'm coming home.' He says, 'Are you really sick?' I say No. He says, 'Oh, you just don't want to go to English. Okay.' So I go to the beach. My mother would never let us do that. Alicia even had the nurse call him directly once. He says, 'I don't like doing this,' but he does it all the time."

To Patty, this is an example of her father's being "passive—or at least just letting me do what I want, when my mother wouldn't." Patty would perhaps prefer that Steve put his foot down a bit more.

Steve never mentioned these continual small indulgences; indeed, he perceives himself as having only recently let up on his daughters: "I've been trying to give them more leeway, be less intrusive. I think I was a little overly involved in discipline. I tended to press a little bit too much about how things were going at school, at home, with their friends—and I've tried to ease up a bit. And I find they've been more responsive."

The bottom line is, as Alicia succinctly puts it, "A smile will get you a lot farther with your father than your mother—and that's a fact.

"He's nicer with us. He's the one who lets us stay up late. Money isn't as tight as it was when we were younger, so if we need a new pair of jeans, we say, 'Daddy, I have only two pairs of jeans,' and he'll say, 'Okay.' "

Perhaps Steve enjoys these little indulgences because he is feeling, at last, his success in the masculine role of provider.

"The other night," says Patty, "I said, 'Mom, I spent my allowance, can I have some money to go swimming?' She said No. I asked my Dad and he just said, 'How much do you need?' I don't think she liked the idea that I went to my father after she said No."

Is this, after all, just a less direct version of Smile for Daddy, the message that led Holly Flax into passivity in two marriages?

Smile for Daddy certainly says Let Daddy Do It.

Could Steve, then, be unconsciously polarizing his daughters into some stereotyped aspects of femininity, despite his own credentials as the husband of a feminist and his own daughters' testimony of his ambitions for them?

He certainly is aware of them as feminine, and has been since they were small. Today, he thinks Patty is the more feminine "because she is more successful in personal relationships. Feminine means softer. Patty comes across as softer, and easier. Although I have recently come to realize that underneath all that softness she is wily, and astute, and competitive."

The question is, what has he really made of their femininity until now—all these years before he saw Patty as wily and competitive?

The feminism is fairly new, after all. He is still pleased that his daughters can be "very caring." Recently, when he got home late one night, Patty took the time to come down and help him with dinner. He doesn't, he says, take that sort of thing for granted anymore.

Well, is this just your passive, sappy American Daddy, letting his daughters run roughshod over him?

No. Clearly, there is something else going on, something he doesn't admit, perhaps even to himself.

I think he is a man who worked extremely hard as the oldest son of immigrants, and fulfilled all his parents' goals. And I think he had two beautiful, smart, talented daughters and he said, somewhere so deep inside himself he is not aware of it, "These are *girls,* they don't have to live the way I did. I can give them some of the indulgence I would like, all these years, to have had myself."

This is how daughters serve the secret, Inside, feminine parts of Daddy.

So he is giving them messages, some of them very clear.

On the surface, he gives them the message his culture expects: Do well in school, as I did. And because today it is assumed that middle-class daughters might take up a profession, he also tells them to do that.

But the message is mixed. He has recently told them he wants them to have fun, to enjoy the best years of their lives. His daughters, as we saw, feel a bit confused by this. And resentful. What does he mean? Even when he was giving them the message to be high achievers, they could tell something was odd. He did too much of the work for them. And then he helps them cut school, despite the fact that he is big on responsibility.

Daughters don't *have* to try. Daughters don't have to slave to carry the family's name into the upper middle class. Daughters can relax and let Daddy do it.

That seems to be what Steve is telling Alicia and Patty. And in so doing, is he really indulging his own envy of the daughters who—as he sees it—don't have to carry the burdens he did? If he had been a girl, he could have married well and that would have taken care of the family requirements. He certainly wouldn't have had to slave to get high honors and then become a successful CPA.

Steve is vicariously living out the feminine side of himself through his daughters. And, just possibly, he is avenging the loss of some dream of his own by not taking their dreams seriously.

Unfortunately, in the process he is undermining them as people. They have certainly bought his message: Marry well and skip the effort. But they don't, underneath it all, seem too happy about this. They keep wistfully mentioning theatre or dance, their already forfeited dreams.

On one level, as an analyst pointed out to me, Alicia's desire to marry a rich husband who will support her while she does a little amateur set designing represents a determination to make a husband support her dreams even if her father wouldn't. And her method, I hasten to add, is very much in line with her father's message that it's easier to marry well than to try to do it yourself.

When mothers live vicariously through their sons, they usually do it by spurring them on to high ambition and achievement, partly because those are usually the things they themselves gave up to take on the feminine role. Unfortunately for daughters, when fathers live vicariously through them, the result may be to emphasize all the passive sides of femininity—everything Daddy had to give up in order to become what he felt was acceptably masculine.

Steve Appleman, then, has produced a couple of Princesses, ripe for the marriage market but completely uncertain of anything else they might do because they are confused. And they are still Daddy's Girls, following his directives rather than their mother's example.

They might, eventually, turn to her model. Or they might find mentors in college or even in marriage who will take them seriously and tell them to get out there and do something, that it *matters*. In the meantime, they sound like the sort of pampered, spoiled kids men are always disparaging:

"I don't," says Alicia, "want to pay my dues. I don't like paying dues."

"We don't," says Patty, "pay our dues very often. We get around them."

Which of course is exactly the problem. It's just what a man, their father, really wants them to do, because there were too many dues he had to pay.

The Pygmalion Syndrome

*M*y father had some definite ideas about the kind of girl he thought I should be. Protected, a little dumb, always ready to please him. Always smiling.

"My dizzy blonde," he would say fondly, in his rare moments of affection, even smiling at me.

I got the idea. He liked me best when I was entertaining—a little R & R after the daily wars of the office world.

And I, waiting as ever for him to take some notice of me, would play the role whenever I had a chance. Make myself foolish for his amusement.

All of this was odd, because he also expected me to get straight As in school, and certainly I was intended for a Seven Sisters college, the women's equivalent to the Ivy League school all my brothers went to (it was still for boys only).

My father inculcated in me a gentlemanly code originated by his sex, not mine, and belonging to a different class, a different era.

"A lady," he would say, "has her name in the papers only three times in her life: when she's born, when she's married, and when she dies."

What a world of self-assurance lay behind this impossible demand! A lady would grow up secure in the bosom of her father's family and would, eventually, be passed decorously along to a husband. She would have no need of vulgar self-promotion because she would have no need to make her own way.

This was an odd philosophy for the son of an antiques dealer renowned through several states for her sharp deals and fine furniture.

My father's pleasure in my foolishness was an odd contrast, too, to his military view of life. He saw it as a forced march, a continual battle against all forms of self-indulgence—meaning pleasure, or even relief. Self-denial was the epitome of virtue.

When I was about nine—just before my mother died—my father and I were out for a drive in his old Studebaker, crossing the Gettysburg Battlefield on a heat-baked day in June. (We were visiting my grandmother, his mother, the antiques dealer, who lived in Gettysburg, where my grandfather had taught at the college and my great-grandfather had been head of the theological seminary.)

The car gave out on a little switchback hill, mercifully (I thought) in the shade, near a large, moss-covered rock. But my father would not leave me there. We would do a forced march together down the hill and along an endless open stretch of flat, hot road to a farmhouse, where my father would call my mother to pick us up in my grandmother's car. He set a brisk pace, and every time I complained, he told me it was better not to stop and rest in the sun, because it would just be much harder to start again afterward.

I will never forget the sudden plunge into cool, deep shadow when we got to the farmhouse. The farmer's wife brought out a pitcher of iced tea while my father was phoning. I had the glass in my hand, cool with ice, wet with condensation, when my father appeared and said, sharply, "It's better not to drink anything. We have a long, hot walk back and it will just be harder with a belly full of water." (Short of cursing, he loved to use a kind of army-camp vernacular, even with me. The words seemed abrupt and alarming. He put the emphasis on *belly* and I instantly saw myself expiring in the sun, my belly burst open from drinking iced tea, or contracted with terrible cramps.)

There was no question of waiting at the farmhouse, or even of leaving me there. An officer never abandons his equipment or his troops. A daughter stays with her father at all times. We marched back, interminably.

I don't think my father was ever aware of the contradictions in what he expected of me.

The military view was possibly fairly well suited to the training of the kind of lady he imagined, who could sit with her back ramrod straight, never touching the back of the couch, all afternoon while the gentlemen smoked cigars and drank Bristol Cream Sherry. A lady like my grandmother.

A forced march was good preparation for marathon bouts of writing papers and studying for exams in college, when we kept ourselves awake on black coffee and the Dexamil provided by a girl in my dorm whose father was a doctor.

But none of this had any relationship to my father's notion of me as a sort of Lolita tucked away for his amusement, always ready to be "on" when he wanted me to be.

Although, come to think of it, entertaining the officers was always part of the military life, too.

Even today, I arrange my work into forced marches: a free-lancer approaching a deadline is like nothing so much as a soldier on the march, unless it is a nun in retreat.

I am suspicious of change of pace. If I stop, take a break, it will be difficult to start again, hard to go on.

Worse, I am suspicious of my needs for variety, for pleasure, for affirmation of my femininity. The femininity he defined for me didn't seem as though it would take me very far in the world. It certainly didn't get me very far with him, although I cherished each tiny crumb of his affection.

In return, he demanded of me unswerving devotion, absolute loyalty.

My father could never bring himself to approve of me when I was feeling really good—because, I think, he knew I wasn't thinking about him. I was taking myself out of his private scenarios, the ones fathers spin about daughters but seldom admit.

I was involved in my own life.

He used to quote me a line from Kipling's "If" that said no one should count too much, but he never forgave me for going all the way to Boston to college. He refused to come to my graduation because I seemed so completely to have left him.

He had a quote for that, too, from *King Lear:* "How sharper than a serpent's tooth it is / To have a thankless child!"

I had been hearing this one since childhood. In college I read *King Lear* and discovered this quote was part of Lear's curse upon Goneril, his oldest daughter, who has been taking care of her father—retired, idle, but used to command—and his hundred riotous knights and squires. Finding them a strain on her household, she has just asked her father to move on, even though she swore she loved him "Dearer than . . . liberty . . . / No less than life," in order to get a third of his kingdom.

Goneril and her sister, Regan, are always interpreted as wicked daughters, monstrous, even; but I have a lot of sympathy for Goneril in this scene. Her father blackmailed her into extravagant flattery, demanding to know which of his three daughters loved him most, and when the youngest, Cordelia, refused to flatter him, he disinherited her.

Wouldn't I have flattered my father to gain a third of his kingdom?

There is something odd about the total devotion my father demanded of me—as there is about the total devotion everyone still thinks Goneril and Regan owed their incredibly demanding father. Their crime, it seems, was that they promised to take care of him (at no matter what expense to themselves) and then reneged on that promise. (Of course, they also schemed with their husbands to take control of the kingdom, but that too seems less heinous when you consider that Lear had given up the throne.)

And my father's insistence on devotion was contradicted by the fact that he kept telling me I should be independent.

My father was a crazy mirror in which to try to see myself. But I had to see myself, somehow, in whatever mirror he provided. It was the only way I could find out who I was.

When you are grown up and somebody responds oddly to you—say, frowns at you when you tell a good joke—you are supposed to have a strong enough sense of yourself to think, "What is wrong with that person?", rather than, "What is wrong with me?"

But when you're little, every important person in your life is a mirror in which you see yourself. And the reflection in that mirror—their response to you—shapes your identity.

In the end, my father was not one mirror, he was a whole series of mirrors, and the images I saw in them canceled each other out.

We have for some time blamed mothers for giving double messages: the famous mad mothers, the "schizophrenogenic" mothers, who are said to put their children, especially their sons, in double binds at an early age. Why would a father want to do such a thing to a daughter? What happened to perfect love?

My father was the older of two sons. His father, my grandfather, was a scholar who spoke seven languages and read nine, including Sanskrit. He was one of those fin-de-siècle Universal Men. He got his Ph.D. in physics at twenty-one or so, and eventually became head of the Engineering Department at Gettysburg College, where he also started the art department, using reproductions he himself collected on his travels to Europe and mounted on stiff paper.

My sense of my father's father is that he was a gentle, retiring man whom I would very much like to have known. He died when I was very small. I have only one almost-memory of him, playing Chinese Checkers with my brother in his study, under the light with the green glass shade. The study I knew well, since my grandmother, in a typical nineteenth-century gesture, kept it intact until she died many years later. She even left everything as it was in the little attic storeroom behind the study, full of arrowheads and old boys' books.

When she died, my grandfather had a final joke on my puritanical father, who was appalled to discover a collection of erotica in several languages (including Sanskrit) behind the books on one of the shelves in the study. My father, I am told, threw them all out.

Probably my grandfather failed my father. As a father he was a classic withdrawer, retiring into his study at every possible moment when not presiding over the dinner table or grudgingly sitting out in the parlor for guests. He probably almost never openly displayed any emotions, and his habitual abstraction might have looked very much like sternness to a small boy.

Did he invite my father to come with him on long tramps to collect arrowheads? I don't know. I do know that he left my grandmother to rule the house, and she did, running it as household and antiques shop both, so that you never knew from one visit to the next whether the Virginia sofa or the Sheraton highboy would still be there.

My grandmother was a tiny red-headed lady whose own grandmother had smoked a clay pipe on the frontier in Carthage, Illinois. She herself was an ironbound individualist who died at eighty-six in her own house, having once walked back from a nursing home because, simply, she couldn't stand it. My father, her dutiful son, visited her regularly every other Sunday until she died, bringing her a bottle of Bristol Cream Sherry to serve after dinner when the men brought out the Havana cigars she liked because, dried, the butts repelled moths.

She was every inch, as they say, a lady. She wore a pince-nez and my father was definitely her son visiting in her house—there was no jolly masculine condescension to a little old lady.

How I envied her power! As matriarch, she had reached the peak of female power, like the prerevolutionary Chinese mother-in-law who, having outlived all the other women of the clan, ruled her sons, their wives, their children, and children's children. And my father, having himself been dominated by a powerful mother (made powerful by the willing abdication of her husband from family affairs), grew up to be the classic proud, touchy, fiercely patriarchal male, determined to keep all the other women in his life absolutely under his thumb.

This is the way of all male supremacist societies. Look at Iran, or any other Islamic country; look at India, or even Israel. The dominated daughter grows up to become the dominated wife, whose only chance at power (and revenge) is to control her sons, ensuring the continuation of a breed of males who regard control over women as the *sine qua non* of masculine identity.

And what about her daughters? Unfortunately, it's quite likely that such a mother will reject them—they are, after all, painful reminders of her own powerlessness. Her rejection will drive them into the arms of Daddy, who will seduce and dominate them in his turn, until they too grow up to become mothers who dominate their sons. The cycle is a deadly one, and mothers are always seen as the villains, as if they were superhuman beings who function completely independently of any social or family context.

In his book *Family Constellation,* Walter Toman says that a man who grew up as an older brother of brothers will become a better father to his sons than to his daughters, since he has no experience with girls as sisters, but that he is "inclined to overcontrol both of them and manipulate them beyond necessity." That certainly describes my father.

The daughter of such a father who is (as I was) the youngest sister of brothers is supposed to be an exception, though. "If it were not for his sons and later on for his daughter's suitors," Toman points out, "their relationship might be called perfect. She is feminine, submissive, and invites a man's help and protectiveness in ways that can hardly be resisted. . . . Secretly the father wishes that she would never marry but stay with him."

The last part describes my father perfectly—he was a man who got angry whenever I left home. In fact, my father was so controlling, and so possessive, that I was in desperate rebellion against him and against his fatal, seductive power.

It is true that I grew up tending toward submissiveness. I thought men were people who did just what they wanted at all times, and were especially not in any way responsible to a daughter or younger sister. So I was, willy-nilly, often unnecessarily submissive with men, and hated it. I would end up in a quarreling, brother-sister kind of relationship (always an easy one for a little sister to fall into) or else in a continuous desperate bid for independence. Either a man was going to control me, or I was going to control his access to me; there wasn't any in-between for a long time.

And because my father was remote, angry, and emotionally withdrawn, I was drawn in turn to remote, angry, controlling men who had little love to give anybody. I became a sort of perpetual Little Match Girl, asking feebly for support and love that the men I chose simply did not have to give—and wouldn't give if they did. Outside the relationship, I cultivated extreme independence, so that everyone (including, often, the man I was involved with) thought I was very fierce and tough.

Anne Roiphe has called daughters like me the "under-fathered," but in truth I was in some ways over-fathered. My father wanted me to be Antigone, or even worse, Iphigenia. He demanded nothing less than total devotion—total sacrifice of my life to his needs.

And he terrified me.

What I have to think about are the ways in which he encouraged my femininity and coaxed me into heterosexuality despite the fact that I was afraid of him, while at the same time leaving me angry because, like any emotionally incestuous father, he was using me, manipulating me. He would entice me and then retreat, as if to distance himself from my emotional needs. The result, for me, was a seesaw of hope and disappointment, of promise and rejection.

I need to see how I identified with my father as a powerful being, and how that too often clashed with my femininity. But the femininity he defined for me seemed foolish and useless; it was men who had power and worth.

Which is why I have always had so much trouble with love and work, and why I came late to learn to be a woman.

Once again, writing about him, I wonder: Will I be adequate? Can I possibly match his vision of himself, rock-hard and dapper, standing in the back of that motorboat, a combination of Steve McQueen, Humphrey Bogart, and Al Capone?

He is hugely pleased with himself.

Yet his view of me, his daughter, includes his fear of my power—though never, if he can help it, more than potential power—to shatter his smugness, remind him of his condition as eternal son to a strong mother.

Perhaps it was because my father, like so many other men, had never resolved his problems of relationship with his own mother that his reactions toward me, as a female child, were so confusing and contradictory.

On the one hand, he lectured me just as he lectured my brothers on the evils of vanity (Never use the word "I" in a letter, he would tell me), on not caring too much for the opinion of the world, on being self-reliant. On the other hand, he kept for me a special—if thin—vein of silliness, flirtatiousness, even charm. It was for me he would smile warmly in exchange for a compliment; he very rarely smiled for my brothers. It was with me he would get foolish and fond, and call me his "dizzy blonde," in mock exasperation. It was with me he loved to sit on the porch on summer evenings before dinner.

When I was five and we went out to a hotel for a breakfast treat of waffles, he arranged for "Happy Birthday" to be played over the loudspeakers; later, when we went to the zoo, he bought me my first helium-filled balloon. I kept it bobbing on the ceiling over my bed until it collapsed to the floor.

I believe he thought of himself as an indulgent father—and of me as indulged, self-indulgent, even spoiled. He wanted it that way.

But I had to be very careful in the way I approached him. He liked his women to be well under control. He didn't like surprises, and above all he could not tolerate demands because they threatened the veneer of outward control he fought to maintain. He liked me to be docile, foolish, and pretty.

He didn't want me to have any problems. When I did, his essential contempt for the femininity he believed he cultivated in me came through. "Be tough-minded," he would say, if I ever complained about anything at all; if I felt unhappy, for instance, about something that had happened at school.

I knew what it meant. It meant that I wasn't tough enough to "take it," and that, of course, was because I was a girl.

But, as a girl, I wasn't supposed to be tough-minded. Wasn't supposed to be serious about myself, or about anything I did. The last thing in the world he wanted was for me to be tough-minded in relation to *him*.

Because I found, early on, that his macho pose, his masculine ease of manner, depended on my continuous empathy and sympathy, *on my identification with both his image of me and his need for me to support him in his image of himself.*

So we are seduced; so we first feel our power as women. And we do not recognize the terrible limitations of an identity, a femininity, that is shaped by Daddy's vision of us.

My father needed me to flatter him as Lear needed Goneril and Regan to do so. And if I defect, from him and from other men, am I monstrous, as Góneril and Regan were? If I refuse that ancient feminine role, the seduction of men by flattering their egos, what does it do to me?

When I fall into this trap, I see myself with Daddy's eyes rather than my own.

Which means that I don't really see either him or myself.

In *To the Lighthouse,* Virginia Woolf created two major female characters: the earth-mother, Mrs. Ramsay, is the center of her family and of a whole collection of guests who assemble on an island for their summer holidays. Mrs. Ramsay arranges all their lives, and soothes, cherishes, and nurtures her philosopher-husband, Mr. Ramsay, in very much the same way as she cherishes and nurtures her six-year-old son James.

The artist, Lily Briscoe, is the onlooker, always on the fringe of things. A perpetual daughter-figure, Lily watches Mrs. Ramsay nurture the men, and rejects her role, her continual pitying of the men, who are sterile creatures and would not be able to enter at all into relationships, into the emotional flow of life, if Mrs. Ramsay did not respond to them, for "the whole of the effort of merging and flowing and creating rested on her."

Mrs. Ramsay appears to come alive only when she is relating in this way to other people, especially to men. Alone, she feels herself to be "a wedge-shaped core of darkness, something invisible to others," that is periodically illuminated by the light from the lighthouse as it sweeps across the dark bedroom where she sits. Even alone, she is both illuminated and obliterated by the male, phallic, lighthouse light.

Lily is working on a painting. She refuses to waste herself in rescuing any man just "so that he may expose and relieve the thigh bones, the ribs, of his vanity, of his urgent desire to assert himself."

Lily has chosen not to live in that dark place, not to be visible only in a male light. She has chosen to inhabit a world in which *she* sees things and paints them, rather than a world in which she is lost in men's lives. Yet she is unable to finish her painting. Her vision is sterile. There is a hole at the center of the picture, and the composition will not coalesce.

Years later, Mrs. Ramsay is dead and those left have come once again to the island. Mr. Ramsay comes upon Lily on the lawn where she has set up her easel for yet another try. She is aware of his deep need and longing for a word of sympathy from her—for a connection. She struggles with herself, with her desire to give him *nothing,* and finally, finally, gives in and compliments him on his boots.

With that gesture, she has acknowledged her kinship with Mrs. Ramsay, with the ancient feminine role of connecting, of creating relationships. And she has her reward. When she turns back to the painting, she has a vision of Mrs. Ramsay sitting in her old seat just inside the window, "casting an odd-shaped triangular shadow over the step." The shadow, the wedge of darkness, the core of Mrs. Ramsay's being, becomes a brushstroke on the canvas that, finally, completes the composition and the painting.

Mirrors and mirrors. In Virginia Woolf's brilliant image, the men are emotionally, socially sterile without the women, and the woman, the artist, is sterile in her work if she refuses to make at least a gesture toward feminine interaction with a man. Mr. Ramsay, the father figure, is modeled on Virginia Woolf's own father.

We are drawn, drawn into empathy; but if we go too far, we lose ourselves.

Lily Briscoe did not want to become Mrs. Ramsay. Yet she was not a man, could not assert herself in Mr. Ramsay's style. She was looking at their relationship and could find no image for herself.

All the simple theories of role-modeling, which have daughters simply imitating their mothers to learn how to be a woman, have left Daddy out of the picture altogether. Certainly, we identify with our mothers. But we are also looking very closely at their relationships with our fathers. For instance, if Mother seems to be enjoying herself, then we have good reason to want to grow up to be like her. But if she obviously isn't, then that identification becomes problematical.

Does he value her, or does he seem to want her there only to serve him? Do they fight? Am I a pawn in their power struggle? Does she use me against him, or does he use me against her? Or both?

When my mother and father were locked in argument, shortly before she died, he knew well how to get at her through me. He vetoed my French lessons because he disapproved of the teacher's politics. My mother bought a piano—she wanted me to have the usual girlish accomplishments—but he forbade me to have lessons because, he said, he couldn't stand the racket of my practicing. And when my mother died and we moved, the piano was left behind.

If he wanted his way, he was both patient and vindictive.

I think I am only now, at this late date, getting over my fear of him. Yet the fear had as its effect not my turning altogether against my father, and against men, as it so easily might have done. Rather, his power, and my fear, made me desperate to have him love me but very confused about how to manage this.

And the fact that he defeated my mother, was so much more powerful than she was, made me want very much *not* to be like her.

Daddies do catch us all at the moments of greatest disaffection from our mothers. The first time, we're in the height of our oedipal crush, when all we want to do is replace Mommy and marry Daddy.

Then later, being daughters, we never quite give up our love affair with him even through our heedless girlhoods, even at the height of tomboyishness. What we are very likely to do at that point is to identify with him.

But we've already found we aren't going to grow up and *become* him, so we do the next best thing. We turn our identification into empathy with him and fierce loyalty to his masculine principles.

This is the point at which daughters become "pals" and find they grow up understanding men better than women—liking men better than women.

Empathizing with Daddy, we feel most ourselves.

How I loved it when I sat next to him and filled his pipe. He needed me much more than he needed my mother, obviously.

And, in return for my devotion and my loyalty, he would treat me specially. I would always be important in his eyes, and in the eyes of any other man who came along.

What a trap this can be! He is so conveniently there, and if he and Mother play me off against each other, how easy it is to use him in an alliance against her. Who cares if she is hopelessly nagging; he understands me.

We hardly ever think about the returns we really get from Daddy, as long as he's there to elevate us.

At eight, I would roller-skate up and down the long side porch, following the shadow lines of the banisters. I knew I was driving my mother, who was trying to take a nap upstairs, crazy. I was also being like my father, on the move, free to leave, free to come back, skates and banister-shadows my train and railroad track. If I were he, she'd have to pay attention to me.

But oh, I didn't want to be her, lying upstairs in the bedroom with her perpetual headache, her afternoon nap.

From the height of my alliance with this superior person, my father, I could look back on my mother—this person who had formerly controlled every aspect of my existence, who had decided when I ate and slept and shat—and pity her. She, after all, was only Daddy's wife, no relation to him really. I was his flesh and blood, his *family*.

So we forsake our allegiance to our own sex and we give it to Daddy, the mirror of our independent selves, the polar opposite of Mother. We grow up seeing ourselves through Daddy's eyes rather than through our own, anxiously measuring ourselves against his expectations, looking for the approval that will show us we've succeeded.

But my father held me at arm's length. In adolescence, when I especially needed him, he was conflicted by urges toward both seductiveness and avoidance, and by an obsessive need to control me. He wanted, finally, to prevent me from growing up into that attractive and threatening woman who would leave him.

I would take with me a piece of his control over the universe. I would take away one of his links with humanity, with the world of emotions that he himself had renounced, in his struggle to become what is considered, in our role-obsessed culture, acceptably masculine.

I was the female part of himself, isolated, alienated, cast off into the world of the Other, the world he had renounced in order to become a man.

My father had exquisite taste. When he came home from World War II, he brought beautiful Persian rugs and intricate inlaid boxes full of tiny silver spoons, Persian miniatures on ivory panels, silk handkerchiefs, a sandalwood box for me lined with blue silk and filled with necklaces dyed lavender and pale pink, made of tiny nautilus shells.

He brought me a Bokhara prayer rug, suitable size for a five-year-old girl. Some handkerchiefs were embroidered with the insignia of the Persian Gulf Command. That corner of the Army will forever be identified for me with exquisite taste.

Yet my father had to repudiate it. This taste ran in our family; but since my grandfather, none of the men has been able to reconcile it with his masculine image. My uncle gave up photography, at which he was very good, simply, I believe, because he loved it and couldn't admit this love to himself. It didn't match his self-image, man-image.

When my brother's son was small, he once chased a Frisbee into a field and came back holding a buttercup in one hand and the Frisbee in the other.

"Come on," my brother yelled gruffly. "You can't throw a Frisbee while you're holding a buttercup. Make up your mind."

Choose: choose the Frisbee, because that is masculine. Throw away the buttercup.

The beautiful things were brought home from the war to gratify my mother and me. Spoils of war to adorn the women, to indulge them. And within that narrow sphere, my father could indulge his own femininity— as long as it was projected onto the women.

My father was tremendously self-indulgent, but he denied it—accusing me instead. And he took his denial out on my brothers, for whom no discipline was too great.

So he pushes and pulls. Smile for me, he says. Be pretty; entertain and nourish and satisfy me; sympathize. But don't grow up to become a threatening woman like my mother, or like yours. Remain innocent and controllable. *Never leave me.*

Because as long as you're part of me, I've got the feminine part of myself under control. Handy, available, but nonthreatening.

My father and I were equally boxed in by his aversion to femininity. I believe his alienation from all that he considered feminine alienated him from himself, from his own emotions, making him murderously competitive with his·sons.

I believe that the force that drove up his blood pressure until it killed him was compounded of bottled-up rage, anxiety, and tremendous frustration that he could not make the world run his way; that in the end even I, the daughter from whom he expected devotion, had left home and seldom returned. He had alienated all his family.

Yet the world—the world of work, of opinion, of psychology and religion—run as it was by other men, never demanded that he change, that he come to terms with his alienated self.

It was always so much easier to blame the women. And to give your daughter double messages.

CHAPTER FOUR

My Heart Belongs to Daddy:
How Daddy Shapes His Daughter's Identity

*N*ot long ago, a friend of mine was complaining to me on the telephone about her mother, who was driving her crazy, always wanting to know what she was doing, how she was getting along, whether she was dating anyone steadily yet (my friend was recently divorced).

What was worse, though, were the mixed messages. For instance, it was of course wonderful that my friend had been promoted to associate editor, but men haven't changed all that much. If she's *too* ambitious, won't that perhaps scare them away?

"This," says my friend, "from a mother who used to brag about how her daughter got straight As."

That was funny, I said, because I had just been making some discoveries about how fathers often give mixed messages to daughters—and have been known, in fact, to drive us crazy as competently as any mother.

There was a long pause, then my friend said, in a distinctly chilly voice, "Speaking as a Daddy's Girl, I have to tell you that it's always been my *mother* who drives me crazy."

A great many of us are Daddies' Girls. We like our fathers better than our mothers. They don't pry into our affairs; they don't ask us whether we have a boyfriend, or when we're going to get a decent couch.

Fathers are more *reasonable* than mothers. Of course, what this boils down to is that we can, usually, get around our fathers more easily. "A smile," said Alicia Appleman, "will get you a lot farther with your father than your mother." When Alicia and Patty found out they could always manipulate Steve into five dollars or the car after their mother automatically said No, there was no way they weren't going to put themselves firmly in Steve's camp.

When we were growing up, middle-class Daddies usually came with very attractive perks. They were likely, for instance, to have had more money to give out in the first place. It was, usually, ultimately Daddy's money that bought us the cashmere or Shetland sweater sets with which we one-upped our friends. (When we went with our mothers to buy them, we used the second charge card, the one issued to our mothers—

or even to ourselves—under his name.) Daddy's career had put us into a nice house, a good neighborhood, the right schools. We drew our sense of status in the world, of entitlement, or privilege from *his* status—and from the things he gave us.

If we were working class, things happened a little differently. Our mothers were more likely to have worked too, and may well have taken over Daddy's paycheck on Friday nights even if they didn't work. It wasn't so much a question of the privileges he enabled us to take for granted as it was of simply learning that he was boss. We learned this in the middle class, too, of course, especially when he refused us the charge card. ("What do you think, I'm made out of money?"), but more often Daddy's authority was disguised by indulgence.

Working mothers in every class were still likely to have had dinner on the table when Daddy came home, and to have let us know that even if they were earning some money Daddy was still the man on the Outside, completely important and necessary to our mothers' sense of identity and the fitness of things.

So we learned, from our fathers and our mothers, both the advantages and the inevitability of Daddy, this man on the Outside, who held title to the whole world even if our mothers, like Holly Flax's, could lay claim to dominance Inside the smaller world of the family.

And yet, even before we really understood the politics of the wide world, we had our own reasons for wanting Daddy on the Outside.

Daddy is, remember, our first hero, the man who, we believe, will rescue us from our intense, ambivalent involvement with Mother and make us feel separate and autonomous. At the same time, he is the focus of our increasingly erotic excitement and the stimulus for our earliest heterosexual fantasies.

He obviously plays an important role in shaping our identities. Yet this role, which goes far beyond those of hero or sex object but is closely linked with both, is perhaps the least understood aspect of the whole relationship.

Theories about identity, and the process by which a young girl makes the identifications that determine her behavior and mold her image of herself, are many and various. Does she, for instance, like Pavlov's dogs, respond to reward and punishment? Or does she imitate the appropriate sex-role model, her mother, and so become feminine? These are the two theories most people are aware of; indeed, the phrases "sex role" and "role model" have become clichés. And while daughters most certainly do identify with their fathers as well as their mothers, we somehow assume that mothers, since they are "feminine role models," will automatically have more influence.

One young father told me he was glad he had had a daughter because he thought his wife was a much more responsible person than he. She was working full time while he was writing a novel and holding down a part-time job, a model he didn't think he would want his son to follow. "But of course my daughter will model herself on her mother, so that's okay."

"What if she models herself on you?" I asked, and received a thoughtful silence.

Identification is, in fact, a subtle, complex process that goes on all our lives. Psychologists and psychoanalytic thinkers frequently disagree about how it works, and they are constantly coming up with new theories about how we become the people we are. One of these ideas actually has a fairly long history in psychoanalytic theory, but recently it has taken on new importance for understanding how daughters' identities are shaped in the context of our passionate attachments to our fathers.

The Identity Triangle

We enter the Identity Triangle when we look past Mother to Daddy—when, as I described in Chapter One, we are lured by his glamour, his power, the excitement of his Otherness, to begin to identify with him as a way of separating from Mother. So even before we fall in love with him, Daddy becomes an important person in our universe.

The research of Dr. T. Berry Brazelton at Harvard has shown that infant girls younger than six months respond differently to Daddy's body and to his voice. The psychoanalytic theorist Dr. Ernest Abelin, who has developed much of the idea of triangulation, points out that by six months, when the infant is first differentiating herself from Mother, Daddy becomes both interesting and essential. Then, as the baby grows into a toddler and discovers the excitement of moving around under her own steam, Daddy becomes identified with what another psychoanalytic theorist, Dr. Phyllis Greenacre, has called a "love affair with the world."

The full-fledged toddler begins, explains Dr. John Ross, "to identify with Daddy as a being perceived to be different from herself and different from her mother, who exists in relation to the mother but is not the same as her." In other words, if we are having a hard time telling ourselves apart from Mother, the addition of a third person, Daddy, provides the contrast that makes us able to see Mother more clearly. As we look from one to the other, as we perceive their relationship to each other and respond to their different ways of handling us, we begin to develop a sense of ourselves as a person who isn't, in fact, quite the same as either one of them.

For boys, who must "disidentify" from Mother much more completely than girls, Daddy becomes a crucial element in the Triangle too, and he offers for them the same lures of autonomy and independence he holds out for us. But for boys, of course, direct identification with Daddy, and with Daddy's world, points the way to the future. We may want to claim all Mommy's love that Daddy seems to get, and be bigger than she is, and be able to walk away from her whenever we want. But little boys can actually look forward to doing so, and their claim on all this is compensation for the pain of giving up their infantile closeness and identification with Mother. As they bury their mother-identification along with their passionate oedipal love for her, they bury their Identity Triangle, too. From then on, they identify with other boys and men in a simpler, more linear fashion. "I am masculine, not feminine," they can say, and so resolve identity conflicts in an either-or way that, for the moment at least, makes their identities much more clearly defined than girls'.

But daughters don't give up Mother. We go on loving her, and identifying with her as our most important image of adult femininity. We *add* our identifications with Daddy to make the Triangle.

And then, not only do we discover that, inevitably, we're never going to become Daddy; we also begin to discover that we're not even supposed to be like him. Just as we're thinking about our own autonomy, he's telling us our future lies in a *relationship*—with him.

And we have already begun to figure out for ourselves that since we can't become him, we need to enter into an alliance with him in order to feel more singular, more separate from our mothers. So we enter wholeheartedly into the Triangle.

It may be that the minute we realize we need Daddy to rescue us, the minute we understand, however unconsciously, that we must depend on our attachment to him to separate from our mothers and that our future lies in a relationship with him, we become heterosexual. And feminine. So we fall in love with him, and when we add erotic excitement to the excitement of his power and autonomy, we're well and truly hooked.

When we fall in love with Daddy, our Identity Triangle becomes more complex because the lines of love and identification run along both sides, from us to our mothers and back, and from us to our fathers and back. But Daddy's side of the Triangle becomes very special. We are idealizing him, and we continue our passionate attachment to him until well into adolescence—sometimes even into adulthood. *This means that the object of our love, and our idealized image of independence, power, and authority are one and the same: Daddy.*

Even so, nothing about attaching ourselves to Daddy at this stage in our lives indicates that we will grow up to be passive nonachievers. Fran Nobile, after all, was immensely attached to her father.

But our idealization of him makes us very vulnerable. Even as we create a Daughters' Myth of the knight in shining armor who has the weapons to free us from Mother, we need very much to feel that our knight loves us. Otherwise, how will we ever feel that he *has* singled us out?

As Dr. Ross puts it: "It does seem, for whatever reason, very important for daughters to be adored by their fathers, as little children. It validates them. The father mirrors their value."

Indeed, even if Daddy fails us, as he too often does, it is much easier for us to blame ourselves ("I wasn't lovable enough") than to blame him. For if he fails us and we admit it, what do we have left? There is nobody to stand as a boundary between us and Mommy, or between us and the Outside world, the world of Daddies. We are caught between two overwhelming forces—without weapons to deal with either.

So our identification with our father takes place within the context of our passionate attachment to him. It is part of a relationship that has always had an erotic side. And this erotic aspect of the relationship extends its influence into every other aspect. The need to enjoy Daddy, says Dr. Ross, "becomes elaborated in terms of needing his love and approval for other pursuits."

So there is always this complication in our identification with Daddy: the man who symbolizes independence must also validate our identity as an attractive female. He sets the seal on our heterosexuality. *But does he also validate our autonomy?*

Even as we attach ourselves to Daddy, we still want to feel we are capable, competent, able to take care of ourselves and master at least our own corner of the world. We are as ready as boys to become interested in a challenge, and we respond just as much to the excitement of achievement, of success. We like to move our bodies around, to climb and run, and we want to come and go as freely as possible.

Are we going to be encouraged by the Daddy we idealize to experience these things, or not? Well, that depends on Daddy. Because he, too, has some definite aims for us and, more than likely, as we shall see, his aims are not the same as ours. And since we turn to him at the height of our idealization, when he seems the most powerful, when we are most caught up in our relationship with him and most vulnerable, what *Daddy* wants is the crucial element.

For the rest of our lives, our ability (or lack of it) to integrate attachment and autonomy in our lives will depend to a large degree on just what Daddy wants from us. If he doesn't encourage our bid for independence, we are thrown into our first conflict between autonomy and attachment—the conflict that will later become the familiar feminine one between love and work. If he does encourage us, then we may be lucky enough to avoid this conflict altogether. On this stroke of good or ill luck, on this turn of the wheel, our whole future may depend.

Reciprocal Identification

What happens is that Daddy becomes the mirror in which we discover our feminine identity. This is not a brand-new idea, but it reemerged in the 1960s, when study after study showed that, as Dr. Michael E. Lamb of the University of Utah puts it, "the more masculine the father, the more feminine his daughter."

Our identification with Daddy is usually not direct, as a boy's is, but reciprocal. Daddy gives us cues to the kind of femininity he finds pleasing in us, and we respond by shaping ourselves into the image he demands. In part, he does this through his own particular masculine style, as my father did by being a pipe-smoker and letting me fill his pipe. In part, he does it through many more-or-less subtle messages.

Because we so very much want Daddy to love us, we are extremely sensitive to all his cues about what kind of behavior will please him, as Helene Deutsch, the first person to notice Daddy's importance as a mirror for femininity, discovered in the reports of her women patients.

Mothers, of course, are our first mirrors. As tiny infants, we need Mother to mirror our needs with love, care, and sensitivity. If she does that, we start life feeling we are basically okay. A little later, but still before we turn to Daddy, we are mothering dolls, earnestly replaying our first relationship, with ourselves in the position of power.

Mother also mirrors our biological sex, so that when we work through our early childhood confusion about which sex is which, we end up firmly identifying with her as female.

If our father or another man is around, we identify with our mother as a woman who has a relationship with this man, Daddy or a father figure; and if she seems at all happy, we take cues from what seems to work in attracting him.

Traditionally, this was pretty much all daughters were expected to do in the way of identification: sort out our biological sex, learn to attract a man, develop mothering skills. Today, if we are lucky, the role model our mother presents us with will open up beyond diapers and dinner—if our mother is, for instance, a lawyer or doctor or small businesswoman or beautician or electrician or painter or welder or writer or social worker.

But there always has been that other leg of the Identity Triangle, with Daddy at the other end instead of Mother. When we look to him for a mirror, what do we find?

Daddy's Little Girl

Most often, Daddy wants us to be feminine, with all that implies to him—to this particular Daddy, with his own particular history. And then, he is idealizing us at just about the same time we are idealizing him.

He couldn't, as a small boy, control his mother. He can't, as an adult, always or maybe even very often control his wife. He can control us. We are, in the words of Dr. Tessman, his "controllable ideal little girl."

He sees us as fragile, delicate, sensitive, beautiful. None of these traits is threatening. We enhance him: *he* has sired this delicate creature. Out of his strong masculine body came the seed to make another sex, a sex completely different (he fondly imagines) from his own. He is fascinated, attracted.

So he sets out to mold us into his image of the ideal woman, to teach us what being feminine means.

Only, too often, his idea of femininity involves a lot of stereotypes. Psychologists have found, over a period of years, that Daddies see their daughters as stereotypically feminine from a very early age.

Dr. Lamb writes of a 1974 study in which both fathers and mothers saw newborn girls as "soft, fine-featured, little, inattentive, weak, and delicate." But fathers were more extreme about these judgments than mothers, seeing daughters as "more beautiful, pretty, and cute than sons," despite the fact that newborn girls are "physiologically more mature and more robust" than newborn boys.

Yet, as Dr. Lamb points out, these traits are "clearly desirable," meaning they make females desirable to males. A father who sees his daughter as weak and inattentive will be more attracted to her. These traits—or a father's illusion that his daughter possesses them—are survival mechanisms for infant girls because they "enhance paternal involvement with daughters."

Indeed. And for about the first year, fathers seem to treat sons and daughters very similarly. But by the second year, fathers spend twice as much time interacting with sons as with daughters. Dr. Lamb suggests that this may be to force daughters to spend more time with their mothers. But it may also be because fathers identify more with sons and want to be with them, because they feel their masculinity is both more enhanced and more challenged by a son.

Nevertheless, remember, Daddy is at this point much more *exciting* to a little girl than her mother is—just as he is to a boy. By two, for instance, most boys choose to play with their fathers rather than their mothers, and so do many girls. Others may alternate between the two; not until age four do girls consistently choose to play with their mothers.

By two, toddlers are fairly competent on their feet; between two and three, they consolidate their sense of their gender identities. Fathers have fallen into place in the Identity Triangle, and a child's relationship to Daddy has become, in a sense, the prototype for later moves away from Mother toward the world.

At this stage, according to Dr. Ross, characteristic interaction between fathers and children has become sex-typed. He describes a father with his two-and-a-half-year-old son in a nursery setting: "like the other fathers, Jake does not face his son but sits to the side and slightly in back of him." A son faces out into the world, and his father encourages his autonomy as a sign of his masculinity. The son also avoids face-to-face contact; father and son communicate through impersonal activities, such as hammering nails into a piece of wood.

A three-year-old girl, Nancy, and her father are a very different story. For play, Nancy chooses her father over her mother most of the time. She, too, loves building things with him, and she, too, gets tossed up in the air. But "for the most part, Nancy will seek to engage her father more directly, sensuously, and somewhat flirtatiously. She will face him. . . . Or she will fit her body to his, languishing there, close against him. . . . And she will talk more with her father, her language development having progressed more rapidly than that of most boys."

Nancy's father, suggests Dr. Ross, must cope with two different responses: he is attracted to his daughter and he identifies with her. If he is anxious about either of these responses, he may start avoiding her. But if he is not too anxious, if he is able to enjoy his daughter, he may be giving her messages that tell her to be "as girlish as possible." So he "abets and quickens a little girl's thrust toward womanhood, long before the goal is in any way comprehensible to the child herself."

Helene Deutsch is today held in low repute by many feminists, who feel that she placed too much emphasis on passivity and masochism in women. She did, but she also saw very clearly how much the environment—and especially parents—contribute. She wrote forty years ago about how fathers treat sons and daughters differently, using language a feminist might use today:

> We have seen that children of both sexes ask the father as the representative of reality to help them liberate themselves from the mother. This request is sometimes granted to the girl with regard to activity, but never with regard to aggression. Has anyone ever seen a father romping with his little daughter in any manner except lovingly? Does he ever encourage her in competitive struggles? The bribe offered to the little girl by the father, as a representative of the environment, is love and tenderness.

Many researchers since have observed that the father treats his daughter differently from his son. He tells his son what to do and has definite expectations of him; but he is likely to expect a great deal less from his daughter. "In learning situations," writes Dr. Lamb, "fathers seem more concerned about making the situation enjoyable than about ensuring mastery of the task, and they apparently seek to protect their daughters from failure." Some fathers, like Steve Appleman, get too involved;

others withdraw completely. "Overall, then, the message conveyed to young girls may be that success is to be attained via affective relationships rather than through independent achievement."

So our fathers encourage us to find our earliest sense of self not in exploration of the world, but in a relationship with another person. Intimacy with Daddy is useful and necessary. It's part of his job in "seducing" us into heterosexuality. But it's also where our conflicts begin. We turn to our Daddy in our bid for independence, autonomy, selfhood—and, too often, our bid stops short, right there in Daddy's lap. He's not a bridge out into the world, he is the world.

So the little girl's conflict between Daddy's love and tenderness and her own autonomy arises not from any innate fears of loss of love, but from the man who has the power to make her feel important and singular. She does, in part, give him this power, it is true. She is vulnerable to Daddy's message; but he doesn't have to give it. He can tell her he loves her when she is strong, independent, and competitive, as Fran Nobile's father did.

If he does that, she will learn a very different kind of heterosexual femininity than if he simply wants her to be pretty and passive, like Holly Flax's father.

Heterosexual Femininity

Heterosexual femininity is what we learn in our relationship to our fathers. "Maternal" femininity—the mothering part of our personalities—we learn, says sociologist Dr. Miriam M. Johnson of the University of Oregon, from our mothers. Dr. Johnson is one of the people who developed the idea of reciprocal identification, and she saw that the maternal aspect of women's identity is different from the "heterosexual," which includes every aspect of femininity that is geared to relating to men "in terms of their masculinity."

Heterosexual femininity is what Daddy "seduces" us into when he "seduces" us into heterosexuality. Usually, he doesn't even have to work very hard at this because we are so eager to associate ourselves with him.

The only problem is that the heterosexual femininity we learn in our relationship with our fathers does not just provide a way of relating to men in personal relationships. It helps form the basis for our adult interaction with the Outside world, the world of male dominance hierarchies, of achievement, of money and power.

On its deepest level, heterosexual femininity includes everything I discussed in the last chapter: how we feel about our feminine sexuality, whether it's good, just okay, or a serious liability, something to be hidden, something dangerous or "Bad." Or whether it's okay in some circumstances (with a husband) but not in others (with a boyfriend, perhaps). Part of this knowledge may also involve a sense of whether it's okay to wear "sexy" clothes or whether we should always be "modest."

Heterosexual femininity includes whether we feel comfortable with a man, or with men—and under what circumstances. How are we used to behaving with a man? Do we smile a lot? Do we flatter him, or discount our own needs in order to empathize, and identify, with his? Do we think he is basically more important than we are?

Since we were babies we have been responding to thousands of tiny, subtle cues on these things. And, of course, we learn from our fathers things like whether it's okay to disagree with a man, or to say No; or whether we have to say Yes and then get around him indirectly, if we can.

Heterosexual femininity includes our sense of whether or not we have permission, relative to our fathers (and therefore to other men), to allow ourselves to develop—and display—such personality traits as determination, assertiveness, self-reliance, competitiveness, initiative, ambition, dominance, or leadership. It may even include whether or not we think we can allow ourselves to admit—let alone use—traits that we are born with, like intelligence and talent. It includes whether we take what *we* do seriously, or only what Daddy does; whether we feel competent and able to deal with the world ourselves, in our own cause, or whether we only feel strong and competent next to Daddy, because he deals with the world. Whether, in short, we need to keep a Daddy on the Outside.

Finally, heterosexual femininity includes all the things we *expect* from a man. Do we expect him to hail cabs, take us out to dinner, earn more money than we do? Do we expect him to be the provider while we build a nest, or to be a hero who will rescue us from our own muddled attempts at coping with our lives? Or do we expect him to disparage us, or even knock us down? If we "provoke" him, will he yell at us, strike us? Do we have to please him all the time?

Of course, we are going to pick up a lot of cues from our mothers, and our sense of how they relate to our fathers, and these cues will influence our sense of our own possibilities quite a bit. Remember, too, that the cues we pick up from our mothers are rooted not just in their knowledge of their husbands, our fathers, but in what they learned from *their* fathers—and what the line of women behind them back through time learned. Women pass on what works with men, whether it is ultimately positive for women's own identity or negative, like suppressing our intelligence to please a man.

Helene Deutsch has pointed out that we also may imitate our mothers in order to get our fathers' approval. So, ultimately, it is still the fathers who are the ultimate validators and shapers of our heterosexual femininity.

There remains a third aspect of femininity: feminine style. This includes how we wear our hair and make up our faces, whether our skirts are long or short, full or straight; how we walk and talk and our style of flirting. Feminine style might be part of heterosexual femininity (if Daddy loved us with curly hair as children, we might go on curling our hair as adults); but it can also be picked up easily from mothers, teachers, girlfriends, movies, television, or magazines. Girls who grow up without fathers don't have trouble with this aspect of femininity; in fact, it may very well be the girl who is most insecure about her heterosexual femininity who is most sensitive to cultural cues about style. A girl who feels secure in her father's love might feel perfectly free to choose shop instead of home economics and risk the label "masculine." Fran Nobile certainly didn't feel her femininity was threatened when she pumped gas one summer.

All the traits we think of when we talk about someone who is "typically feminine"—passivity, dependency on men, insecurity about being competent in the world, and so forth—belong to women whose personalities were molded in a family in which women defer, or expect to defer, to Daddy, the Outside man.

If this pattern is changing today, daughters of fathers now in full flush of a new kind of fatherhood will have to tell us, in ten or twenty or thirty years, what it was like.

When a father is an equal-time caretaker of his daughter, as several I interviewed were, the turn toward the father at two or three years old is likely to be less extreme, less desperate, because a daughter's embroilment with Mommy will be less consuming. One father I interviewed said that when he is away, his daughter always says she misses him and wishes he were there to read her a story; yet when his wife, who also travels frequently, is away, the daughter asks for her. In short, he said, "She plays both ends against the middle." This isn't all that surprising since we do know that when a child has both parents around, she—or he—tends to want them both around all the time. After all, who wants to have to choose?

Such a father and mother may also have less of a stake in hanging onto their daughter as part of themselves. A mother who feels like an autonomous person will not cling to her daughter; nor will a mother who is happy living her own life want to deny a daughter hers. Similarly, a father who experiences his own femininity more directly, through nurturing an infant and small child, will be less likely to expect his daughter to live out the secret, buried, Inside parts of himself. He will be more able to see his daughter as a separate person rather than as a supportive element in a relationship designed to keep him afloat.

Everything is changing today, and new patterns of family will eventually produce new patterns of identity in women and men.

The daughter of the future, though, will still learn her femininity as much through interaction with her father as from direct imitation of her mother.

Little girls who grow up with fathers include in their femininity from the very beginning a sense of masculinity, how it works, what it expects from femininity. If we have a loving relationship with our fathers, this sense is very strong and pleasurable. The relationship, it could almost be said, becomes part of our identity.

Too often, unfortunately, it becomes the whole of it.

No wonder so many of us grow up and *continue to feel that we have arrived at autonomy when we are in a relationship with a man.*

Historically, women were considered to arrive at adulthood when we married and had children. As daughters, we were subordinate to our fathers, and dependent on them; as wives, we were subordinate to our husbands and, legally at least, dependent on them.

So the move Outside our father's house led straight Inside to the center of a new family, in which we switched from the daughter's corner of the Identity Triangle to the mother's, but otherwise found our position little changed.

A life defined by attachment to father or husband has been the pattern for most women in the world through all of history. Only within the last 150 years or so have women—feminists, for the most part—questioned this pattern by daring to suggest that women might venture on their own into the Outside world: the world of work, of writing, of exploration, of success and failure, of achievement, money-earning, and public recognition.

By daring to suggest, in short, that women might be autonomous beings. Selves.

Yet our struggle toward selfhood continues to be made more difficult by the messages our fathers give us.

Let Daddy Do It

The general message that we "be as girlish as possible" is not going to be delivered in the same way by every father. But as he strives to shape our femininity in relation to his masculinity, Daddy is going to be motivated in part by his culturally conditioned ideas of the nature of that relationship.

As a small boy, for instance, he probably shaped his masculinity at least as much in opposition to what his culture considered feminine as he did in imitation of masculine models. Now, when he has his chance to mold a daughter into his image of ideal femininity, he may want to polarize her into someone very different from the masculine identity he has developed. This is called "complementarity."

His ideal femininity is designed to be different in order to *fit in* with his masculinity.

Consider:

Dr. Nobile, doctor, dominant male, father, wants his daughter to be his opposite number—Mother.

Holly Flax's father, sole breadwinner, debater of politics with his sons, wanted Holly to be his opposite—passive, pretty, and nice.

Steve Appleman, superachiever, oldest son, Hope of the Family, wants his daughters to be his opposite—self-indulgent and dependent.

My father, the tough guy, wanted me to be the dizzy blonde—and thought of me as a Golddigger.

If part of Daddy's pleasure in his daughter is that she is controllable, part of his unconscious aim will be to mold her into a femininity that will enhance his sense of his own masculinity. If, for instance, independence, competency, and control are all important aspects of his masculinity, he may feel that women cannot or should not possess such traits. Furthermore, he wants his daughter to love him (although her love for him is not as critical for his self-image as his love is for hers), and he may believe that her love, too, should serve to enhance his masculinity.

So he may give her a series of messages that all add up to Let Daddy Do It. The substance of this message is that if a daughter is passive, dependent, unsure of her own competency in the world, Daddy will feel strong and masculine, no matter how many doubts he may have about his masculinity in other contexts. His daughter's identity is shaped to help him feel like a man.

When Steve Appleman finished his daughters' themes, he was saying, "Let Daddy Do It."

He was saying the same thing when he told them they could cut school. "Daddies have to work hard every day," was the message. "You don't. Let Daddy Do It."

When the father of the conventional Princess showers her with money and clothes, he is saying, "I can take care of you: I'm Daddy. Let me do it."

My father's restaurant ritual was giving me the same message.

Ultimately, this was what Dr. Nobile was saying when he wouldn't let Fran play softball because boys should use the field, boys who needed to learn to be competent so they could grow up to be Daddies.

(Actually, this is a variant of Let Daddy Do It that might be called Your Brothers Can Do It But You Can't. The point is that boys are learning the skills that will enable them to say "Let Daddy Do It" to their own daughters.)

The classic Let Daddy Do It message is Smile for Daddy, the message Holly Flax's father gave her, the one Gretchen Cryer and Nancy Ford immortalized in the song of that name in their hit show, *I'm Getting My Act Together and Taking It on the Road.* To get your act together, as Holly Flax has done, means to defy Daddy's message—to say, "No, thank you, I can take care of myself." This is not always the easy thing to do. It is made much more difficult by the implications of Let Daddy Do It. Because inside this message are a number of others.

Message #1: "I'm Superior, You're Inferior."

This says that Daddy is superior because he can do all the things we can't, and can give us all the things we can't give ourselves.

If we're inherently inferior, why try?

It sounds a lot like the small boy's attitude toward girls. And the small boy, we know, often feels that if he *isn't* superior to girls, more competent, more privileged, and so forth, his identity is compromised.

So, too often, does Daddy. Dr. Nobile was acting out of this conviction when he took his son up the ski slope to compensate him for failing to be (as yet) superior to his big sister.

This message is one of the most maddening a father can give a daughter because there is almost no defense against it.

My father would say, "I'm superior to you and there is no way you'll ever catch up because you'll never grow up to be a Daddy."

If you'll never catch up to him, you might as well latch on to his coattails.

Message #2: "You'll Hurt Me," or, "If You Can Do It, I Can't."

On one level, Daddy is saying, "You will wound me, injure my self-esteem, if you refuse to let me take care of you, if you become able to manage your own life."

This message is a familiar one. How many of us have been counseled by prudent mothers to be careful about wounding a man's ego? What they really meant was that he is supposed to be the only one with an ego, with a sense of himself as competent, independent, master of the world. How many of us were taught little tricks to make boys and men feel masculine next to us? Holly's mother was teaching her this when she sat silently while her husband involved Holly's brothers in discussions.

Whether we, or they, are consciously aware of it or not, we get a lot of these messages first from our fathers.

Think about it.

If Daddy takes us to the playground on weekend mornings and we get into an altercation with a little boy, will he be likely to encourage us to fight back? Or will he scold the little boy for fighting with a girl? If we get into an argument with another girl, will he tell us both that fighting isn't nice?

If he does these things, he is letting us know that for him, femininity means remaining passively attached to a powerful, competent Daddy (who feels powerful and competent because we're passive).

There is a threat behind this message. In addition to sensing that we will wound his self-esteem if we learn to take care of ourselves, we become, ever-so-secretly, afraid.

Message #3: "You'll Lose Me," or, "If you learn to take care of yourself, you won't need me."

If Daddy's sense of masculinity in relation to femininity is that men take care of women, then a woman who can take care of herself may threaten him. He may let his daughter know that his love is conditional on her needing him; his support might be withdrawn if she becomes too strong, too competent.

Such a father has no trouble bonding with us as infants, when we really are helpless. But how about when we are growing up, becoming lean and strong, able to learn to ride bikes, climb trees, play softball?

We are sensitive to the message that we may lose Daddy if we involve ourselves in these things. And the suggestion of power in the message that our behavior can help make Daddy feel strong or weak is seductive. So we may, like Holly Flax for the first part of her life, give up on any idea of individual initiative, settling for the illusion of power Daddy holds out when he asks us to sacrifice our own competency for the sake of his ego.

The terrible thing about all these implications of Let Daddy Do It is that they happen so naturally. Each serves to maintain the bond that our supposed fragility fostered when we were born, keeping Daddy protective while we are growing up and after all still do need him.

Then, at the moment when we are idealizing him as our rescuer, his dreams and ours may meet. He would like nothing better than to be the rescuer we seem to him not only to want but to need. So a pact is struck, all unconsciously, and the structure of our future relationships with men, and with the world of men, is given shape through a mutual emotional seduction.

And there is a further irony.

While women have begun to struggle against some of the implications of Let Daddy Do It, one reason Daddy does want to do things for us continues to be because that is how he gets to live out, vicariously, the femininity he gave up on his way to masculinity.

Daughters and the Secret Side of Daddy

While we are trying Daddy on for size, identifying with his attractive masculine perks, he is vicariously identifying with us.

Through us, he has the chance to live out those forbidden, feminine parts of himself, the parts he had to deny in order to become whatever his particular corner of the culture labeled "masculine." His delight in us, in our femininity, helps him compensate for the things he lost when he turned away from Mother—the softness, the tenderness, the expression of feelings.

These things, or the yearning for these things, he has kept hidden away. He doesn't show them in the locker room, or at work, or playing poker. He may sometimes show some of them to his wife, but more often he may feel it necessary to keep up a masculine front with her: she is the one with the feelings.

With us, with his daughter, he can make connection with *a feminine person who is part of himself.* He may identify with us secretly, like Steve Appleman. Or he may do it by being openly playful and tender with us.

With us he can, as my father did, indulge his own love for beauty without admitting that that love is part of himself.

If he indulges us, again like Steve, he may be vicariously indulging himself, making up for all the leisure time, the fun, the pleasure he feels he lost out on in the struggle for manhood, the push to earn a living, to achieve.

My father, the tough guy, wanted me to be the silly, dizzy blonde he could never be.

Dr. Nobile, dominant male, Catholic, and father, wants his daughter ultimately to be a mother, something he could never be, and might, as most men do, secretly envy.

Holly Flax's father wanted her to be pretty, passive, decorative. His image of masculinity required that he refuse his wife's help in maintaining a standard of living they both demanded. Maybe he would have liked to be able to be pretty and decorative himself.

If the secret feminine yearnings of all these fathers seem to be satisfied by the same feminine images they have demanded as their polar opposites, that should not be surprising. What else would we envy, yearn to be, except our opposite—the person we can never be?

But once again the apparently perfectly natural working out of things ends up not working out very well for daughters. *It brings us right back into that state of semisubmergence inside a relationship that we wanted to escape when we turned to Daddy in the first place.*

Because if we embody the secret, Inside, feminine part of Daddy, then he doesn't want us to be separate from him. Doesn't, in fact, even *perceive* us as separate from him. We not only belong to him, we are part of him.

And if we are his ideal, controllable little girl, living out the image of femininity with which he presents us, we are also really a part of him—of his fantasies of masculinity and femininity.

No wonder men have always taken the devotion of daughters like Antigone for granted.

No wonder daughters like Goneril and Regan, looking out for their own interests, are regarded as treacherous and wicked.

And no wonder we, the daughters, confuse our identities with Daddy's vision of us, confuse our autonomous selves with ourselves in the *relationship*—and so feel we exist only when we are lost in empathy with his needs, in vicarious identification with his power and accomplishment.

Everyone and everything—our mothers, our fathers, history, religion, the structures of the family and society—has taught us that this is our true destiny.

Femininity, then, became by definition not an autonomous identity but a self-abnegation, part of a relationship in which other people, men, feel whole and nurtured as long as we remain the secret, Inside parts of themselves, and in which we feel whole only as long as Daddy loves us.

Daddy's Mixed Message: "Don't Go Too Far"

Daddy is confused, so he confuses us.

That's one way to look at it. Because a lot of those messages Daddy is giving out to his daughters are not only subliminal; they are mixed.

"Smile for Daddy, and I will love you and take care of you," is pretty straightforward. So is "Get good grades and I will approve of you."

But what about: "Get good grades in school, but don't plan to go to college"? This is one our mothers may have gotten, or their mothers. Today, we are more likely to hear: "Get into college and do well, but then get married"; or: "Get a job, but nothing *too* serious. Don't be ambitious"; or: "It's nice that you have a talent, but don't take yourself seriously." Or even, "Go to law school, become an associate, then drop out to start a family."

All these messages say Don't Go Too Far. Their effect on a daughter is devastating. Not only do they discourage us from identifying with Daddy; they engender a natural and inevitable resentment in girls and women, who are continually told they must either limit themselves or lose their fathers' love. Having been given a taste of self-validation, of achievement, even of freedom—having had a brief chance to compete with peers and test ourselves against reality—we are asked to give it all up, to enter voluntarily into the world of relativity. There we can judge our own situation only by the positive or negative response of another person: first Daddy, then a boyfriend, then our husband.

Increasingly, though, daughters don't obey this message. They fight it, as one daughter of a traditional Catholic father has done by coming to New York to work in advertising against the wishes of her father, who pushed her all her life to get good grades in school and today truly does not understand why she did not stay home in Indiana and get married like her sister.

She, meanwhile, is in despair because she feels so completely unsupported by this father who always wanted her to achieve before. The pull backward is strong—every step she takes into the world of work is fraught with danger because his support is missing. She is daring *terra incognita,* the place on the edge of the maps where medieval cartographers used to write, "Here Be Dragons," the place where, before Columbus, people thought you fell off the edge of the earth. How much easier it would be to turn back, go home, get married! Then she would feel secure in her father's vision.

Colette once wrote that there was no bravery to equal that of the young woman who went alone into the household of a stranger, a husband, often much older, and in the days of formal courtships known (if at all) only through his public image. A bride entered the unknown world of his private life, where, moreover, he had almost total legal control over her, not to mention physical and psychological dominance.

Daughters who got mixed messages from their fathers are facing the same kind of unknown world today when they move into forbidden or disapproved territories on the Outside. Will the world welcome them or will it punish them for daring to go beyond Daddy's stated limits? It is, after all, Daddy's world; and if he has forbidden it a daughter will inevitably fear that his world will reflect his wishes—and perhaps carry out his punishment.

This might well be one explanation for women's "fear of success," first discovered by Matina Horner among women college students who, in a psychological test, wrote stories in which a woman medical student was penalized or victimized for daring to be first in her class, over a male student. It might also account for the later finding that, as the numbers of women in a given field increase, women's fears of success decrease.

But the Outside world is not on the whole, even today, tremendously welcoming to women. And even if they make a good start in such fields as business and law, women still find that in a few years they are falling behind again, when men select other men for partnerships and promotion.

Mothers who work, and who enjoy work, do provide an image of a possible self on the Outside—and studies have shown that daughters of working mothers have a less stereotyped view of what women can do than daughters of traditional nuclear families. But Daddy, who as a small child was intensely loved and nurtured by his mother, and who receives similar, if less intense, nurturing from his wife, will naturally want loyalty, empathy, and devotion from his daughters. One of the ways he can get these is by giving mixed messages.

A large study of preschoolers and their fathers reported by Norma Radin of the University of Michigan, one of its authors, found that with daughters (but not sons), fathers showed "contradictory behaviors such as meeting explicit needs and ignoring explicit needs or requesting and ordering aversively."

The study was designed to see how fathers affected the intellectual development of small children. Fathers were found to have a lot of influence on their sons; but, thinks Radin, "the ambivalent message coming from the father to the daughter tended to alienate her and reduce the likelihood of the girl's using him as a model for problem solving, intellectual striving, or vocabulary development."

Dr. Lamb, who reports the same study in a later book, suggests that "fathers may simply be ambivalent about the appropriateness of independence and achievement in girls, and their ambivalence may translate into inconsistency in the patterns of father-daughter interaction."

Both are probably right.

Fathers aren't sure what they really want from us or for us. For one thing, change has come very fast. Even as he sends his daughters to his own university, Daddy can't quite give up thinking of us as females under his protection and control. Education for girls may no longer be intended solely to bring a professional son-in-law into the family, but Daddy probably still wouldn't mind if that happened. The Appleman sisters seem to have gotten that message.

Just as it is extremely difficult for fathers to see their daughters as people who are sexual beings, so it is extremely hard for them to see their daughters as people who need to feel competent, to achieve and be recognized, to gain mastery over some corner of the world; in short, as autonomous.

The idea that we might be so is still very new. In 1981 the *New York Times,* which has always been a voice of male authority in America, commented on a new study showing that "women who work enjoy greater self-esteem and suffer less anxiety and depression than women who do not work." Said the *Times* reporter, "The idea that work plays a central role in life satisfaction is not new but is given a novel twist by research showing that it applies to women as well as to men. The customary thinking has been that satisfaction for a woman comes largely from her role in the family and home and not in the outside world. . . ."

Indeed. Daddies, always the most conservative people within the family (after all, they have to represent the world of reality), have on the whole held the customary view.

If Daddy is unconsciously identifying with his daughter as someone he can indulge, who doesn't have his masculine need for achievement, and if this image of her also reinforces his masculinity, how can he identify with her as an autonomous person? And if he can't identify with her, how can he encourage her?

Many men have trouble with this. Rosabeth Moss Kanter, in *Men and Women of the Corporation,* showed that while a sponsor or mentor is essential for any corporate woman who hopes to rise to power (as it is for a man), it is hard for her to find one because male bosses have trouble identifying with a subordinate female. On the other hand, a boss may choose to sponsor a younger man because he sees himself in his protégé, just as Dr. Nobile identified with his son and took every opportunity to help him along.

Some fathers, of course—like some bosses—have even worse problems dealing with daughters. My father, for instance, went far beyond mere mixed messages. He went all the way to the double message in which you can't win: the "damned if you do, damned if you don't" kind. Like: "Smile for Daddy, but I despise all this weak, passive femininity. Give me a real man, anytime." My father's corollary to this one was: "Be tough-minded because the only people I respect are tough-minded men. Too bad. You lose because you can't be a man."

This double message drove me crazy, as it was intended to do. It meant that whatever I chose, I would lose.

If I chose to be feminine, I would be the kind of person he despised.

If I chose to be strong, tough-minded, like a man, he would not take me seriously, would not even recognize my efforts, because he could only recognize them in another male.

I was, you will say, an extreme case.

Well—yes and no. Because as I studied the transcripts of my interviews, I discovered that many fathers had given their daughters mixed, if not double, messages.

I have come to believe that, as much as anything else, it is Daddy's mixed messages that make us "feminine" by forcing us to fall back on empathy, loyalty, and devotion—on *attachment* to Daddy because we can't get any consistent signals from him as to what he really wants from us.

If a father is endlessly inconsistent in his messages, if there is no way to win, why try? This, surely, is part of what has happened to Alicia and Patty Appleman. It was certainly part of what happened to me when I became an infamous underachiever in college. And, in fact, a 1979 study of depression in female college students found that inconsistency in a father's love was twice as likely to lead to depression in his daughter as a mother's inconsistency.

If Daddy is unpredictable in his moods, as many men are, if he puts you in no-win situations, as my father did, a daughter has no choice but to abandon herself to empathy, to cling to him in a loyalty and devotion that are rooted in fear.

"You have to learn to read his moods," counsels the wife of the irascible Marine pilot in the movie *The Great Santini,* when her daughter despairs of winning her father's affection. The wife spends the entire movie reading his moods and interpreting them to his children, while he acts out his destructive competitiveness with his son and his fatherly desire to avoid his daughter altogether.

This is a fairly extreme situation compared to, say, the Appleman or Nobile families. But if part of a daughter's devotion is rooted in her own desire to hang onto Daddy as a ticket away from Mother, part is also, all too often, rooted in fear and anxiety.

Both the fear and the love, the anxiety and the idealization, are the legacy of Daddy's daughters.

Daddy's Alter Ego

The attachment to Daddy matters a lot. Holly Flax smiled for Daddy and idealized him because he was nice, and because he was Daddy. He wasn't around much, physically or emotionally, and those moments of tenderness when he said, "How'd you get to be so pretty, how'd you get to be so nice?" were magnified into talismans by which she lived the first thirty years of her life, right through two husbands.

There was another ritual in her life, too; one that, twenty years ago, would have translated into "Make your husband happy."

At ten, she loved to make little desserts for her father, who always told her how delicious they were and what a terrific cook she was.

So when Holly grew up and stopped smiling for Daddy and began to want to take care of herself, food was what she naturally turned to, with its associations of doing something for Daddy that would win his attention and approval.

She started her own bakery. Food is love. She managed to heal her conflict between attachment and autonomy by taking Daddy with her into autonomy.

It's too soon to tell what Alicia and Patty Appleman will ultimately make of their father's mixed messages: I'm betting that at least one of them will take a chance on herself eventually and that her training in getting what she wants from her father will prove to be useful in getting her own way from other Daddy-types, like managers or bosses. So she won't lose her father, either.

Writing this book has been one way for me to bring Daddy with me on my own journey into autonomy.

But possibly the luckiest among us has been Fran Nobile. Come motherhood, she will have to weather a lot of paternal disapproval to go on working. But she has her husband's support, which makes a big difference.

Fran had the least conflict growing up because she has been able to identify with her father yet maintain *a strong feminine identity that did not exclude self-assertion, leadership, or dominance, competitiveness, achievement, and disagreement with Daddy.*

Fran's message was mixed, too, but it was the least crippling. Dr. Nobile came the closest of all these fathers to recognizing his daughter as an autonomous person because he recognized himself in her.

Steve Appleman has come close, too—and Alicia and Patty might yet make it into autonomy, might yet trust themselves. But his attachment messages, being covert, are harder to fight than Dr. Nobile's openness about his "be a mother" expectations.

As the product of a passionate relationship with her father, Fran prefers to be involved with a man, but she has chosen one who does not feel threatened by her desire to go on with her autonomous work life. She has managed, in fact, to carry her privileged daughterhood into her marriage. Because she felt sure of her father's support while she was growing up, she married a man she fully expects to support her, too—not in the old-fashioned way, as an expensive object, but in the new way, as an autonomous person.

She has, in short, been able to combine attachment and autonomy. It wasn't an easy struggle, and her father wasn't always entirely on her side. But in that odd twist between selfhood and relationship, between being an autonomous person and being an object, that daughters find themselves going through with fathers and other men, she has found herself, and come out whole.

CHAPTER FIVE

Good Girls:
And Other Accommodations to Daddy and His Messages

*O*ne of the points that struck me in the course of interviewing for this book was how often, when I asked about things like adolescent rebellion, or fights with fathers, or defying a father, the answer was, "I was a good girl—I never gave him any trouble."

I was a good girl, too. In the fifties, there were only two choices: you were either a Good Girl or a Bad Girl.

The most basic distinction between Good Girls and Bad Girls was sexual: one was a virgin, the other was not. This distinction was already beginning to break down, but it still carried vast resonances in the form of all kinds of social and personal expectations.

A Good Girl was quiet, obedient, cheerful, supportive of her father, loyal to him, and devoted to his interests. She never argued with him, although she often did with her mother. Indeed, the more she disagreed with her mother, the more loyal to Daddy she became. She was a good student, although that certainly didn't mean speaking up in class, asking questions, or arguing with the teacher. It meant taking lots of notes and passing tests.

If a Good Girl was working class, she got a job after high school and planned to marry soon. If she was middle class, she went to college and planned to marry soon.

Our notion of Good Girls hadn't changed much from the 1930s, when Katharine Hepburn played an archetypal Good Girl in the movie *Alice Adams.* Fred MacMurray, her rich boyfriend, decides to marry her after he overhears her fiercely defending her father, accused of stealing the formula for a superglue he developed while slaving as an employee for a stingy boss who wouldn't manufacture it. Fred knows a loyal daughter will make a loyal wife. That's what it's all about.

Bad Girls, on the other hand, were disobedient and rebellious, ungrateful to their hardworking, long-suffering fathers, who spent all their time earning money so their daughters could grow up as Good Girls. Bad Girls smoked, chewed gum, wore eyeshadow and too much lipstick. They argued with their fathers, made noise, could not be depended on for absolute loyalty, and, as a natural consequence, were bold and brassy and liable to sleep with boys. (Good Girls did sometimes sleep with their boyfriends, but only Bad Girls got found out.)

The possibility of Badness was always intriguing to Good Girls, but we learned very early that the consequences would be stiff. A woman I interviewed for this book, who never would have dreamed of going as far as Badness, told me a story about how she decided, quite consciously, to be a Good Girl.

As a child, she had always cuddled up to Daddy and smiled for him just the way he wanted. If she did this the right way, if she waited until he was in the right mood and then sat on the arm of his chair and caressed him, she could get just about anything she wanted out of him, and if (or maybe especially when) her mother had just forbidden it.

Then, at fifteen, she started to get emotional, to "act up." She was trying—clumsily, as adolescents do, but sincerely—both to grow up and to hang onto her parents.

As an adolescent, she was once again confused by her close attachment to her mother, and she needed her father to affirm her specialness, to make her feel singular and important. She needed his approval of her womanhood, of her almost-grown-up sexuality. But that was beyond him.

One day, she looked at her mother and felt as though she would choke. Was she about to turn into *this woman?* Was there no room for herself?

"It was always at the dinner table—I would start crying and screaming and say I was fat and ugly and looked like my mother. He would get very upset and say, 'You're not fat and you're not ugly, and you shouldn't feel that way.' "

But this, needless to say, did not console her. She would run from the dinner table to her room, slam the door, and cry.

Her father couldn't stand these messy emotional outbursts. "You can imagine," she told me, "in a quiet house where the children were very controlled, all of a sudden I was having these outbursts of hysteria."

Her mother would tell her father, "She's just going through a stage. Ignore it." Her father "would alternately ignore it and get hysterical himself. He expected my mother to fix it, but she couldn't. She just kept telling him I would grow out of it, which of course made me feel terrible.

"One day he stood up and yelled, 'Either she goes or I go!' He went flying into the den and slammed the door. He spent the night in there.

"I was much more upset about that than my mother was, because he stood up to her and that *really* scared me. He was going to send me to boarding school. After that I became a Good Girl again, because I didn't want to go."

Her mother said that she shouldn't take her father seriously. "Why are you getting upset?" she would say. "You know you're not going anywhere, and neither is he."

Intellectually, she knew her mother was right, "but emotionally, it was still very upsetting. *I thought I had gone too far."*

Going Too Far: title of a book of radical feminist essays by Robin Morgan. Title of the voice that says, inside, "Now you've done it, now you've gone too far."

When I ask women what they are afraid of, what their father's anger means to them, it is very hard for them to find a reply. "I don't know," they often say, but they do. It means annihilation; it means the withdrawal of that mirror by which we see ourselves as singular people, the one Daddy carries around with him and flashes for us when we make him happy.

The truth is, we have as hard a time separating from Daddy as Daddy does in letting go of us.

If he's either secretly or openly threatening us with loss of love for Going Too Far, then we have to find some way to accommodate ourselves to his demands. What we do is to internalize Daddy's expectations and come to see them as necessary, inescapable. Part of ourselves, and of our own demands and expectations for ourselves. His vision of us—the image we see in the mirror he holds out for us—becomes our own vision of ourselves. It is no wonder that it sometimes seems we are willing to pay any price to keep him our Prince so we can go on being his Princess.

Too often, the price is Goodness.

Conscience develops by stages in both boys and girls, and both go through the stage of moral development in which Goodness means pleasing your parents. But according to Maccoby and Jacklin, girls "tend to conform more readily than boys to directives from parents and teachers." Boys from an early age pay less attention to requests or commands from adults. Lawrence Kohlberg of Harvard University has suggested that girls enter the "good child" stage earlier than boys and stay in it much longer.

Freud claimed that women have a different, much less developed superego, or conscience, than boys do. Again, this is supposedly because girls remain in their oedipal attachment to Daddy much longer than boys do with Mother, and are therefore much more dependent on his love. Girls, Freud said, fear loss of love more than anything; their goal then becomes to please Daddy rather than to obey a more abstract sense of justice or a more impersonal moral code.

When boys, on the other hand, give up Mother and choose to identify with Daddy instead, they also acquire an impersonal, masculine conscience, ready to pass moral judgment without being swayed by the feelings they left behind with Mother.

Since Freud, however, there have been many new ideas about this process. It is true that girls remain passionately attached to Daddy far past the time when boys have renounced their attachment to Mother. But we remain attached to Daddy for some of the same reasons that boys give up their attachment to Mother. For each of us, the prize is growth away from Mother, toward identity and adulthood.

It is also true that we form our identity through attachments and relationships to adults in a way that boys do not. As Dr. Nancy Chodorow, a sociologist at the University of California and author of *The Reproduction of Mothering,* points out, "mothers tend to experience their daughters as more like, and continuous with, themselves. . . . By contrast, mothers experience their sons as a male opposite." This means boys have been pushed to differentiate themselves from Mother from an early age, whereas girls "come to experience themselves as less differentiated than boys, as more continuous with and related to" other people, especially adults.

And then, of course, we have our own special reasons for being sensitive to Daddy's cues. If he gets angry when we attempt to assert ourselves and differentiate ourselves from Mother, it means he is refusing to support us in our efforts to become autonomous. And without his support, his love, we feel rejected. If the loss of Daddy's love feels like the loss of the whole world beyond Mother, if it carries with it the threat of isolation, we are certainly going to strive to be Good.

So we come to construct our feminine identities as accommodations to Daddy, as strategies to keep Daddy and his successors attached to us so that we don't have to face the terrifying isolation with which we feel threatened if we Go Too Far.

For men, though, there is generally speaking no such thing as Going Too Far, especially in terms of ambition. The farther they go, the more attractive they become to women, and often to other men. Little girls learn that the price of autonomy and ambition—of independence in the Outside world—is loss of attachment, is in fact rejection by Daddy and other men. Little boys, as they grow up, find increasingly that *they are rewarded with attachment for autonomy and achievement.*

Consider the hardworking executive. He's up at 6:00 A.M., at his desk by 8. His days last ten, twelve, fourteen hours, and he takes work home. He travels frequently. In his corner office, at his immense, empty desk, he looks as though he might be lonely.

But every night he is met at the suburban station by his wife, who has supper ready for him. She also has a receptive ear, a soothing word, an enthusiastic response. The sheets on his bed are clean; his socks and underwear are neatly stacked in the drawer. In the morning there is coffee and breakfast and a warm ride to the train.

In the office, there is his secretary, ready with coffee and all the day's appointments neatly laid out. She buys his presents, arranges his trips, screens his phone calls.

On the plane, there is the stewardess; in the hotel, perhaps, the call girl.

He is seldom alone.

Or consider Freud, the lonely pioneer of psychoanalysis. He had a built-in support system in his struggle to discover, articulate, and establish a new discipline and an entirely new way of perceiving the human psyche. And at the center of the system were women—starting with his mother, continuing with his wife, and ending with his daughter, who carried on his work.

He walked across the hall from his office to his home each noon and evening for a meal in the bosom of his family. For his intellectual nourishment, there were numbers of disciples and followers, many of whom settled in Vienna to be near him. Between patients, family, and followers he must, in fact, have hardly ever been alone.

Women, we have been told, are dependent on men, while men are independent citizens. And it is true that until very recently men have functioned with much greater ease in the Outside world, so that they have indeed seemed to be more independent.

But the reality is that one reason men have always been able to be so at ease in the world of work is because they have always had women on the Inside to give them the nurturing, sex, and emotional support they need to sustain themselves on the Outside. Little boys learn early that they will have this support to compensate them for the pain of giving up their passionate attachment to Mother. As soon as they become firmly established on the Outside, in the world of males, they find that they can move freely back and forth between Inside and Outside. And every time they come back in, first to Mommy and then to her replacements, their girlfriends and their wives, they are welcomed and nurtured and fed and made much of and sent back into the world ready to fight another day's battles in the classroom or the boardroom, on the team, the assembly line, or the subcommittee.

Furthermore, men are dependent upon women for their emotional lives, as well as for the support they need to carry on their work.

If this sounds strange, consider that retired widowers who don't remarry have a much higher mortality rate than those who do. Having relied on their work associations rather than personal relationships, and on work itself for their self-esteem, they become completely dependent on their wives when they retire. Wives have usually been in charge of the couple's social life, and any nonwork relationships the men have were made through wives. So when wives die, the men are like beached whales. Widows might have trouble with the Outside things like money and odd jobs around the house; in retirement communities, men are in great demand to do things like fix the plug on the toaster. But the widows are not socially and emotionally isolated because they talk and communicate their feelings in ways that men do not, unless to a woman with whom they have a sexual relationship. Even then, most men rely on women to interpret their feelings to and for them. (Married men in general have been found to be healthier than unmarried men, while for women, ironically, the reverse is true.)

Women, in short, are not more dependent on men than men are on women. Men only appear to be less dependent because they can take women's support for granted; because they can control the terms of their dependency; and because, until now, they have been able to control the very people—women—on whom they depend.

In *Making Good: Conversations with Successful Men,* Jane Adams reports that men on their way up the corporate ladder feel it essential to acquire a wife first. Once they've got her, their personal and emotional life is taken care of; they can focus their energies on "the real business of living"—success. They view the emotional servicing their wives provide as "their reward for being strong, capable, successful providers."

Such wives would traditionally run the household, raise the children, and keep the family social life going, as well as provide the men with sexual and emotional refueling.

If some women today are less willing to provide such total care, men would still like to have it. Writing in *Esquire,* Gail Sheehy reported that young male executives today are wary of getting married because women can't be *depended* on any more; we aren't willing to devote ourselves to husbands, to sacrifice our own lives for their careers. In short, a woman with a career of her own might not want to pick up and move, as my mother did, whenever her husband's job demanded it.

These men are certainly not offering support and nurturing to the women with careers. Nor is the husband who has an affair because he feels his wife, busy pursuing her career, is no longer *there* for him. Nor, of course, is the father who tells his daughter not to Go Too Far.

If women's function has been to nurture men, to be loyal and devoted to their interests, then for women to conceive of a goal more ambitious than, say, teaching or social work has been considered selfish. And selfishness was and is one of the hallmarks of Badness, just as loyalty and devotion have always been hallmarks of Goodness. How could we, then, follow personal goals with a clear conscience?

Nor has this feeling of conflict between attachment and autonomy diminished in more than a small percentage of young women. More typical is the young woman in a 1980 career-counseling seminar who described her feelings of self-condemnation over her plans to get a graduate degree. She felt selfish, she said, and worried about whether she was letting her boyfriend down.

For men, on the other hand, Goodness has never been a moral imperative, much less a personal one. After all, the traits of Goodness—devotion and obedience to a particular person—are, outside of the military, inimical to the competitiveness that is so essential for success in the world. When men are loyal and devoted, it is more often to a cause or a group than to a person.

Boys have always been expected to be a bit Bad, to sow some wild oats, before buckling down to society's demands for a steady job, a family, and general conformity. In this way they show their mettle, prove what they are made of, and assert their individuality. A boy or young man who fails to sow a wild oat or two is considered dull, unlikely to get very far in life.

Rakes and scamps have always fired the romantic dreams of American girls, partly because they are livelier and sexier than Good Boys and partly, no doubt, because the girl who dreams of becoming an earth-mother also dreams of the power of nurturing. She would love to tame and reform a confirmed Bad Boy; a certain amount of Badness in a man, in fact, inspires loyalty and devotion in many women.

For girls, though, there was never any moratorium, no sowing of wild oats, because the usual result of such behavior—illegitimate children—came home to disrupt the structures of the legitimate family and threaten the fabric of society. Even today teenage pregnancy is a problem few middle-class families are prepared to face, although the sexual revolution has made sex commonplace among teenagers.

Nor was there any image for girls of the noble rebel, who could defy a father as a revolutionary male defied his king. Right through the 1960s we still believed in the dictum Shakespeare put into the mouth of the tamed Kate at the conclusion of *The Taming of the Shrew:*

> Such duty as the subject owes the prince
> Even such a woman oweth to her husband:
> And when she is froward, peevish, sullen, sour,
> And not obedient to his honest will,
> What is she but a foul contending rebel,
> And graceless traitor to her loving lord?

Kate's career as a shrew started with her rebellious daughterhood; substitute the words "daughter" and "father" for "woman" and "husband" in this passage, and you would get the age-old definitions of Good Girl and Bad Girl.

After Shakespeare's day, numbers of rebels (some of them female) changed the political picture until the first sentence of Kate's dictum became invalid. With the fall of princes, or their conversion to constitutional monarchs, subjects became citizens, for whom absolute obedience was no longer a duty.

Wives' duty to husbands continued in the prerevolutionary mode, though, right through the nineteenth century, and so did daughters' duty to their fathers. Our rebellion came first with a demand for free choice of husbands; only gradually in the twentieth century has it come to include things like an education, an apartment of our own, and the right to such masculine prerogatives as ambition or a career.

Even in Shakespeare's day, the nobel rebel could redeem himself by winning, in which case he became the prince. In subsequent centuries, he could become an artist or actor or even chairman of the board, and in America the rebel and the Bad Boy could always become millionaires. Money and success redeemed any number of sins.

But well into the twentieth century girls were kept Good because we believed there was no possibility of redemption if we fell into Badness.

Today, of course, we are not quite the Good Girls we used to be. Girls commonly cease to be virgins by fifteen or so. They take drugs, run away, get abortions. They also go to Ivy League colleges, get M.B.A.s, and join Fortune 500 Corporations, or become truck drivers, telephone repairpersons, and carpenters. Women today think of their bodies as their own and their sex lives as nobody else's business.

Yet vestiges of Good Girlism cling to us all. Girls often sleep with their boyfriends in order to please them and hold onto them, rather than because they really want to. Runaways might learn something about independence, but they might also end up as prostitutes, totally dependent on their pimps.

If women were not, on the whole, still Good Girls, none of us would stay with husbands who batter us and/or force sex on us. We would not so often quietly, even unconsciously, mute our ambitions, truncate our careers, fear success, and otherwise succumb to conflicts about work, about developing an independent identity. We would not feel, obscurely, *selfish* about wanting to work or go to graduate school or even save ourselves from a relationship with an abusive man. We would not still wonder, as we too often do, whether if we take care of our own needs and ambitions, we will lose our boyfriend or husband or lover and end up alone.

And the threat of loss is very real, because men still demand our devotion. "It's okay if you work," says the older husband, "as long as I get my dinner on time." If we leave them, we live alone and wonder whether it was worth it, and look for a new man who might, just possibly, be able to give us more room.

"Why do you want to spend Saturday afternoon playing soccer with a bunch of other women?" demands the young machinist or executive trainee of his girlfriend, herself a telephone installer or executive trainee. "Why can't you come and watch my soccer practice?" (There is still, usually, no question of his coming to her practice.)

If she goes off to her own soccer practice, she feels good about it. But she also wonders how long this will last, how long before he will find someone more willing to devote herself loyally to his cause.

At thirteen, I wanted to be a cheerleader. (I didn't make the squad.)

At nineteen, I wanted to be an earth-mother. I used to refer to my generous expanse of pelvis as a "baby making machine." What else were big hips *for?*

I had an assortment of feckless boyfriends who used to stop by and tell me all their problems. I would cook for them and sleep with them, after I went out and lost my virginity during my nineteenth summer. I did it as my father's daughter, cold-blooded, tough-minded. I felt it had become a burden to me.

My motives were mixed. Partly, I wanted to grow up, and I felt that losing my virginity was a way to do so, by ceasing to be a Good Girl, a dutiful daughter. On the other hand, I knew or felt that the time had come to add sex to sympathy as a way of pleasing men.

In any event, I risked my father's label "whore" and took the plunge. Times were changing.

But as a full-fledged earth-mother I wasn't any less a Good Girl than I had been at fifteen, getting good grades in school and writing poetry only in secret.

I still kept the Lily Briscoe part of me hidden away. She was a Bad Girl, I would have felt (had I known her yet), because she wasn't devoted to men.

Now it may be that my position as youngest child in a family of men made me more disposed to loyalty and devotion than the average girl. That's what theories about birth order suggest. But I'm not sure I agree.

I think most of us willingly settle for being Good Girls because the penalty for rebellion, for failing to please our fathers, seems too great to pay. What is at stake, after all, is our sense of self-esteem. If that is immensely dependent on feeling adored by Daddy, and if a Good Girl is what Daddy adores, then you could see that our first and greatest source of self-esteem is precisely this sense that we are—or at least appear to be—Good Girls.

The gap between being and appearing to be is enormous. It is the gap into which the sense of a separate self enters. If Daddy gives us his love freely, as happened to Fran Nobile, we have some room to maneuver, even as Good Girls.

But if Daddy is the more usual passive, or distant, or controlling, or even rejecting father, problems arise. We become considerably more compulsive about being Good Girls because we are so terrified of losing his love. We may become the kind of Desperate Achiever we'll be seeing in a later section, who can't untangle the knot of her relationship with her father sufficiently to allow herself freedom to have an emotional life of her own; the kind of woman who can work but not love. Or we may even become Bad as a way of hanging on to a rejecting father. But more than likely, we'll become the kind of woman who hesitates to choose between her man and her own goals; who may, in fact, not be able to see any difference between them. She's a subspecies of Good Girl I call:

Little Me

Very few of us have escaped at some time in our lives feeling like Little Me, or failed, however briefly or abortively, to attempt to play it out by asking a man to face the world for us. To take care of us.

Little Me comes out in incidents as trivial as one I remember: I was walking in the country with a man, a good friend and casual lover. I had on flat shoes, and as an ex-tomboy I had certainly scrambled up and down a great many banks, bluffs, and steep slopes in my time without any assistance whatsoever. But when we came to a moderately steep little hill, I suddenly wanted, very much, for him to walk partway down the hill, turn, and hold out his hand to help me down.

He didn't. He scrambled down ahead of me, unheedingly. I felt crushed; even slighted. He had ignored me.

Did that incident have anything to do with the withering of our friendship?

Where had I learned this strategy, acquired this feeling, this need? Certainly not from my brothers, with whom I competed mightily.

I was set up for it by my father, when he refused his tenderness to me except when I played "the dizzy blonde"—his very own Little Me. It was inevitable that I would fall into the same game with other men. And when he had made me feel inadequate by telling me I should be tough-minded at all times, making it clear that all the traits he respected could only belong to men anyway, he left Little Me as my only option. That was what he had labeled me, whether I liked it or not.

My mother set me up for it because she kept losing her arguments with my father. My stepmother reinforced it when she told me the best thing that ever happened to her was to marry my father so she could quit her job.

Little Me is a response to the seduction, the charm, the delight of Daddy's power. The power with which he is supposed to reach his hand out to us from the Outside world and help us down hills. As my father handed us out of taxis.

We are predisposed toward Little Me as infants and toddlers when Daddy tosses us in the air, then cuddles us in his lap. All we have to do is lie back and enjoy it. Then we discover that this man, who has so much energy and strength, is not going to use it against us. That he is, instead, going to protect us.

It is immensely comforting to feel protected, to feel that Daddy is on the Outside, between us and a world that is, to say the least, confusing, and often dangerous, violent, and threatening.

It is pleasing to know he provides for us. If he is an indulgent Daddy, we feel our power in "seducing" him into giving us what we want. The first time Daddy, with an indulgent smile, agrees to buy us the toy or dress that Mother said we couldn't have, we sense the beginning of a female power that, we are taught, can take us a long way.

We attach ourselves to this power, and make our attachment to Daddy's power part of our own identity. We can do things in relation to his power, to his authority, that our brothers can't. We can tweak him on the ear, cuddle up to him, purr.

Sons, as a rule, can't. Their job is to learn how to *become* this power, this authority. But our job is to seduce it, and to be seduced by it.

It's a powerful lure; next to Daddy's power, what can we do but play Little Me? And it's all too easy to get stuck in the role because, in general, we are denied access to Daddy as a source of support for autonomy and as a person with whom to identify. Rather than identifying with him as a competent, problem solving, rational person, we learn to say, "I can't do it. I need Daddy to do it for me."

Actually, Little Me is an accommodation of despair, however much it might be masked by a sense of entitlement. But some women carry it off beautifully. They always have.

Consider the three classics: the Golddigger, the Princess, and the Secret Little Me.

The Golddigger bats her baby-blues at Mr. Sugar Daddy and says, "Oh, aren't you big and strong and handsome and rich. I *know* you're going to treat Little Me just wonderfully!"

The Golddigger has always been the Little Me with the most highly developed sense of self.

Why? Because she always demanded a *quid pro quo* for her devotion and loyalty—or at least the appearance of devotion and loyalty. Like the courtesan of nineteenth-century France or the hetaira of Greece, to whom she is closely allied, she knows how to drive a bargain with a man.

Men often complain that women are Golddiggers. But secretly they like the Little Me with the big demands because she makes them feel—as she is supposed to do, was in fact trained to do—big, strong, handsome, powerful, and rich.

Women are called Golddiggers with some contempt, because supposedly they are parasites. But in fact the offer of sex, nonstop admiration, and the prestige of appearing in public with a gorgeous young female is far from nothing.

It's what every sugar daddy wants.

What really galls men about the Golddigger is the fact that she demands a fair exchange for her efforts. She won't promise eternal loyalty and devotion in exchange for nothing more than his name. She keeps her own name—and ends up with the diamonds, too.

The Princess is a tamer, more respectable version of Little Me than the Golddigger. She is domesticated, designed for marriage.

The Princess demands a lot from a man, and she knows how to get it. Holly Flax did very well when she finally turned her Smile for Daddy lessons to good account and married a rich and indulgent man.

The Princess does promise loyalty and devotion; but only as long as the man is rich and powerful enough to give her everything she wants and needs, as her father did. She loves feeling special in this way, and she knows it's the way he loves making her feel special. The Princess is a specialist in status-by-attachment. Little Me says we are more important, more worthy, more valued and valuable when we are attached to a man than when we are not, so that alone we easily feel a loss of self-esteem. Possibly, like Mrs. Ramsay, we in fact feel less like a *self* than when we are acting in and through a relationship with a man.

But in reality such an attachment to Daddy, and to other men, comes at the expense of a sense of our own competency, even of our own sense of self.

Traditionally, Little Me was the basic identity of most wives. They were told, by their fathers and mothers, that men needed to be the providers, that the masculine ego could only thrive in such a role. Little Me was the obvious accommodation. In return, wives received the chance at power through motherhood, a source of power much devalued these days but one that women like my grandmother or the matriarch of the Chinese clan knew could be very real.

Yet many Princesses, for example, don't, as wives, *look* like Little Me at all. They appear to be quite powerful personalities, and may in fact hold considerable power in many areas. They may possess the power of emotional manipulation over their husbands as well as their children. They may have real, if nonpaying, power-in-the-world as the heads of volunteer organizations, charity drives, and church or synagogue groups. And these days they may well earn money as writers, lawyers, businesswomen. They may even be feminists.

They have evolved a special form of accommodation I call:

The Secret Little Me. This is any woman who defers to the men in her life—her boyfriend, lover, husband—in the same way she learned to defer to Daddy, yet who appears to other people to be a competent, even powerful person. She may, in fact, be powerful in the Outside world in her own right. But somewhere along the way she got the message that only as long as she played Little Me in her personal relationships with Daddy and other men could she be a competent, achieving person in other areas.

The Secret Little Me is usually a woman of talent and intelligence, energy and drive. The catch for her, though, is that she really believes her power comes from the man to whom she is attached and that he will let her, so to speak, use his power only as long as she defers to him. This is the basic shape of her heterosexual femininity.

The Secret Little Me is really a woman who has never outgrown her little girl's belief in the magical powers of Daddy. Given a relationship in which that part of her feels securely under Daddy's care and protection, she is able to use other parts of herself to function perfectly competently in the world. But the loss of the attachment makes her feel the magical source of her power has abandoned her.

This was what happened to an actress I interviewed who had gained a considerable reputation in repertory theatre. The only daughter of a bank executive, she was married to a lawyer. She was known as a strong person; younger actresses could always rely on her for help and advice. But when she and her husband divorced, she fell apart. She began drinking heavily, canceled a commitment for a summer tour, and became morose. She told me she had simply lost all her self-confidence. Her husband had been proud of her acting career, but he had taken care of all its business aspects and had usually dealt with her agent and arranged her schedule.

Within a year of her divorce, the actress remarried—a widower who had been a friend of her husband's and who was also a lawyer. As soon as their relationship was established, seven months after the divorce, she stopped drinking and became her "old self." She had regained her feeling of power.

The Secret Little Me, then, says that as long as we are attached to a powerful man, we feel powerful, able to deal with the world. Alone, we feel anxious, empty, inadequate; powerless. We don't believe in ourselves.

Being afraid you can't make it in the world without a man is not an uncommon problem; many women hesitate before the possibility of divorce for precisely this reason. But generally we think of this as a problem of the traditional Little Me, the woman who, for instance, gave up her job and her own activity in the world when she married and/or had children.

The Secret Little Me not only keeps her job; she may actually advance her career while maintaining her marriage. The point is that a relationship to a man whom she perceives to be powerful—and to whom she relates in private as Little Me—is an inherent part of her identity. Without the relationship, she feels lost.

Today, when the *New York Times* wedding announcements say, "Susy Jones, lawyer, to wed John Doe," and, "Susy plans to keep her own name after the marriage," the Secret Little Me would seem to be an outmoded aspect of women's identity. Let us hope so. But one way or another, it entered the identities of most women over thirty, as a set of cautions and proscriptions, as excessive anxiety about dealing with the world, as an inability to do without a man, and as part of our fear of success. As a confusion between ourselves and ourselves in a relationship with a man.

Some psychoanalysts, among them Helene Deutsch and Edith Jacobson, have noted this confusion in women. Jacobson remarks that women's ego ideal—which might also be called "Who I want to be when I grow up"—tends to become enmeshed or bogged down in relationships. Deutsch observed that women often got enthusiastic about ideas they apparently received from a man but which, in fact, when she probed more deeply, turned out to be ideas they had originally had themselves. "Creative women," Deutsch wrote, "frequently cannot value their own ideas until they receive them from someone else."

Although Deutsch connected this observation to women's biology, to the need to be impregnated, as it were, by a man, in my view this is a perfect example of the Secret Little Me at work. A woman whose original ideas were neither valued nor perhaps even credited by father, mother, male peers, or teachers would have to attach herself to a male who is more powerful and who is above all *visible* in the world. Recognized. Then she can share, at least vicariously, in his recognition, even while remaining herself a "wedge of darkness."

Iris's story is a case in point. She decided, after twenty years in the suburbs as a good wife and mother, to leave her second husband because he objected to the increasing amount of time she was spending on a job in television. She wanted to become a producer. Her youngest son was an adolescent, her daughter hardly ever turned up for dinner, and her husband worked six days a week. So she no longer felt guilty about spending so much time away from home.

She moved into the city, leaving a housekeeper to run the household. She was, for the first time in her life, free.

The first thing she did was to find a man, a producer, to be her mentor. She became his assistant, and she made dozens of important contacts, even though they were in his name.

Then the mentor relationship turned into an affair, and she began to wonder just where it would lead. Her lover managed to be out of town on her birthday and refused to come near her when she had the flu, and she began to miss her husband.

To her friends, she wondered out loud about giving up her mentor/lover and launching herself, finally, on her own career. But secretly, she didn't believe she could make it. She lay awake nights in anxiety. And she didn't much like being poor.

Nor did she like being taken for granted.

Her father had been a generous man: "He loved giving presents to everybody. He never asked for anything in return. He would go out to the store and get these gorgeous nightgown sets, one for my mother, one for me. And he took us on vacations. These were delicious, wonderful things and we all enjoyed them. They were all gifts from the provider."

Not only that, but he had talked to her all the time: about his job, about how her mother was incompetent and she shouldn't grow up to be like her.

" 'Be controlled,' he would say, 'don't get hysterical the way your mother does.'

"The message was clear. He was telling me, 'You don't have to be like other women. You're smart. You can do something with your life, *and I can help you.*' "

Iris was overwhelmed. And afraid.

She was afraid to open her mouth to this powerful, seductive male, her father, who certainly wasn't interested in what she really thought or felt. She felt she had to appear to be what he wanted her to be—calm, controlled, mature.

Inside, of course, she felt anything but calm or mature. But she couldn't tell her father what she felt; her own thoughts and feelings were clearly unacceptable to him, just as her mother's "incompetency" and "hysteria" were. And since Iris was going to grow up to be a woman like her mother and not a man like her father, she began to believe that she, too, underneath her veneer of control, was just as hopelessly incompetent and hysterical as her mother.

At some level, she believes this still; she gets excited very easily and you can hear the hysteria creeping into her voice. But she never quite gets carried away with it because on top there is always this immense control that translates the hysteria into action, and whenever she really panics she does what her father and mother both taught her from the beginning—

She runs to a man.

Her mother always told her that her father was more than just a good provider, that he was a source of strength. And when Iris divorced her first husband, at twenty-four, Daddy handled everything. Iris was actually a little angry when it turned out she had to deal with certain details, like visitation rights to the children. Her father had really promised her that the ex-husband would just disappear.

When she left her second husband, it was natural for her to seek a new father figure, one who would take care of everything, since her father was long dead by this time.

Iris became a smiler. She smiles all the time. When she gets nervous, she smiles even harder, to placate that father in her head. But at the same time, she gives the impression of being extremely competent. Her smile often looks positively triumphant.

And that is because she really believes in her father, in his power to take over for her, to rescue her. Like the actress, she has never lost her small girl's faith in the magical power of Daddy.

But unlike the actress, who needed a man only to deal with the business aspects of her career—to front for her with the Outside world—Iris needed a man who would himself embody her own goals.

This has been an old story for women, an old expectation for daughters. Even the Appleman sisters want to marry men who will give them big houses and comfortable lives, rather than getting those things for themselves. It's no accident that one catch phrase of feminism in the early 1970s was "I'm becoming the man I wanted to marry." This did not mean we were giving up heterosexuality, although some women did; it meant that we were going to do for ourselves what we had been raised to believe only a man should, or could, do.

But Iris's confusion went deeper than social prescription. When she thought about her own goals, her own ego ideal, she saw, not the award for best production nor the money she could earn and the things she could buy with it. She didn't even think of the satisfaction she would feel at fulfilling her own ambition.

She thought of Daddy.

If Daddy validates you, mirrors your worth as a feminine person, how do you find the strength to step aside from that mirror?

When Iris left her mentor/lover, she returned to her husband. Better that than stepping off into unknown territory, alone. She might never come back. So she never became her own woman. She still didn't even have an image of who that might be.

If Iris had had, from girlhood, the image of a powerful female, perhaps a successful rebel, her story might have been different. If her mother had not herself been a Little Me, her story would have been different, too, but for a different reason. Her father would never have been quite so powerful, so overwhelming an influence on her.

Yet Iris's mother, like so many of our mothers, probably had herself had very little choice in the matter. She may have been dominated by a powerful father, may herself have had a mother who could offer her neither defense nor support.

Little Me and the Secret Little Me are accommodations passed along from mothers to daughters, too. Up until now they were very nearly the only options available to heterosexual women in the postindustrial West.

The one image of independent womanhood most of us possessed was the spinster. The spinster's origins were honorable; in the Middle Ages, she was a woman who earned her living by spinning. She was probably married, since married women could belong to guilds and all women performed work of one sort or another. But as marriage laws and customs altered to abridge the economic independence of women, so that their only socially honorable state was one of married dependency, a spinster became, in English law, literally a single woman. Any woman who earned a living, the law inferred, must be single.

By the nineteenth century, marriage was considered to be the only possible means of fulfillment for women. To be a spinster was to be a failure as a woman. Louisa May Alcott, successful writer or no, was always very conscious of her spinsterhood; in one novel she described "that sisterhood called disappointed women."

There is virtually no tradition of spinsterhood among Jews, whose marriages in Europe would have been arranged. Among Catholics, spinsters became nuns, a reasonably honorable occupation. Among WASPs, spinsters could be governesses or schoolteachers or they could keep house for their fathers; whatever they did, they were more or less permanently arrested in daughterhood, and Goodness was their only option.

Today, the term "old maid" is gradually fading away, as women become more sexually assertive and remain sexy well into what used to be middle age. Nevertheless, as girls very few of us think that when we grow up we want to be alone. Why should we?

College-age women have expressed their fear of ending up with careers but without husbands or children. Only for women is this choice necessary. Only for daughters is it usual to be awarded Daddy's love, approval, and companionship on the condition that we not be independent, that we remain forever Good Girls, forever Little Me.

And if we refuse, if we think about rebelling—about separating ourselves and finding out who we might become as our own women—as often as not we are stopped cold by a new label, a negative identity that frightens us as adolescents and as adults. Even today, we risk becoming:

Rebels and Bad Girls

Even though I was a Good Girl, I thought I was Bad, because in my fantasies I was bold and rebellious, stood up to my father at all times, and forced him to respect me.

I don't think he would have understood what I meant by respect. To him, with his old-fashioned notion of virtue, respect was what a man gave a Good Girl or Woman. It was a sign of her sexual virtue: virginity before marriage, faithfulness after. Respect meant not "taking advantage" of a girl's virtue or a wife's fidelity. It meant, in short, not trying to go to bed with a female.

What I meant was intellectual respect.

I longed to have my father see me as *I* wanted to be—independent, a girl of integrity who would stand up for my convictions, fight for the right, conduct myself at all times with honor. But of course he could not possibly see me in this way because I was a girl, and for a girl, these things simply didn't count or even, really, exist.

What I also meant by respect was support. I wanted desperately to feel that he supported me—me, not some stereotype daughter, some perfect little Barbie Doll who didn't give him any trouble.

I wanted him to tell me that he supported my right and my ability to be somebody who was not like my mother and stepmother; that I could have ideas of my own and he would still love me; that he would even support my right to disagree with him. Desperately and earnestly through my adolescence I argued my point of view: the people who were questioned by McCarthy and his committee were not necessarily evil; Truman was right to prevent MacArthur from invading China; maybe you *could* tell if some Communist was trying to brainwash you.

I left copies of Emerson's essays open around the house, with strategic passages underlined: "What I must do is all that concerns me, not what the people think," from "Self-Reliance" and one of my father's own favorite themes. Everything Emerson said was so close to what my father said all the time that he could not, surely, fail to wake up and see that I, too, needed to think for myself, hold my own counsel, believe my own thoughts.

What I hadn't noticed was that Emerson was speaking entirely of men. My father thought I was mad. Here I was, an earnest little bluestocking, and all he could see was whether I was Good or Bad. (Emerson, undoubtedly, would have been as bewildered as my father. He too had a daughter, but she was devoted to him.)

On the other hand, I was in love with my father. If I wanted desperately for him to see me, it was because I was convinced that he—and possibly only he—*could* see me. Because only his view of me counted. He alone had the power to lift me out of my dreary daily skirmishes with my mother and then my stepmother, skirmishes in which, it seemed to me, two women who had renounced their own dreams were determined to make it impossible for me to realize mine.

Furthermore, I believed that my father and I were linked by a deep bond of sympathy, originating in our unspoken but (I was convinced) completely shared grief for my mother, and our equally unspoken but shared belief that my stepmother was an altogether unsuitable replacement. (She was, in fact, eminently suitable.)

I dreamed of all our shared ideas and feelings, and remained stubbornly loyal to my father's vision. It didn't occur to me that there was anything wrong with his view of the universe—he might be a bit odd about the Red Menace, but that was common enough in those days. Surely self-reliance was the best virtue. One should not demand too much of anyone (especially of him); women *were* likely to be untrustworthy (they made demands on men, they asked them for money); the masculine virtues of honor and courage and tough-mindedness (whatever that was) *were* absolutely the best ones, and a woman ought to follow them as well as a man.

The contradiction between wanting to disagree with him and to be loyal to his view of the world was never evident to me. The two things meant the same—I wanted him to see me, approve of me, give me permission to be myself.

Because I really wanted to be a Good Girl, as Fran Nobile had been able to be. Good Girls were rewarded: Good Girls got the cars and personal telephones and real cashmere sweater sets.

Since my father was stingy, he made me feel I was a Bad Girl from the start. I didn't deserve his attention. But worse: since his absolutism left me no options between rebellion and submission, I was in a paralyzing bind. If I rebelled, I would Go Too Far, beyond the pale of my father's approval and authority, and therefore by implication beyond his—and his world's—protection. I would be an outcast, because the unprotected daughter had no place to go but down into Badness: to shoplifting, promiscuity, and prostitution, to drink, drugs, and general disintegration.

This was what my father believed, what his cautionary tale about whores told me—and it was what his world had allowed him to believe, and go on believing.

To me, rebellion meant indulging my life's passion: writing. It meant putting down on the page the things I really thought and felt. It meant separating myself from my father.

To him, any separation at all, even to the extent of expressing my own opinion, meant disobedience, disloyalty, treason. Just as it had in Shakespeare's day.

All I had to do to fall from grace was to refuse to meet his impossibly contradictory demands that I be every conceivable kind of Good Girl. The minute I refused him my empathy, my loyalty, my devotion, the minute I ceased to nurture, I was labeled.

It is not surprising that it took me twenty years to open up enough space between my father and myself so that I could begin to feel possession of my own bit of turf.

Many, many women never get that far in a lifetime of trying.

Part Four

THE VOICES:

One Does, The Other Doesn't

Sally, Denise, and
Dr. Thomas Archway

A Good Girl Rebels

Jack and
Carolyn Rosenthal

CHAPTER SIX

Work and Love: When Fathers Help

Daughters Succeed . . . and When They Don't

One Does, The Other Doesn't

Sally, Denise, and Dr. Thomas Archway

*N*ot long ago, the Reverend Sally Archway and her sister, Denise, two years younger, got together to talk over their childhoods. One of the things they agreed on was that their parents used to say that Sally was the smart one and Denise was the pretty one.

Today, Sally Archway is an ordained Episcopal priest. Denise lives at home with her parents to save money while she works as secretary and looks for "some direction" for her life.

"Mother always said I was going to grow up like her," says Denise, "fall into being a housewife and raise kids. And my sister would be like my father—she'd be the successful one, have a job, be a professional. Sally knows exactly what she wants to do. She's a very strong, capable person, and she's very intelligent—very sharp, like he is."

"Denise," says Sally, "is what *Seventeen* magazine said you have to be to be attractive. She has long hair, she is extremely thin, she's lithe. Dad and I were the two intelligent ones. I refuse to believe I'm anywhere near presentable."

In fact, Sally is more than presentable, she is very attractive. She is a lot like her father: tall, for one thing—he is six feet one inches, she is five feet nine. And smart. But of course she is willowy where her father is broad and solid, and her hair is blond and curly where his is close-cropped gray.

Dr. Thomas Archway, who is a senior physician at a large western clinic, also says his daughters are quite different: "As a very small child, Sally always wanted to be the ringleader, always wanted to be the boss. She was physically large, and tended to command her playmates."

He and his wife could see from the beginning that she was exceptionally intelligent. They "recognized that she was bored with school in kindergarten and first grade," and when they had her tested, it was recommended that she be skipped two grades because she was physically and socially, as well as intellectually, precocious.

So Sally has always been goal-directed and her father "fully expected her to be a professional of some kind—teacher, lawyer, doctor." Denise, he says, is "a very different person. She's quieter and less assertive. Anything that happens is all right, and if today isn't too good, tomorrow will be better. She just kind of floats along." She has, in fact, "no career ambitions at all. She's dying to get married."

Sally, he agrees, is more like him.

Parental labels have a way of influencing children's lives because they reflect parental expectations, even if they also reflect accurate observation of children's different temperaments and physical styles. Labels influence children's images of themselves and, as we saw with the Applemans, your image of yourself begins affecting your view of your future quite early in life.

"At the time," says Denise of her mother's prediction, "I thought, 'Yeah, that's probably true.' Now it upsets me because I think it really has affected me. In the back of my mind, it's always, 'Just get married and don't worry about it.' "

Not that she doesn't want to get married; but she thinks motherhood can only be a woman's main activity in life "for a while. I don't want to have the kids grow up and all of a sudden have nothing."

Today, Denise is thinking of going to Europe with her boyfriend. Her mother, who now teaches full time, thinks she should get a skill, perhaps become a computer programmer (which is the other thing Denise is thinking of doing). Her father is saying, "You're only young once," and why not go to Europe?

It's fascinating how two daughters in the same family can have such different images of themselves and their parents.

In nearly all Sally's childhood memories, for instance, her father is present and always active, doing something like mowing the lawn. Most importantly, she remembers doing things with him; she especially loved going to the clinic with him on Saturday mornings.

Denise, on the other hand, says he is not a central figure in her childhood memories; he was not, after all, home very much. Her most vivid memory of him is of floating with her sister on an inflatable rubber raft during a vacation. He is "holding the raft, and we would just go la-de-da through the waves." A daughter's memory of being safe and passive —just floating along—while protective Daddy steers the raft. Sally never mentioned this scene, although Denise was sure she would. Denise never mentioned visits to the clinic. When I finally asked her directly, she told me she only went once or twice, and then not until she was twenty.

Birth order is held to be crucially important in the creation of ambitious and achieving women. To be the oldest or the only child means, it is said, that a daughter will be more likely to have a special relationship with her father, be treated more as a son would be.

But, in fact, as Margaret Hennig and Anne Jardim point out in their influential study of successful women executives, *The Managerial Woman,* what is important is the special relationship, not birth order.

Callie Opal, remember, was a second daughter who became her father's companion—and also, in the context of that family, the most ambitious child.

Still, Dr. Archway may have been more present in Sally's childhood life, even though he was certainly the same workaholic father he was for Denise, simply because she *was* the oldest. He taught Sally to ride a bike, for instance; and then she, the older sister, taught Denise. On the other hand, if Sally felt a special bond of temperament and intelligence with her father from the beginning, she would selectively remember him more than Denise would have, because her memories of him would have more importance for her.

He says he spent a lot more time with Sally when she was little, and much of it was outdoors—"walks, picnics, that sort of thing." You can tell that he feels a strong identification with this daughter who is like him in so many ways, even though, as he also points out, he is probably closer to Denise, who, after all, has been at home much more. She lived at home through high school and then came back after college.

In any case, as I pointed out in Chapter Four, this extra attention in early childhood—focused attention—is something boys usually get rather than girls, as is the inclusion in Daddy's activities.

Not that Sally was treated as a boy; she and her father agree on that. Actually, her parents had been expecting a boy, because Sally's mother had taken part in an experimental program to determine the sex of unborn children from saliva tests and so forth, and had been told she was carrying a boy. The program was wrong, but no one seems to have been disappointed. Sally thinks they were just glad to have a healthy child after four years of trying. Dr. Archway says he thinks girls are easier to raise than boys. For one thing, "You can raise them without getting involved in some of the problems that you can more easily refer to their mother"; and for another, boys can be more troublesome when it comes to things like drinking or racing around in cars.

In any case, it was Denise who became the classic tomboy. She takes after her mother, who is the athlete in the family, a golfer and skier. Denise rides horses, hikes, backpacks. Sally was a good deal more conventionally feminine in her interests. She plays tennis, but she remembers sewing in the family room while her father read or watched TV or built a fire. (Today, she likes to have a fire in her own fireplace.)

When Dr. Archway went to the clinic on Saturday mornings, Sally would go along to sit in his office and open his mail. She was Daddy's Girl, and this meant being with him. She loved it.

But the memory that made the biggest impression on her was going with him while he talked to everyone who had to work on Thanksgiving and Christmas, from the nurses to the dishwasher. "I was filled with pride," she says, "because everybody obviously admired him so much for thinking enough of them to come in on a holiday. He really has that touch, of recognizing when other people put themselves out." (Years later, Denise had the same feeling of pride and pleasure when she went with him. But she went only once and, of course, she did not identify with him in the same way.)

Sally Archway was ordained in 1979. Her father still doesn't completely understand it, since he and his family were never particularly religious, but the things he showed Sally on those holiday rounds seem to have had a lot to do with her vocation.

What she saw was a man whose work "is at the center of his life. On Christmas we would open our presents, then go to the hospital, and then come back for dinner—very much what I do now, as a priest."

She saw a man who, by her own account, was comfortable with his authority, who had developed a style that was "caring, nurturing, and, above all, recognized the other person."

She saw, furthermore, a man who radiated warmth and friendly communication at work in a way he found difficult to do at home. Although he was unfailingly supportive of both Sally and Denise, he was also, as Denise describes him, "very laid back, very quiet," or, as Sally described him, "noncommunicative."

Both girls saw, in short, an American institutional Daddy, a man who came alive in his work. But only Sally identified directly with him.

Yet, Sally told me, "When I called him to tell him about this interview, he said, 'I don't have any influence on you at all.' I said, 'That's absurd, what are you talking about?' He said, 'Children are like weeds. You let 'em grow and you take what you get.'"

When I visited Sally's office in the Southwestern church where she is an Associate Rector, I was first struck by bright colors—an orange bookcase, an Indian painting on the wall, and Sally herself wearing a bright green sweater over her clerical collar. Her voice on the phone had been so efficient that I, as full of subconscious stereotypes as anyone else, was not prepared for this tall, glistening young woman in dirndl skirt and sling-back sandals. By the time we had finished our lengthy interview, I was convinced that this woman is doing the thing she is ideally suited for, and that she has, moreover, managed to integrate both her father and her mother into a clear sense of identity that admirably serves both her own needs and those of her Church.

Maybe the key to Sally Archway is in both sides of her father—his unfailing support, which left her with a strong sense of confidence in her own abilities, and his emotional distance, which made her hungry.

On one level, Sally's background seems very similar to those of the successful female executives described by Hennig and Jardim: in addition to being first-born with a sister and no brothers, her father is a professional and she had a special relationship with him. Certainly, to some extent he took her into his world, and he was definitely a role model.

On the other hand, she says, her father did not *expect* her to be, necessarily, a winner. He was, she remembers, "equally supportive whether we won or lost, whether or not we were on the honor role, as long as we sort of tried.

"The one thing we both remember in terms of direction from him was, 'I don't care what you do with your life—whether you become a jockey, or a receptionist, or a doctor, or an Indian chief—but you have to be able to support yourself.' "

This does not sound like a demand for high achievement; in fact, it sounds like no more than the standard expectation middle-class American fathers have had of their daughters for the last twenty to forty years. But for Sally there seems to have been another message underneath, in a pattern that is the opposite of Steve Appleman's. Unlike Steve, Tom Archway really did expect more of Sally.

He says: "I fully expected her to be a professional of some kind—teacher, attorney, physician—although I can't recall ever being very specific about it. I think the general attitude was, 'You should get as much education as you can, you're obviously smart and capable, and a lot of other people aren't as lucky.' "

This is a classic WASP or Protestant attitude: you owe something in return for your intelligence and your privileges. It creates a sense of duty that has been giving WASP daughters the rationale for professional vocations since at least the nineteenth century.

So Sally had her father's support, and his expectation that she would do something serious with her life, something on a professional level. She knew she was smart, and that her parents approved of this. On the other hand, there was still that hunger, a need for emotional warmth, a communion that she didn't quite find at home.

On the whole, the distance between Sally and her father seems to have been a kind of companionable silence, perhaps exemplified by the image of them together in the family room—she sewing, he making a fire—neither saying much, if anything. This distance, this mutual autonomy, provides an excellent foundation for a daughter's future professional life.

It is, of course, essentially a masculine style of relating. It is the style called "instrumental," based on doing things rather than on communicating feelings. When, for instance, Sally was applying to medical school before she decided to enter the seminary, he helped her fill out the applications. "But I can't remember him communicating on a personal level what he thought of that. It was all objective, 'You ended this sentence in your essay with a preposition.' I felt good about that; I had asked him for that help, and Daddy and I work much better when we have something between us, when we have something to discuss, or when we're doing something together."

The way most fathers feminize their daughters, as I pointed out in Chapter Four, is by relating to them expressively—more warmly, more emotionally than they do with their sons. And Denise, more than Sally, finds her father warm and sympathetic. When she and her father were visiting Sally recently, for instance, they were drawn together: "I can't tell you how many times I grabbed his arm, or leaned against him, or went up and hugged him." She finds that now, living at home as an adult, she can talk to him about the men in her life and "he cracks little jokes and laughs—he's very casual. He'll say, 'Tell him to go jump in the lake.'"

But Sally, as an adolescent, found that even while she was being encouraged to assert her autonomous self, she was hungry for emotional warmth. She found it, not through boyfriends or cheerleading, two of the traditional girls' routes, but at school, and more specifically in the Church.

Both she and her parents were excited about the private boarding school to which Sally went because of its high academic rating. Tom Archway now says, wryly, that they "didn't pay enough attention" to the fact that chapel was required every day. Sally remembers that her parents "figured I was smart enough to persevere through the religious aspect." One of her father's sayings was, "Baptism is giving reality to myth," so neither daughter had been baptized.

Sally found herself, as well as the Church, at school. First, she loved the school: "I felt challenged, supported, and nurtured, and in the midst of that I started going to chapel every day because it was required. I also got very involved with volunteer tutoring in a ghetto school, through the chapel. I saw the impact we had, and the fact that we were doing it through the Church somehow got translated into the idea that the Church *can* do things in society, and wasn't just this sort of place where you wandered away from everything to sit and think esoteric thoughts."

This discovery of the Church as an effective institution was, of course, tremendously important because Sally had such strong memories of being with her father in his institution, the clinic. (In fact, she declared a pre-med major in college and went as far as completing the application process for medical schools before she realized she didn't want to be a doctor, which was a profession her father would have understood perfectly.)

At twelve, Sally decided she wanted to be baptized and confirmed as a member of the Episcopal Church. Her father thought it "a childish phase that would pass." When a chaplain wrote a note asking if he had any objection to her confirmation, he scrawled on the bottom, "I don't if you don't," and sent it back. He meant it "facetiously—what does this kid know about being confirmed in the Episcopal Church? But the chaplain took it seriously."

As she remembers it, when she first told her parents of her decision to go to the seminary, "We were sitting at the dining-room table. My mother said, 'Oh my God, you're entering a convent!' I said, 'No, that's not true, I can still get married and stuff.' And Daddy said, 'Roosevelt said we all have four freedoms. Roosevelt was wrong, we have five. And the fifth freedom is to screw up our lives.' "

Sally's voice, when she quotes her father, deepens and she speaks in slow, solemn tones. She is satirizing him, gently. She can do it now. But, at the time, "I felt . . . empty." And she lets out her breath in a great sigh. "It was one of those comments, like 'The only person you can trust less than a Republican is a born-again Christian.' Where do you start? He comes on with a statement like that, and I can't get back down to ground zero."

As the daughter of a father who spoke almost entirely in sayings, I know exactly what she means—and how she felt.

"I wasn't going to argue," says Sally "You can't argue that no one has the freedom to ruin their own life."

Eventually, though, when Sally did "confront him, and ask, 'Do you really think I'm doing this awful, terrible thing, and why do you have no respect for my religion?' " his response was: "Everybody needs a crutch. And if your crutch is going to be your faith, that's your concern."

What, I ask, is his crutch? "Probably his career. He is very much a workaholic, and gets his identity from his career. He is very good at what he does, and extremely popular with the entire staff."

Then she qualifies her sense of what her father meant by "crutch": "He is a great humanitarian, in the sense that if someone needs something, he will never put that down. He'll put it down for himself, and he might sort of subtly let you know that he thinks there might be another way. But he would never grab somebody's crutch away from them, which makes him beloved by the staff, I think. So he was almost nonjudgmental—it was, 'Well, people need a crutch to get through this world, and if that's going to be yours, that's fine.' "

So Sally had to choose her career independently of her father's full understanding; but not, and this is important, in defiance or rebellion. *She never had to choose between her father and her career* because, while "it was an issue he was not going to understand, he never said, 'If you do this you're breaking with me.' " And, in fact, "it ended up with an agreement that they would never understand why I'm an Episcopal minister—my mother keeps saying, 'How could I have had you?'—but they will support me."

This support is crucial. Without it, it is very hard for anyone—daughter or son—to make a career choice and follow it through without costly, if not crippling, personal conflicts. Someone, somewhere, has to tell you that it's okay, that you have permission, to do what you want to do.

Men get a general acceptance, even an imperative to achieve, from the culture at large. Women, however, who are only just beginning to receive such permission from the culture at large, have until now depended greatly on getting it from their parents. And Daddy, as representative of the Outside world, has, it seems, had the most power to make a daughter feel she has or does not have this permission.

Tom Archway's memory of exactly what passed between himself and Sally when she told him she planned to become a priest is slightly different. "I was astounded," he said. "I was talking to her on the phone—she had been a pre-med student, and I really thought she was going to go through the application process, although I thought her credentials were probably borderline. She said, 'I've decided not to go to medical school.' I said, 'Well, that's pretty interesting; what have you decided to do?' She said, 'I don't want you to laugh, but I've decided to become an Episcopal priest.' I said, 'Well, that's really very interesting because there's no such thing as a woman Episcopal priest.' And she said, 'There will be.' "

He is an extremely impressive man: tall, solid, obviously strong and competent. When he talks, he often puzzles a bit over his words, searching for exactly the right ones. He has, actually, quite a considerable understanding of Sally's career choice, in his own terms. He obviously has thought it over. "I think," he says, "it meets her needs, and I'm pleased with it because she's obviously accepted and successful in it."

But he doesn't think he contributed to the decision, and he is a bit bemused by it, as Sally said. "It's strange. I don't go to church myself, and I find it difficult to really relate to what's going on. If she had become a doctor I could understand that, because I know the system, and the politics, and the career ladders that are available in medicine."

He can see that her first decision to go to medical school would have been perfectly natural. But he doesn't see himself as, particularly, a mentor. He remembers teaching Sally to ride a bike, and he certainly sees her as more like him than Denise is, but he doesn't see the influence of his example at the hospital. She was, after all, in his words, "pretty small," and, although he thinks she might have learned "something," he doubts that she would consciously have modeled herself after him.

But she has.

Take the matter of authority. Many women have had trouble assuming authority because it has been, in the past, so exclusively a male preserve. The boss has traditionally been male, and the male boss's ability to command respect has been enormously enhanced by the fact that most people have grown up with a model of the father as the ultimate authority.

How does a woman step in and assume the authority that comes, not just from Daddy, but from God the Father, the ultimate Daddy?

One thing she does is look at her own father: "The way he showed his authority when he appeared on Christmas Day to talk to those nurses. It was not an untouchable authority. It was caring, nurturing, and above all recognized the other person. He was in a position where he could stay home on Christmas Day, but he recognized that other people couldn't. I definitely feel I work with my authority the same way."

And then there is the matter of choosing a vocation that becomes the center of your life, even of your identity, as Tom Archway's work is at the center of his. As Sally puts it: "I think I had a good pattern for that." And as she points out, her own holiday rounds as a priest are remarkably similar to the ones she went on with him every year from "four until I graduated from high school."

Identification with her father has been, for Sally Archway, an extremely productive way of adapting herself to the world in which she found herself.

Of course, she was lucky. The first woman minister was ordained in 1977, two years before Sally graduated from seminary. Then there was that early relationship, that time spent with Daddy at the clinic: "My perception of myself was very much that I was Daddy's girl. That meant being with him, it didn't focus on me. I would be opening his mail—he wouldn't be going with me to buy roller skates. Daddy's girl meant being supportive of him. I was entering *his* sphere." Excellent training for a woman who ends up in the Church—or in a corporation, or a law firm.

Excellent training for a priest.

But the Church, she feels, has also given her something her father didn't. The Church has saved her from the WASP curse of emotional isolation.

Her father, the son of a rancher, enlisted in the Navy right out of high school. His destroyer escort was sunk in the Pacific, and he spent ten days in an open lifeboat. It took months to recover from wounds and exposure.

The experience, says his daughter, "changed his life. It made him decide that if he was going to make it, it was going to be on the strength of his own will and perseverance—and he expects that of others."

Such experiences can intensify the split between the private man, whose emotions would have to be held tightly in check, and the institutional man, for whom both activity and a goal offer relief from emotions.

Sally's father didn't mention his war experience to me—and this is a characteristic of such a man. My father always said it was simply not done to talk about what you did in the war, and his experience was cushy compared to Tom Archway's. Not to talk about what you did, and especially not how you felt about it, is part of one masculine image.

A daughter who identifies with such an image, whose father relates to her in a more masculine style, might well miss the warmth a daughter like Denise is able to elicit.

As I have said, Sally's relationship with her father is based on mutual respect, on their sharing of activities rather than feelings and personal experiences. "The time that Dad and I got back on board," she said, "after I had done this unfathomable thing by going off to seminary, was when I started working. I could say I had this committee meeting, and I'm meeting with the vestry, and we're making some plans to deal with the floor space of the church. I could deal professionally with him again—and that goes back to the fact that we're always able, I think, to deal with each other better when we have something between us."

Since she feels emotionally more distanced, a daughter like Sally might also idealize her father more than one like Denise. Denise, after all, was raised to be a companion to a man, not to emulate traditionally masculine achievement patterns. Since her father was—and is—warmer with her, she feels much closer to him than Sally does, and finds it easier to confide in him and joke with him.

It was Denise who shocked both Sally and her mother by refusing, one night, to move out of Dr. Archway's favorite chair in the family room, where she was ensconced when he came home. According to Sally, he said, "Get out of my chair," and Denise said, "No." To everyone's surprise, he let it go and sat in an ordinary chair.

This is the kind of everyday assertion of privilege daughters can, traditionally, assume with fathers. But Sally, for whom her father is very much an ideal, says: "I wouldn't have been there in the first place, or I would have moved as soon as I heard him come in." Her father is "someone I look up to, whom I admire, and whose way I'm not going to get into."

Which is interesting in view of her image of God. As a woman who has been strongly touched by feminism, she finds that in her preaching she tries not to refer to "God the Father" a lot, "using 'God' instead of 'the Father,' or trying to really concentrate on Jesus' humanity." She has been told that her preaching style is feminine because she uses "feminine" examples out of daily life. "A lot of how I deal with the term 'God the Father,' and with communicating, I think, is sort of who I am and how I preach and how I hold the baby at the baptism—which I'm told is much better than any man."

But on a personal level: "Emotionally and psychologically, God sort of fits in with the way I see my father, caring, but distant. Caring, but non-communicative. Although my God has a much better sense of humor than my father." (Here she laughs, as she does often in the interview.)

"I think my main thing is having a total trust and faith. I really do believe that my God is not going to desert me. If I'm really forced to it, I have no qualms about using the word 'father,' and yet a lot of my perceptions of God are not what I've learned from my father or any other male figure."

In fact, when God *is* most like her own father, "It's God at His worst, in some respects, and yet God at His most real. Even though I'm a priest, my God is very distant from me at times. There is no question that I feel that caring, and yet not a word."

Perhaps it is this poignant recognition that underlies her conception of her ministry as helping people to reach God. "I see what I'm doing very much as service to the people—helping them to learn who this God is, helping them to figure out how they fit into this community of the Church, and helping them, in some ways, say their prayers. There have certainly been times when I've needed help to say my prayers, to get any sense of a contact with God."

Although she doesn't make an issue of her feminism, Sally Archway's emphasis on the humanity of Jesus may, in the end, be far more influential. If she can identify with Jesus, she finds it perfectly natural to suggest other kinds of identifications to her congregation.

"Last Easter," she said, "I was talking about the women going to the tomb to discover that Jesus has been raised, and I said, 'We, like those women, might have felt. . . .' Two men came up to me afterwards and said it was the first time anyone had ever asked them to feel like a woman."

Interestingly, Sally finds that the people who most easily accept her priestly role are men who, like her father, "have to deal in their own professions with women who, they are beginning to realize, are capable, can deal with authority, can handle clients—partners in law firms, doctors with hospital practices."

Tom Archway describes himself as "kind of a women's libber before there was women's lib" because, of course, hospitals have always employed large numbers of women. In the late forties and fifties, "there were a lot of social pressures against women working," as well as a severe nursing shortage. So he found himself campaigning for women's right to work—whether informally, to their husbands at parties, or in talks before service clubs.

His own wife, he adds, "does pretty much what she wants." She focused on mothering while the children were young.

When I asked Sally whether she sees herself, today, as more like her mother or her father, she said: "A little of both, and becoming more like my mother. Although if you had asked me two or three years ago, I would have said, 'Oh, my father's daughter, all the way.' "

Why, I asked, had her feelings changed?

Three reasons. First, she felt she had personally been "working through a lot of mother-daughter stuff. My mother and I now have an excellent relationship, and we communicate a lot on a lot of different levels. We still get extremely fed up with each other, but we can go out shopping and have a good time, or we can sit down and talk about how hard it is to give my father support, and feel our bond with each other.

"Second, I am sure this is connected with my getting a job, and getting my own house, and moving away from home. All that needed to happen before I could relate back to her. She is very supportive and very proud, as is my father."

And, third, she feels her mother has changed, has become more the sort of person Sally can relate to. Sally saw her as a "housewife, when I was in college and seminary. She's gone through a real transition. She was everything I was not: athletic, sporty, very gregarious at parties. If someone were to take their shoes off and dance on top of the coffee table, it would probably be my mother. I always found that embarrassing.

"Now she's becoming much more independent, so I've gotten to know her better. She's no longer just this sort of bohemian type—she's taken on a personality of her own. She's teaching emotionally handicapped children, and is very good at it. Last year, she took her first vacation away from my father and hiked from Cuzco to Machu Picchu in Peru. She has that kind of adventurous spirit."

By finding these links with her mother, Sally has, in a sense, completed her Identity Triangle. From the beginning, her Triangle was different from her sister's because she identified more directly with her father than with her mother. This doesn't mean reciprocal identification wasn't important to her; it is always important to daughters. What it does mean is that her father's messages told her she could be feminine and still identify with him. While she clearly does miss the warmth and flirtatiousness Denise gets, she received the benefit of his respect; he took her seriously.

This is not at all the same thing as rejecting her femininity. If she had felt rejected as a female by her father, Sally might not have the serene sense of herself she has today. She would be more conflicted, and possibly far less successful in her work. Like Dr. Nobile, her father was telling her that she could selectively identify with him; unlike Dr. Nobile, of course, he never said Don't Go Too Far. He gave her no mixed messages.

But while Sally certainly identified with her mother as a biological female, and while she has undoubtedly incorporated some of her mother's nurturing qualities into her identity as a priest, she couldn't identify with her mother as a woman whose main role seemed to consist of her relationship to her husband and children; who was, in short, an Inside woman. For Denise, on the other hand, direct identification with her mother has always been important, partly because her father's messages told her that he wanted her to be the same kind of woman. For her, reciprocal identification with her father reinforced direct identification with her mother.

Perhaps daughters whose mothers don't offer a model of the kind of woman they want to become themselves, daughters who find their ego ideal shared with their fathers instead, have conflicts about their identifications with their mothers precisely because they are afraid they might, after all, grow up to be only Inside women. It's tricky to handle the task of identifying with your mother just so far.

But once you have achieved your ego ideal and feel secure in your identity in the world, it is easier to turn back to your mother and find ways in which you can identify directly with her. Sally's mother has made it even easier by changing her own life; she has become more nearly the kind of woman Sally could have directly identified with all along. But Sally herself also feels more comfortable with traditionally feminine interests like shopping, or the emotional life of the family. Inside stuff.

Hennig and Jardim found a similar pattern among the top corporate executives they studied. Those women, too, had only partly identified with their mothers, who had embodied the image of the nurturing Inside woman. At a time when sex roles were quite rigid, the executives had had to go to extremes in order to fulfill their identifications with their fathers. In their first years on the job, they had had to suppress all outward signs of feminine style and heterosexual femininity and act like asexual "automatons." This was the only way they could avoid conflicts about roles and identity, both in themselves and with their male bosses and peers. (Even today, young women are counseled to "dress for success" in man-tailored suits and plain shoes.)

But by their mid-to-late thirties they had all reached the highest levels of middle management and, among other things, they began to relax. They felt more secure about both their job performance and their acceptance by male peers. What they did then was to take a "moratorium" from their single-minded devotion to work, to the ego ideal they shared with their fathers. They all plunged into a period like adolescence, during which they explored the pleasures of feminine clothes, makeup, social life. These things had previously been forbidden them, to some extent, by the rigid standards of the workplace, but they must also have been identified in the executives' minds with their mothers, who had no independent lives. Indulging in the more frivolous aspects of heterosexual femininity—even outside of work—would have seemed to lead toward marriage and a life as Little Me. No woman trying to make it in a man's world could afford to start the sequence. The cost, in anxiety, self-doubt, and conflict, would be too high.

But once they had clearly established an identity in the Outside world, they no longer feared they might turn into Little Me; in the course of their moratorium, half of them married widowers or divorced men with children, and the rest felt they were ready to marry if they met a suitable man. So these previously father-identified executives were able to turn back to their mothers and identify directly with at least some aspects of their roles as Inside women.

Sally Archway will never have to take a moratorium because she has been freer to integrate feminine style, heterosexual femininity, and father-identification from the beginning. Partly, of course, this is because sex roles have become less rigid; consider her green sweater and sling-back sandals. If women had been allowed to be priests thirty years ago, they would undoubtedly have had to wear black man-tailored suits and sensible shoes.

In adolescence, Sally felt very conscious of herself as a young woman: "I remember taking great pride in being seen with my father. I looked older than I was, because I was tall. He is a very, very good-looking man, so I remember dressing up, and knowing that I looked older than I was, and going out to dinner with him when he would come for fathers' weekends at school, and feeling that I looked very sophisticated."

As an Episcopal priest, she certainly has not had to behave as an automaton. She dates, and she has always assumed that marriage and motherhood will be part of her life, although men sometimes do have a little trouble integrating their images of her as a woman who is a priest. She told me about a man who, after asking her out, said he wanted to fix dinner at his house but didn't want to compromise her.

"I almost," she said, "canceled dinner. That Virgin Mary concept. You have the authority of a priest, and the only way a lot of men can relate to that is in the authority—or the image—of the Virgin Mary."

Her father doesn't have that problem; although he does think that the demands of her vocation will make it hard for her to marry, unless perhaps to another priest. He can cite examples of successful women doctors combining a medical practice, marriage, and motherhood, but he thinks the priesthood takes even more time and attention than a medical practice, and that very few men would have the understanding necessary to cope with a wife in such a job.

But he is extremely proud of her: "I think she'll do very well, although

I'm not familiar enough with the system to know exactly what progress means—possibly assuming some kind of administrative role in the government of the Church."

And then he makes a remark that shows you for sure that, whether he understands her choice of vocation or not, he is completely behind her:

"I don't know whether she'll be the first woman bishop or not, but she's probably got a shot at it."

Just like that. A father talking about his daughter.

A Good Girl Rebels
Jack and Carolyn Rosenthal

C arolyn Rosenthal is a businesswoman, the daughter of a businessman, and the oldest child. Once again, it seems, the oldest daughter gets ahead.

But Carolyn has two younger brothers, and you would think that this might have canceled out her advantage with her father. In fact, he says he always thought Carolyn would be a social worker and his oldest son would be an executive. But it didn't work out quite like that.

She is full of energy, and wears her red hair in a cloud of curls around her face. She is completely confident of her ability, of her career, and of her ultimate success.

"People," she says, "have always expected I would be successful. People have been telling me for years that I would be a vice-president, at least. I sort of think, well, maybe I will."

Her father says, "I don't think she's going to be President, but I would like her to be a vice-president."

Carolyn is part of a generation, the one that went to college in the second half of the sixties, that had strong ideals. She didn't want to work for a corporation like her father, so she went to law school and spent four years with Legal Aid as a criminal defense lawyer. Then, in her late twenties, she began to think about her future. Legal Aid didn't have a lot to offer, and after she looked around for a while, she realized that law was a good background for business. She went to work for a small, up-and-coming electronics firm that was beginning to expand into computers. She likes the freewheeling, entrepreneurial aspects of a growing company, and she loves being in on the ground floor of the new technology.

She lives in a sparsely furnished two-bedroom co-op she bought with her husband, but at the moment she lives there alone. He has moved out while they reassess their marriage.

She is a feminist; the one thing she regrets is that she graduated from college a year or two before feminism came along. But she is far too pragmatic to be an ideologue. She has no little hooks out to catch people and rub them the wrong way, which is the sort of thing that can mess up an opportunity when it comes along.

Until recently, three things shaped her life. First, she was her father's favorite, the one he always encouraged and expected to succeed. Second, as a self-described Good Girl, she has always found that success has come easily to her. And third, she determined, early on, to be more successful at more meaningful work than her father was.

These three things don't seem to add up. How can you feel competitive toward your father and still be a Good Girl? And how can Good Girl traits lead to success?

Carolyn's competitiveness, though, may in part be something else, a way of carrying out her father's messages to her to succeed where he could not.

Jack Rosenthal, Carolyn's father, works in a branch office of a multinational corporation whose headquarters are in Chicago. He went to an Ivy League school, and after the Army got his first job. At thirty, he got an M.B.A. (His wife, a music teacher, supported the small family for the two years; Carolyn was a preschooler.) When he took the job with the multinational, he fully expected to make vice-president.

But Jack failed to achieve that final testament not so much to competence as to political ability—the proof that you have the political savvy to get along well on the executive team. When, at thirty-nine, he was transferred to the branch office rather than the home office, he knew he wouldn't make it. And, says his daughter, he is bitter.

"I think," Carolyn says, "that I'm very determined to succeed, and to be good at my work—and, as opposed to my father, to have my work *mean* something to me. This is a reaction. I watched my father gradually come to feel that his job had no meaning for him and was not rewarding, and I said, 'I'm not going to be that way. My job is going to be important to me; it's going to feed my soul, not just support me.' And I decided I would be more successful because I was determined that I would not have that petulant sense of being underappreciated, or underused."

These feelings are competitive, "I'm going to make it where he didn't," but it also looks very much as though Carolyn received pretty explicit permission from her father to have such goals. For one thing, although Carolyn describes her family as "very competitive," she was the only one who developed a competitive style. She won; the older son, the second child, came out second best. "He's a carpenter," says Carolyn. "My guess is he figured out early on that competing wasn't going to get him anywhere. Not that he can't. He's chosen not to. We were always a very rational, idea-oriented family; we were not emotional at all. I think my brother was more emotional. He's just not as hard-edged as my father is, and as I am."

Carolyn "always had the sense that my father related to me as his favorite child, the one who should follow after him." When she was little, she remembers that on the one hand, "there was a certain amount of sexism: the boys did outside chores, raked the lawn, and I stayed inside, with my mother, and helped clean up after dinner." On the other hand, though, "there was never any sense that I wouldn't aspire in the same way, go to school in the same way, or that I wasn't smart."

In fact, she "always knew there was a lot of pressure" on her to succeed, "but I managed to do it. I always thought my father wanted me to be successful in the work world. He paid a lot of attention to me: I was Daddy's Girl. I was special, and smart. He didn't care whether I dated, or whether or not I got married. Whatever I said my goal was, he always told me to aim higher. I would say I was going to be a teacher; he would say I should be principal. I would say social worker, he would say 'head an agency.' "

Jack tells me he doesn't remember saying these things, but he supposes he must have. So, in fact, Carolyn's competitiveness may really be, in part, the fulfillment of her father's own wish.

The fact that she was a girl probably made it possible for Jack to encourage her to be successful in ways that he himself had not been able to. It's easier for some fathers, the very successful and the failed, to groom a daughter than a son as their successor or as the fulfiller of their own lost promise; a son's success in either case may feel too directly threatening, too painful. So although Jack says he wanted his oldest son to be the businessman, he was probably giving him some very different *sub rosa* messages.

The younger brother is "the sweetest and least competitive of us all. He's going to social work school," which makes him heir to Carolyn's original career goal, and perhaps to a secret wish of Jack Rosenthal's.

Carolyn's father is—and was—a nurturer, as his own father had been. Carolyn was "a Spock baby, and as the first child I got a lot of attention. They kept a scrapbook and everything. When my father came home from work, they would obsess about me, and he was very involved in taking care of me."

Her father confirms this. He loved taking care of all his children. He changed diapers, fed them, put them to bed. Now, when all his children have left home, he speaks wistfully of missing having a family around, just as traditional mothers are supposed to do. He tells me he jokes with Carolyn, "and like all jokes it isn't really a joke, that maybe when I retire we'll move near her and I'll take care of her child. I miss having little children. I think I was good at it, and I enjoyed it."

Carolyn thinks that her father "may not have connected with what it really took to be a success. Successful executives work seventy-hour weeks, and that's not my sense of what my father did. Possibly, on some level, he really chose to spend time with his family instead of being successful. He has always made the family a very important part of his life."

Social work was Jack's avocation; he was "President of the Family Service Organization, and on all the boards." He thought Carolyn would become a social worker because she loved working with underprivileged children at community centers. Today, she serves on the boards of directors of two community service groups. "The pattern of social work," Jack says, "I think they get to a large extent from me."

His parents had been first-generation. They ran a Mom-and-Pop business in northern Illinois, and they must have been ambitious for their only son. They could afford to send him to good schools, after all. The best. But he might, just possibly, have been living out their expectations more than his own. The failed executive might, under different circumstances, have been a successful social worker.

In addition to competitiveness, Carolyn had a number of other non-Good Girl traits. For one thing, she is not afraid to make her own decisions. Her father wanted her to go to Harvard or Yale for law school; she chose the University of Michigan because she wanted a more diversified student body.

He encouraged her to think for herself. "I'm opinionated," he says, "and she grew up in a house where we had opinions and expressed them. I grew up in a small town, but I had my own views and was marching to my own music, or my parental or family music, and I think those values got transmitted."

He also encouraged her to be aggressive about asserting her own views—to be, even, dominant. "I always thought I was his equal," she says, "in a very arrogant way. I was fresh. He always encouraged me to give my opinion on political issues. When I was twelve, I told some relatives they were racists. They never showed up at our house again. He thought it was cute."

It may be, of course, that he didn't take her all that seriously in such matters. Or that, like most fathers, he was ambivalent. Still, he calls her "the head of the family" only half-jokingly; her brothers went to her college, although they both got into his university as well. She has, he says, "a lot of leadership and very good judgment and is sensible, and very attached to the family. Her brothers think very highly of her. We all do."

Jack thinks Carolyn is like himself, that they share "professional skills, high standards, organizational ability, leadership. And we both like to make lists." He clearly also thinks she is dominant, although he doesn't see himself as dominating either his wife or his children.

She thinks he does dominate his wife, but not herself. "I am a dominating person," she says; "a fairly aggressive person. I always took a leadership role, and I've never had trouble with that as a woman. That was one advantage of being a lawyer: I had to be an advocate. In court, I had to take a position. I have a sense that I was trained to do that. I grew up arguing the whole time, politicking, taking positions."

With the politicking and the arguing, with the encouragement to take an independent view, came a very special relationship.

For most daughters, one aspect of the Identity Triangle is a degree of competition with their mother for their father's attention. This starts very early, when little girls fall in love with Daddy and play to marry him when they grow up. Mothers have a stake, from the first, in keeping themselves in the picture; sometimes, in fact, they prevent fathers and daughters from developing any real closeness. An argument could be made that this intervention serves a purpose, anthropologically, in preventing incest. Psychologically, it shows a daughter that her mother "owns" Daddy and that the daughter must look elsewhere for her love objects.

But some daughters don't have to compete. "It wasn't," says Carolyn, "a contest between my mother and myself for my father; I just assumed that my father and I had a bond she didn't share."

This sense of feeling entirely secure in their fathers' affections was also a characteristic of the Hennig-Jardim executives' childhoods. You could call it an emotional Princesshood: a father's adoration gives a daughter a sure sense of herself, whether as a charmer of men or as an achiever—or, with luck, as both.

Carolyn and her father would talk about issues at the dinner table. "We ate dinner a minute and a half after he got in the door, and he dominated the conversation. In my family you talk about facts, about issues, about the newspaper. My father would ask, 'Did you see the article that begins on page 12?' My mother was not interested."

So Carolyn, naturally, "grew up with a sense that I was more interesting than my mother, particularly *vis-à-vis* my father. I'm sure I thought I was better than she was—that I was his equal in ways that she wasn't. My father would talk to me about finances rather than my mother, because she couldn't understand it.

"My father and I were the two smart ones. It's not that we had an alliance against her; she just wasn't a strong character. She didn't make a lot of demands. She worked very hard to accommodate him. Her father had been a very difficult man, so she had learned to be very cooled out and accommodating."

This is the kind of response smart daughters are very likely to have toward mothers who can't offer the challenges, the links to the Outside world, that fathers do. Carolyn's mother, as women did then, gave up teaching when Carolyn was four to be what her husband calls "at home" for twenty years, to take care of her children and her husband.

A woman who spends all her time servicing and accommodating a husband and small children is likely to be perceived as a much less distinct personality than a father. The Hennig-Jardim executives, who were all born thirty-five years before Carolyn, saw their mothers as rather vague figures, too. It is, perhaps, an inevitable penalty of full-time motherhood, at least where smart, aggressive Daddies' Girls are concerned.

Given her dominance, her aggression, her independence, how can Carolyn call herself a Good Girl? Because, she says, "I always thought that what they wanted from me, and what I wanted, weren't so different."

For example: at first, being a Good Girl meant, exactly as it has meant to so many girls, never asking for more than you knew you could get. You didn't ask for the moon, you asked for what was allowed.

Carolyn's uncle had a small department store where the family shopped. She knew very early on that she could have anything she wanted, as long as it was in her uncle's store. The catch was that "you couldn't *want* anything that wasn't in that store. You could buy whatever was reasonable. I internalized that idea so well, knew so exactly what was reasonable, that I didn't ever want what I couldn't get."

Unwittingly, Jack Rosenthal corroborated his daughter's description of herself early in our interview: "She was a great kid; there was never any problem with her. One of her nursery-school teachers said her only problem was that maybe she was a little too good."

Lucky for Carolyn that the limits her father set were large ones when it came to careers. In the last chapter we saw what accommodations daughters need to develop when fathers' limits aren't so large.

Whatever the limits, the first rule of Good Girlism is, Never Rock the Boat. Daddy sets the rules and the limits, and you go along. You never Go Too Far.

Was it part of being a Good Girl, never aiming too far beyond what she thought she could easily get, that kept Carolyn focused on social work, a traditionally feminine field, right through college? This was, after all, the end of the sixties. Although women had taken part in the student left and the antiwar and civil rights movements, feminism had not yet made its impact. Women weren't flocking into law schools. And then, despite her father's encouragement to aim high, he did think she would be a social worker. Her mother, too, provided an image of a conventional, supportive wife. Even if Carolyn allied herself with her father, that image of her mother was there in front of her.

"I was," she says, "into being a helper. I wanted to be a social worker.

But then in my senior year in college, I was president of the Student Council." Two fateful things happened during that year of student uprisings and civil rights agitation: "The president of the college left, and the black students took over the admissions office. So I ran all the college meetings—I was leading meetings of twelve hundred people. I began to have a sense of myself as an actor in a bigger pool, that I could stand up and perform in the world. So I thought of law school, and once I decided to do it, I knew I wanted to be good at it. I think the decision conquered my fear of success."

Still, if her father hadn't encouraged her to be aggressive, to aim high, she wouldn't have been president of the Student Council in the first place. Nor would she have been psychologically prepared to grasp the opportunity when it came—to rise to the challenge of leading all-campus meetings, and then to deduce from this experience that she could do something different with her life than social work.

Given her competitive attitude toward her father, her feeling that she wanted to be more successful at more meaningful work than he had been, business was a risky choice for Carolyn. It meant she was, really, taking the first step out of her Good Girl position. To choose social work as her meaningful career wouldn't have challenged her father directly, nor would success in it have been, however subliminally, a confrontation with the fact of his failure. To choose business was to confront him directly, competitively. Despite his encouragement, that can't have been an easy decision.

What helped her was that, once she chose, he did encourage her. What also helped her was that he had given her permission, all these years, to confront him. In a way, she was claiming the ultimate privilege of a daughter by daring to try for success where he had failed.

Even so, she began to become her own person. As she grew into her career, Carolyn started to see that there was more involved in her Good Girlism than knowing when to stop on a shopping expedition. There was a way of relating within the family that involved smoothing over or denying problems.

Being a Good Girl, then, meant that "I grew up understanding that what they wanted of me was to support the myth that they were terrific, and I was terrific, and that I would never have any problems. I would get as much as I could get."

Basically the family, like Holly Flax's, cared about appearances. "I always repressed any sense of being unhappy," says Carolyn. "This is what my parents are like: everything is an act of will. They say their children are terrific, their marriage is terrific, their lives are terrific. Their children never cried. If you willed it, it happened."

This isn't a surprising attitude in a man who was the hope of the family, the grandson of immigrants who must have believed that you could accomplish anything you set out to do in America. Jack Rosenthal was a Good Boy himself, who had learned early to live up to expectations—and who must have been bitterly disappointed in himself when he failed. How better to cope with that than to deny, as much as possible, that there was, or ever could be, a failure? His wife, obviously, agreed to the strategy.

Growing up in such a household, Carolyn learned, she now realizes, "a much more manipulative way of being in the world than my father ever demonstrated. You don't confront things in my family. If you're like I am, you play the game on the surface, and you're clever. Beneath the surface you try to manipulate your way out of all that stuff. If you're like my brother, you just refuse to play the game. But you never confront. A 'this is how it makes me feel' conversation is as foreign to my family as supporting the Arabs. I learned very quickly to do what they wanted in order to get what I wanted."

And this is, after all, what a lawyer does in court, and a good business-person does as well. At work, Carolyn's style is "cajoling, trying to be pleasant, be nice, while being directive."

In fact, being a Good Girl taught her that politics, not simply intelligence, is always the name of the game. Merely being smart "is not the ingredient on which success is based. My father thinks of himself as very smart, and I grew up believing that being smart is the most important thing. It's not. I see, now, that success has a lot to do with how you treat people, how you get along with people, how good a strategist and politician you are. My father disdained all those things. It's as though, having gone to good schools, he *should* have succeeded. To this day he resents the fact that even though he is smarter than the people with whom he works, he is less successful.

"I think this is why he didn't make vice-president. I'm sure he would be impossible to work with. He's arrogant about his own skills, and very demanding."

Given, by her father, a sure sense of access to his world, she was able to apply the skills she learned in order to get along in her family to the Outside world, and use them to succeed.

But today Carolyn feels angry because "My parents have always supported me, always said I'm terrific, but in such a general way as to be of no significance. I don't have any sense that they have an idea of who I am now and how successful I am or even if I'm successful or what it's about. Nothing has any texture to it. He should have some idea what I do, since he's a businessman. But he never asks me, so I feel he doesn't care."

At thirty-three, Carolyn Rosenthal is going through what she calls a "delayed adolescent rebellion. I'm feeling incredibly hostile to my parents."

This sounds a bit different from the "delayed adolescence" of the Hennig-Jardim executives; but in a sense Carolyn, too, is taking a "moratorium"—from her marriage and from her lifelong devotion to her father. It is no coincidence that these things are happening at the same time.

She married a man who is, she feels, like her father, and in the relationship, she says, she identifies with her mother: "What I expected from a marriage was modeled on what my parents had, and that was sort of—a friend. I never saw my mother as sexual, and I had a lot of trouble with my own sexuality until recently. Discovering it. It was gone for a long time. My father was seductive to me in an asexual way, seductive to my head. All you needed to do to seduce me was to tell me I was smart and special, and you had me. But I never had a clear sense of what it was to be a woman.

"I think my mother was a person in the world—I didn't want to see it, but I think she was. In fact, my mother is smart; I didn't see that, either. After I grew up, she went back for an M.A. and now she teaches music again. She can be interesting, too. She was invited to be part of a seminar at the Aspen Institute last year, and she became a center of a whole group of people half her age.

"She was a mother, too. But I think she gave up the woman. I never had a sense of her and my father as a couple, a sexual unit."

But when she describes her relationship with her husband, what emerges is a sense that he is indeed much like her father and that she relates to him in much the same way she always related to her father. Her husband adores her, as her father did, and she sees herself as both dominant and manipulative in her relationship to him, as she was with her father. She believes her tendency is, in fact, "to get some man to do what I want without asking directly."

With her father, she never did have to ask. He was "always a cushion. I never had any sense of making my choice and taking the consequences. You could always avoid consequences. My father did all my errands. He went to the library for me, he took my shoes to be repaired, his secretary typed my papers. It was a sign that your parents loved you and you were special. They did the same with my brothers."

One definition of a Princess I have heard is that "She always has two in help—her father and mother." Jack Rosenthal rejects the idea that his daughter was a Princess because he sees Princesshood in purely material terms, "eighteen dresses and forty-two pairs of shoes," and he was always extremely careful with money. But lavish adoration and taking care of, doing for (not quite the same thing as Let Daddy Do It—there is a difference between having your father write your themes and having his secretary type them after you've written them yourself), are the two other marks of the father of a Princess, and two out of three is a pretty good average.

This kind of devotion usually demands, and gets, a lot of devotion in return. So it isn't any surprise that Carolyn's "adolescent rebellion"—her separation from her father—is taking the form it is. She is ceasing to be devoted, loyal, and nurturing.

For instance: "My father used to call me every morning at eight thirty. He always woke me up, and there would be a ninety-second conversation in which he filled me in on family facts—he spoke to my younger brother yesterday and he said such-and-such. I hated it, but I felt obliged to continue the pattern because I felt I would hurt him if I told him how I felt. You don't want to give them any kind of pain, because their lives are predicated on our being terrific, so if you were less than terrific you reflected on them. You would cause them pain if you didn't live up to their expectations. It would be a significant disappointment."

Her first act of rebellion was to tell her father she hated the morning calls. He stopped calling, but he gave no other response.

Recently, she also turned down a date with her father for the first time in her life. She refused to meet him for dinner, because she had to meet her husband. But her father never asked, "What's the matter?" He just went on talking about family news.

"I was furious. I had a headache. I could have hit him. I don't know what I think would happen if I really tried to talk to him. I can't decide whether I'm afraid he would drop dead out of devastation, or whether I'm afraid he's so vulnerable or dependent on what I give him that he doesn't want to hear about any problems."

Her diagnosis of the roots of her father's side of the matter is that he is "so needy for a sense of himself that he hasn't gotten from his work, that he uses me for it. All he needs is a general sense that I'm doing okay. He doesn't need any specifics because he's just using it to bolster himself. I am continually shocked by how little he asks about my job."

She also feels upset that she and her father have never discussed her separation from her husband. But she believes it must be partly a continuation of an old pattern: "My father has never really liked or been particularly interested in any man I've been involved with except negatively. Once when I brought some guy home he didn't like, he went to bed with a bad back. I don't think he ever connected very much to my marriage."

But Jack Rosenthal wouldn't dream of prying into his daughter's affairs. When I asked him how he would describe his relationship with Carolyn today, on a line from "very close" to "not close," he said, "It's not as close as I thought it would be. It is surprisingly adult, which ten years ago I wouldn't have thought it would be. Say we have dinner: we each talk about what we are doing, and about her brothers, but we are not having the kind of conversation we had ten years ago—warm and close, talking about things that are near to us. I think it's illustrated by the separation. When she and her husband separated, I felt very confused, wondered why, and never found out why. That upset my wife a good deal. I was able to live with not knowing on the theory that she had her reasons for not telling us. I never asked her. The conversation is selective. There are things one stays away from. On her side."

He obviously feels shut out. Yet, caught in that fatal fatherly emotional passivity, he can't ask. And to some extent he blames her.

She feels she has nurtured him and blames him for not seeing her clearly; for not entering her world. Sally Archway, too, always had the sense, when she went with her father into his world, that she was in some respect taking care of him. Nurturing him. He did not, she pointed out, come into her world; go with her, say, to buy roller skates.

It is always the case, since fathers lead away from mothers and inhabit the world Outside, that daughters move out to their world. But even as we learn to achieve, we very often have the sense that we are there to support them, nurture them. Yet we all have to break away, grow up, come to terms with our own separation from Daddy.

And this means anger. Anger because, even if we always saw flaws in Daddy, even, in fact, if there were many ways in which we disliked him, we still deep down thought he was the Prince. As long as he smiled at us, we felt special.

Carolyn has discovered that her father no longer has the power to make her feel special; and now that she is sure of her own identity in her work, she is upset because it turns out that the one thing he doesn't seem to be able to see is the identity she has created for herself.

But she doesn't want to confront him with her feelings. Daughters are chary about confronting fathers. Still. Even when the daughters are lawyers, skilled politicians, seasoned courtroom battlers, successful entrepreneurs.

Carolyn thinks her rage is "inappropriate, because it's pent up from twenty years ago. I should have confronted him at thirteen. My anger is stronger because it's been delayed. I'm afraid of being so angry now that I would say too much and estrange them in a way I wouldn't want to do. So I'm trying to give them a clearer picture of who I am, but I haven't yet told my father, 'You are driving me bananas. Can't you understand I'm going through pain and you're sitting here giving me the rundown on today's paper?' "

Of course she's right. Those theatrical confrontations that make everything all right seldom work in real life. Parents, after a certain age and probably most of the time before it, aren't going to change. One has to change oneself.

But if your Good Girl training has been, in so many ways, really very useful to your career, what do you change?

Carolyn wants to change her private life. She has decided that "the skills that have made me successful as a lawyer and businesswoman—and I must have picked the professions because there is a good fit between my style and my job—are particularly inappropriate and unhelpful in my personal relationships."

She would like, for instance, to be more direct in her dealings with her husband, who still adores her and whom she still sees. But her closeness to her father gets in the way. Under the "asexual" surface, Carolyn has clearly been battling a lot of sexual overload. What does a daughter do when she "wins" her father so easily? One thing she may do is identify with her "asexual" mother, and carry that identification over into her marriage with a man very much like her father. In her marriage, she goes on unconsciously defending herself against sexual overload, and that means she goes on being indirect.

Then there is the problem of her identifications with her mother and father, who represent different values: "My father always wanted me to be successful and my mother wanted me to be happy in a relationship. I always assumed these things were mutually exclusive. I understood that my mother wanted a woman's role for me, to marry and have a family, and my father wanted a man's role for me. I was conflicted. Then, in college, I thought I could have it all. But right now I think I'm afraid that if I'm a success in work, it may be too threatening to be a success in my relationship with my husband, too. My father and mother represent two poles: I can be successful or happy, but not both." Work versus love, even here.

Is it a Freudian slip that Carolyn says "successful or happy," as though the dilemma is deeper than a choice between two kinds of success? Maybe on some level she still believes that, as a woman, she can't really be happy through work but only through a relationship. Or maybe her father never believed success would bring happiness, either; he, after all, tried for success in a field he really didn't enjoy. For him, too, happiness seems to have been located in a relationship with his family.

Carolyn chose to take a moratorium from her marriage rather than from her career. Her feeling is that "I think people would say I dominate in my marriage and I think I have. But I think I approach personal relationships as if I'm still the child, trying to please, to get the most she can rather than coming up front to say what she wants."

She wishes that her husband "were more of a match; I think he's becoming one. The ideal would be an equal. A good fight."

But she won't be able to accept that until she stops feeling like a child. She's getting there: "I have had to figure out who I was, as opposed to what everyone else was trying to make me, and to stand up and be who I am. I guess I'm operating on some confidence that I can learn that in my personal life and still keep my style in my professional life."

It's men who are supposed to keep Inside and Outside neatly separated. But Jack Rosenthal, as we have seen, isn't that kind of man. He was brought up to be, and he never really had the chance to see that he wasn't—to stand up and be who he is. Carolyn, as a woman, isn't "supposed" to be able to have the cool, competent attitude she brings to her work. Women are thought to be too emotional to keep the Inside from intruding in the Outside world where, supposedly, it has no place. But Carolyn found that her successful Outside style intruded on her Inside life. Now she is betting that she can keep her Outside style and open up a new emotional and sexual world in her private life. Just as with the Applemans, in the lives of Jack Rosenthal and his daughter, maybe sex roles have been the root of the problem.

CHAPTER SIX

Work and Love:
When Fathers Help Daughters Succeed ...
and When They Don't

career: 1a. A chosen pursuit: life work: a *military career.*

b. Success in one's profession: *He has a career before him.*

ambition: 1. An eager or strong desire to achieve something, such as fame or fortune; will to succeed.

—*The American Heritage Dictionary of the EnglishLanguage*

*W*hy do some women sail confidently ahead, acquire an ambition and undertake the career that will fulfill it, while so many of the rest of us muddle around in conflict and confusion? As a lifelong muddler, I find myself both jealous of and curious about those clear-eyed, apparently unconflicted young achievers who are flocking into medical and law schools and M.B.A. programs. What is their secret?

College women who aspire to traditionally masculine careers (which includes just about anything outside of teaching, nursing, or social work), or older women who have made it to the top in largely male fields, have only become the subject of study in the last ten years or so. But the evidence to date does indicate that many high-achieving women have strong, supportive fathers, who encourage them to be independent, to achieve, and to take risks.

In *The Managerial Woman,* for example, Margaret Hennig and Anne Jardim provided the most complete exploration to date of exactly how a specific group of extremely successful women—twenty-five corporate presidents and vice-presidents—were influenced and helped by their fathers, and why this support was so crucial to their subsequent success. This was a highly specialized group, successful within one field, business, and one arena, the corporation, and its members were all born between 1910 and 1915. But an earlier study by Margaret Hennig and Barbara Hackman Franklin of younger women, in the 1960–64 Harvard M.B.A.

program, also turned up a significant father-factor, as did several other studies and a number of journalists' books in the 1970s.

The conclusion that an encouraging father has been an important influence for many high-achieving women, however, is just a beginning; it raises a number of questions. Are fathers, for instance, as important when mothers work; or is their influence crucial only when mothers are Inside people and the Outside world belongs to Daddy?

Several studies have shown that when a mother works, her daughter is more likely to think of working herself than is the daughter of a conventional, nonworking mother. A mother who is Out There in the world can show her daughter that the work world is not exclusively masculine, that women can succeed in it, and that access to it can be part of a daughter's birthright. This is even more true, apparently, if a mother does something men have usually done. If she is a doctor or lawyer or truck driver rather than a nurse or social worker, her daughter will grow up in a world in which the Inside/Outside distinctions look flexible and less rigidly sex-determined.

The sociologist Sandra Schwartz Tangri has suggested that college women with ambitions toward traditionally male professions are more likely to identify with their mothers than with their fathers if their mothers work in such fields. And an Israeli study has shown that daughters of successful professional women have become successful professionals themselves more frequently than women whose fathers were their only direct source of identification with career and ambition.

It seems to me that these findings can be explained by the Identity Triangle. If girls love and identify with both their fathers and mothers throughout childhood and well into adolescence and even adulthood, then in the best of all possible worlds there would be no conflict between their identifications with their mothers and those with their fathers. Traditionally, as we have seen, fathers discourage direct identification with themselves in favor of a reciprocal identification that reinforces a daughter's direct identification with her mother—who presents an image of conventional femininity, wifehood and motherhood.

There is no conflict here for the girl herself unless, like Denise Archway and thousands of other daughters today, she comes to realize that some direct, selective identification with her father would help her focus her life on something Outside these roles. Denise feels a bit confused because her father is continuing to reinforce her in a traditional feminine identity—you're only young once, go to Europe with your boyfriend—while her mother, after years of conforming to the traditional model, has suddenly turned into an achiever in the Outside world—and is giving Denise reinforcement to do the same thing!

On the other hand, if—like her sister Sally, or Carolyn Rosenthal—

you grew up identifying directly with your father and find you have to deny your inevitable identification with your mother as an adult woman in the world because you don't want to be a person who relates to the world only through husband and children, you may be relatively uncon-flicted about work but you are bound to have some conflicts, as Carolyn does, about the relationship between work and love. Despite the fact that their mothers actively encouraged them to expand their horizons beyond traditional roles, Hennig and Jardim's executives had a great many such conflicts, although they eventually resolved them.

A working mother would presumably encourage a daughter to identify directly with her as a person in the Outside world as well as a wife and mother. Her daughter, then, would presumably not need to identify as intensely with her father, or to rely as much on his encouragement, in order to work—and she could see that love and work can be integrated.

But if her father opposed his wife's working, and discouraged his daughter from identifying with himself or with her mother as a working woman, the daughter probably would have conflicts. She would also have conflicts if her working mother had them—as she very well might in a society in which the ideal wife and mother still devotes herself entirely to her family. The Identity Triangle is bound to be affected by the larger social context in which the family lives.

The Appleman sisters, for instance, knew very early that they were atypical. Alicia remembers coming home after school to an empty house because her mother was at work. Her friends often came home to empty houses, too, but their mothers were out shopping. Alicia felt "different," especially as a young adolescent, and she resented the fact that her mother had to work. Her mother may have resented it, too—after all, at that time most middle-class wives didn't have to work. So when her own daughters were small, might she, unconsciously, have reinforced Steve's messages with one of her own: "Marry a man who can earn enough money so you can do what you want, because a wife shouldn't have to work"?

Now that inflation has forced large numbers of middle-class wives into the workplace, and feminism has helped create a climate in which their daughters may expect to enter a previously all-male profession or execu-tive-track corporate slot, more daughters of all classes are growing up with working mothers and will expect to work in their turn. Even so, as long as society doesn't fully accept the image of a working wife and mother, daughters will continue to be subjected to conflicting pressures and expectations.

The ideal, presumably, would be to grow up in a dual-career family, in which your father supports your mother's success and encourages you to identify with her and with himself, while at the same time he validates your heterosexual femininity with enough warmth and flirtation. A daughter in such a family would be supported in every direction. She could identify with her mother as an adult woman who has her own life in the Outside world and at the same time is valued by her father; she could both love and identify with her father as well. Such a daughter would probably be more conscious of direct identification with her mother as another woman, but she would be free to select qualities in her father that would help her along her way.

Such a family would also have to live in a society that valued the contributions of working mothers enough to give them the support services they needed, whether in terms of more flexible work schedules, day care, a husband's equal sharing of domestic responsibilities, or some combination of all these. That, as they say, will be the millennium.

In the meantime, most daughters reading this book who are older than, say, twenty-one probably had, as I did, a traditional, Inside mother, and were well along in adolescence before feminism and the economy began to make a dent in traditional feminine role expectations. So for this chapter I chose to focus on two women, Sally Archway and Carolyn Rosenthal, who come from traditional families and who have achieved some success but who have not yet reached the "top." Their lives may help answer some crucial questions: Just what do daughters need to become self-confident, unconflicted achievers, and how and when do fathers provide the necessary elements? Are fathers enough? How do conflicts between work and love affect careers? And what about the thousands of women who, like myself, have received discouraging or conflicting messages from fathers about the value of our achievements? If our conflicts about work reflect the shape of our identities as Daddy's daughters, are those of us without superfathers doomed never to succeed?

I also chose to look at Sally and Carolyn because they are committed to careers. Although millions of women now work, I suspect that the majority do not, as yet, consider themselves to be so committed. Indeed, getting a job is so universally expected of young women today that, by itself, it says nothing one way or another about parental influence. And while it is certainly possible to become successful at a job, there is still an important distinction, in terms of how a woman perceives herself in the Outside world, between working at a job and pursuing a career.

A job is something you do, basically, to earn money. It goes along from day to day, and you don't usually have a goal in terms of the work itself, unless it's a larger paycheck or better working conditions.

A career, on the other hand, is by dictionary definition "a life work," "a chosen pursuit." It usually involves ambition, that "strong desire to achieve something, such as fame or fortune." A career requires commitment to a long-range goal in your field of work; and once a job is perceived as a stepping stone to better things, it becomes part of a career.

Plenty of men work at jobs all their lives, but the fact that they know from an early age that they will have to support themselves and a family for their entire adult lives and that they will be identified, largely, by the work they do gives them some impetus to think in terms of a career.

Women don't have this impetus. Even if they expect to help support their family, they rarely, if ever, expect to shoulder the burden alone. And many wives are still likely to be seen, and to see themselves, more as Tom Jones's wife or Bobby's mother than as Ellen Jones, the bank teller. A major part of their identity is still personal, private, Inside. Only if a job becomes a career is work likely to become a major part of most women's identity.

It is this transition from Inside to Outside, from private and domestic to public, from family-identified to institution- or profession-identified that is hard for women to make, even today. And one reason it is hard is that most of us haven't grown up with a sense that Daddy's world could be our world, too.

Daddy's Crucial Success Messages

Message #1: "You Have Access to My World"

When the Outside clearly belongs to Daddy, when it's a place where men have careers and women only have anonymous jobs, where the names and the titles still usually belong to people like Senator Tom Jones, how does a daughter get a sense that she can make a career in that world, too?

For boys, access to the Outside world is a birthright. Since its institutions have always been run by and for men, boys claim access to them the minute they start identifying themselves as masculine. The two, in fact, are synonymous: to identify yourself as masculine is to identify yourself with masculine institutions: "I'm going to be a fireman"; "I'm going to be in the Army." These identifications may become more sophisticated as a boy grows up, but they don't really change. The adult American male is an institutional man. His identity is usually strongly bound up with the institution for which he works: he *is* a sales manager, or a reporter, or a policeman.

But even if a little girl announces that she, too, wants to be a fireman, she is aware from an early age that her gender identity also puts her squarely on the Inside, the world of mothers and babies. If she sees in her mother only an Inside woman, if she sees her father relating to her mother as Outside man, and if, in addition, Daddy lets her know he likes her better sitting on his lap than showing off her achievements to him, she will not easily acquire a sense that she can have access to that fireman's world—or, indeed, that she would be happy in it. Her ego ideal will include being loved by her father, but only as an Inside woman.

But what if, instead, Daddy gives us a different message from the usual father and, like D. W. Opal or Dr. Archway, he takes us with him into his world? What if, like Jack Rosenthal, he forms an "instrumental" alliance with us that excludes our mother?

When Sally Archway went to the clinic with her father, she both saw him in action and was able to help him. She used a small office machine to open his mail; she went around with him to greet the staff on holidays.

Trivial stuff. Certainly, Dr. Archway placed no particular emphasis on it. Yet it helped shape Sally's life. He took her into his world and he gave her real things to do. It takes, apparently, very little to give a girl a glimpse of the world outside the family.

Would it have made a difference if Sally's father had taken her into his office and then said, "Don't touch," making her sit quietly and passively while she waited for him? Undoubtedly. She would have felt hugely frustrated; angry at him for showing her this fascinating new world and then forbidding her to touch it. And she would have got a badly mixed message: "You can come into my world, but it's still mine and not yours, so you have to be passive. You have no real place in it."

Another woman I interviewed, a sculptor, used to spend entire Saturday mornings in her father's office, where she was given the freedom to use all kinds of small equipment, from staplers to typewriters. Of course she was playing, but if play is a rehearsal for real life, what a difference it makes to play with Daddy's office equipment rather than, or in addition to, Mommy's pots and pans! "When I was five years old," the artist told me, "I assumed I would grow up and take over my father's business." Her father wasn't, in fact, a literal role model; she didn't take over his business. She followed her own interests. But the point of her experience wasn't finding a role model at all; it was being welcomed into a world that was run by and for men, and being made to feel at home in it. Being given permission to do things in that world. It would not be hard, after that, to transfer your sense of access to another institution, as Sally Archway did, or to another kind of career.

Both these women did something else that is interesting: they adapted specific elements of their fathers' institutions to their own uses. The sculptor now uses small equipment of various kinds to make her wooden sculptures; only they are saws, drills, and so forth rather than staplers and typewriters. And she has been quite successful in selling her work to corporations with arts budgets.

Sally Archway, who saw her father as a helping figure in his institution, now helps other people approach God through her institution, the Church. And God, as she conceives of Him, is in some ways very like her father.

She has also chosen an institution that demands as much of her time as the hospital does her father's, in a similar pattern of sandwiching her personal life into long days of meetings, services, and visiting people. She, too, now makes her rounds on holidays, just as her father did, and for a similar reason: she visits shut-ins, as he visited the clinic staff, to let them know someone cares.

If you acquire this sense of access to Daddy's world early in life, you aren't automatically guaranteed that career opportunities will open up later, but you are definitely in a better position to see the opportunities that do arise and to take advantage of them, as both Carolyn and Sally have done. You aren't so frightened of a world of work that still, to many women, looks like *terra incognita*.

The Hennig-Jardim executives had also been welcomed into their fathers' world, joining Daddy in activities such as hunting, fishing, watching team sports, or reading the financial page of the newspaper.

It is both shocking and depressing to think that things like reading the financial pages of the newspaper or discussing important issues might still be considered peculiarly masculine, as though femininity involved a kind of know-nothingism, a complete innocence of any awareness of the realities of the Outside world. But, of course, in its stereotyped form it always has. After all, if Daddy embodies the Outside world for you, then the only way you can connect with it is to focus on your personal relationship with him.

Which brings us to the question of women who made careers in almost any period before the present. When the Hennig-Jardim executives started work, for instance, Inside/Outside divisions were still strict and, in most cases, insurmountable. Their first jobs were, in effect, privileges granted them because of their fathers' business connections.

When they began working, these women passed from the protection of their fathers to the protection of their bosses, in a process that is not without its ironic parallels to the traditional marriage contract in which women were passed from one man to the next. Hennig and Jardim are quite explicit about this protection: each woman's boss became a "sales agent" for her, using "his reputation to develop hers." People who respected him would accept his protegée, but if there were a "direct confrontation," the boss became "a buffer," putting "himself between the woman and her opponent. He was the protector and she the protected."

The boss became, in short, her Outside man as well as her mentor and surrogate father figure. All twenty-five women said their bosses were very much like their fathers, and their relationships with the two were similar. "I really have to thank Jim [the boss] for all of my success," the authors quote one woman as saying. "My dad got me to college and Jim took me from there."

These women were, actually, not unlike those female prodigies of the Renaissance who grew up in their fathers' ateliers and subsequently became well-known painters, or the women mathematicians of later periods who were tutored and sponsored by their fathers. How else but under the tutelage and/or protection of a powerful male could any daughter learn and then practice her art or her science in an Outside world that was exclusively masculine? A room of one's own, before the twentieth century, was usually in one's father's house.

Emily Dickinson never left her father's house; Louisa May Alcott kept coming back. Virginia Woolf, born in the nineteenth century, was given the run of her literary father's library and told to "read what you like." When he gave her a ring on her twenty-first birthday, "It was," writes Leon Edel, "as if there were a marriage and also a laying on of hands, a literary succession. The father . . . performed a marriage between Virginia and the world of letters."

When Virginia Woolf's father died, it was the twentieth century. She moved out of his house and set up housekeeping with various combinations of brothers, sister, and friends, until she married Leonard Woolf. Her brothers were also instrumental in helping her gain access to the Outside world, since they brought it home in the person of their Cambridge friends, who, with Vanessa and Virginia, created Bloomsbury, a principal center of English artistic and literary life. So Virginia Woolf wound up in perhaps the best of all possible worlds for a woman: a literary center of the Outside world that was synonymous with her own home and circle of friends and relations. In the end there was, for her, no separation at all between love and work.

If it's Daddy's world, it's Daddy who has the power to give a daughter access to it. Successful women in previous eras would have been heavily influenced by their fathers, as they would also have been protected and supported by them. Fathers were essential to run interference, to remove external blocks to a career, just as they were essential to give the permission necessary to remove internal blocks like the conflict between femininity and autonomy.

Today, daughters have more access to the Outside world than ever before. In contrast to the Hennig-Jardim executives, for example, who had to rely solely on their fathers, both Sally Archway and Carolyn Rosenthal were heavily influenced by feminism. Sally found feminism in full flush when she got to college, and so was able to become involved in it. "It gave me," she says, "a way to fulfill what I felt within myself: wanting a career, knowing I was somewhat intelligent and competitive. To some extent, feminism really did carry me into the seminary. I thought that women needed to be in the Church."

And feminism, of course, had provided the pressure that made the Church finally begin to ordain women, as it also helped pressure corporations to promote women, law and medical school to accept women, and so forth. So in terms of *immediate* access to their careers—in terms of opportunity—neither Sally's nor Carolyn's father had any real influence. But in preparing their daughters to take advantage of the opportunities that arose, their influence was crucial.

Message #2: "You Can Do It—and You Have My Blessing"

Access to the world is crucial. But we also need something more: confirmation that we have what it takes, and permission to use what we have. Permission, in short, to succeed.

Men, on the whole, receive permission from the culture to use their access to the world to go as far in it as they can. In fact, this permission is more like an imperative, since the most admired men are those who are the most successful, the richest, the most powerful. Individual men may have neurotic problems with this imperative; others may opt out for one reason or another, or may honestly be happier with very modest achievements. But the general cultural imperative stands.

For women, as I suggested earlier, the general cultural imperative is now fuzzy. Although the economy is forcing married women to work, full-time housewifery and motherhood continue to be a cultural ideal. Large numbers of people, from child development experts to conservative religious groups, would like to see women back in the home. Possibly as a result of this continuing ideal, working mothers find few child-care options open to them, so they remain torn between their economic and their maternal responsibilities. Even young women now entering professions as a matter of course find that, in addition to all these conflicts, male resistance to their ambitions increases as they rise beyond entry-level positions. Many bosses, husbands, and colleagues are still saying Don't Go Too Far.

Under such conditions, as Hennig and Jardim point out, a father's attitude can be crucial in helping a daughter resolve conflicts about her identity and responsibilities. Both Carolyn and Sally received clear permission from their fathers, as the representatives of the Outside world in their families, to go as far as their talent and energy could take them. Carolyn's father kept telling her to aim higher, and now that she is a businesswoman, he has told her he thinks she could be a vice-president. Sally's father thought she would enter medicine, a serious and demanding profession; now that she's a priest, he thinks she might make bishop.

Even earlier in their lives, both girls had received another kind of permission. When Carolyn's father discussed the day's newspaper stories with her, when he encouraged her to argue and give her own opinion, he was giving her permission to be independent, to think for herself—giving her, in short, *permission to be separate from Daddy without losing his support.* She never had to choose between his love and her achievement.

But permission to succeed doesn't mean much if it isn't accompanied by confirmation that we have what it takes: we need to know we *can* do it as well as that we *may*. When Jane Adams interviewed successful women for her book *Women on Top: Success Patterns and Personal Fulfillment,* she found that most of them had received this confirmation from their fathers. When she turned to successful men, she found that the necessary confirmation was much more likely to have come from an adult outside the family: a teacher, the father of a friend, a coach. In fact, men tended to discount the confirmation that came from their fathers, perhaps because they felt too competitive toward them. Then, too, men receive permission to succeed from the culture, so they are often able to become successful even when their fathers are absent or rejecting; it makes sense that confirmation of their abilities would also come from outside the family.

But for women, the family is still the place where both permission and confirmation are often found. By discussing issues with Carolyn, Jack Rosenthal told her that he, the Outside man, respected her competence as a person in his world. He listened to what she had to say, and he continued listening even after her brothers came along. Holly Flax, remember, wasn't even allowed to join in her father's discussions with her brothers. Politics was male territory; discussion and challenge, a masculine identity-ritual.

I, on the other hand, was allowed to speak up if I wanted to, but what I said was generally discounted. The response was either a brushoff or a lecture, designed to let me know that my opinions, insofar as they differed from my father's, simply were not valid. I was supposed to go along with Daddy.

Neither Holly nor I got confirmation of our abilities or permission to use them; nor, of course, did we get permission to be separate. Both of us were saddled with that terrible, impossible choice between our own autonomy and our relationships with our fathers.

The Tools of Success

When Jack Rosenthal confirmed Carolyn's competency by taking her point of view seriously in discussions and arguments, he was giving her something else as well. She was acquiring the basic tools she would need to succeed in the Outside world. She learned to argue, to take a position and defend it. She learned to think analytically and to assert her own views with confidence. These are all aspects of the "masculine," "instrumental" style, and, as she herself points out, they were exactly the tools she needed to become a lawyer and businesswoman.

Boys learn instrumental behavior partly from their fathers, but they also learn from teachers, coaches, Scout leaders, and their own attempts to make it on male teams and in male groups and hierarchies. All of their activities from childhood on are geared to learning, as future Outside men, how to estimate risks, make choices, and act decisively; how to win, lose, and stand by the result of their own efforts. And they are usually encouraged in all this by their mothers, as well.

But girls can't pick up these skills from mothers who themselves don't have them; neither do we usually get them from teachers, coaches, or Scout leaders—or, at least, we haven't in the past. All our activities were generally geared to learning a "feminine expressive" style, involving nurturing and a noncompetitive, nonassertive way of dealing with others.

Which brings us back to Daddy. He has the tools, the style, the knowledge—and the authority to pass them on to us. So the very act of passing them on becomes a way of telling us we can do it.

When Sally Archway opened her father's mail at the clinic, or when he helped her fill out medical-school applications—when she was learning that "Daddy and I work better when we have something between us; when we have something to discuss, or when we're doing something together"—she was learning useful skills in instrumental behavior, getting confirmation of her abilities, and receiving permission to use them. For daughters, all these things have very often come from Daddy, when they have come at all.

A Special Zest and Pleasure: The Legacy of Daddy's Success Messages

It seems, then, that we need paternal permission to be separate and independent, to *use* our competency in the world, more than boys do. Boys take differing with their fathers as part of their natural competitiveness, their birthright, while for girls it's a gift.

In *Making Good: Conversations with Successful Men,* Jane Adams reports that men who have reached the top of their profession or business had felt so competitive toward their fathers that they were quite unable to think about them in terms of love until either they themselves had surpassed their fathers in achievement or their fathers had become old or incapacitated. Their fathers seem to have represented an obstacle the sons had to overcome on the way to their own fulfillment. One man used a football analogy, in which the "guys on the other team" represented his father: "If you start liking them or caring about them, you can't knock them down and beat them."

Daughters simply don't see their fathers in the same way. We need Daddy's love for our own sense of self-worth and self-esteem. We know from the beginning, usually, that we can't knock him down, so our principal approach to him follows another kind of wisdom: "If you can't beat 'em, join 'em."

Of course, there can be, and usually are, many other influences on our lives in later years, including other mentors, teachers, husbands, bosses. And if we have no fathers, mothers can do a fine job of encouraging us, provided they themselves feel some self-confidence. But if a father is around, his attitude is important, the more so if our mothers don't themselves have a claim staked out in his world.

After all, a father's first role in his daughter's life is, as Dr. Tessman phrased it, "to help her internalize trust in her autonomous capacities." If he does that for her while she is still a toddler, there can be an enormous energy and excitement built into their "collaboration."

Why? Because when a daughter falls in love with her father, all the joy of that love becomes incorporated into the pleasures of sharing achievement or discussion, arguments or problem-solving.

Fathers, says Dr. Tessman, "provide a special zest and pleasure when work can be related to a shared ego ideal, and women who associate their relationship with their father to their work make clear the basis of the original sharing and the piece of happiness that connects them to their work."

Here is where all that sublimated oedipal love pays off.

Such very strong father-involvement can be compared to the strong mother-involvement that has given so many high-powered men their start in life. Winston Churchill, Sigmund Freud, and many other super-achievers were the apples of their mothers' eyes, encouraged from the beginning to do great things in life. Many of Jane Adams's high-achieving men also mentioned their mothers as a source of family encouragement. Maybe the fires kindled by this kind of cross-sex support are the most powerful because of the powerful sexual passions that are harnessed to the drive to succeed.

But even well below the level of intense involvement, fathers who encourage their daughters to achieve *and* maintain a warm, loving involvement with them give their daughters the best of it, because they are saying that autonomy and achievement can be part of femininity, and that they themselves can identify with such a daughter. That's all she needs, really, to move self-confidently into the Outside world. To work with love.

The Desperate Achiever

There is a special variety of achieving woman who works not with love but for love: the Desperate Achiever.

Take one corporate middle manager I talked to. She was certainly Daddy's Girl, but her father made her into a surrogate son. He could demand high achievement and constant, nose-to-the-grindstone striving without worrying about a real son's potential for rebellion or for growing up to surpass and replace him. As a woman, no matter what she does she will be in a different league altogether.

So this father bound his daughter to him with ties of high expectation and achievement. She got As to shine in Daddy's eyes, but she never sat on his lap.

Today, she sits in an office, a Good Girl, a success, a divisional manager with men working for her, and she talks about how she would throw it all over to get married; only she keeps finding men who are cold, remote, demanding, like her father.

She gets along beautifully with the corporate bosses, though. She can twit the vice-president gently, or compliment him on his new tie. The "sons" in the office, her male peers, wouldn't dare.

The boss doesn't mind a "daughter" acting like a daughter; it reassures him, reminds him of his own power. He brought her along, got her here, and as a woman she will never threaten him with competition. At least, that's what he assumes. She is still a Good Girl; but who knows what decisions she is about to make?

Right now, though, she is feeling that achievement is pretty empty.

Without the spark of loving interplay in which femininity, as well as achievement, is acknowledged and confirmed, a daughter is in trouble. She works desperately hard to please Daddy because achievement is the only way she knows. She doesn't have that basic core of self-acceptance that enabled Sally and Carolyn to choose their own goals and to begin to work through their conflicts. The Desperate Achiever is in danger of remaining a daughter all her life.

She isn't able to separate from her father and establish real autonomy, which might mean modifying his demands to a more realistic level. To do that, she would have to rebel; but she can't. She's afraid she'll lose her father's love.

Part of her problem is that she can't turn toward the other corner of her Identity Triangle. Her mother was probably an Inside woman but, unlike Sally's and Carolyn's mothers, the Desperate Achiever's was unhappy. Two studies, one by Marjorie Lozoff of the Wright Institute and the other by Jack Block, Anna Von Der Lippe, and Jeanne H. Block, of the University of California, Berkeley, describe women who fit the profile of the Desperate Achiever. In Lozoff's study, their fathers are "aloof, self-disciplined, and perfectionistic"; in Block, Van Der Lippe, and Block's, "authoritarian" and rejecting. The women subjects describe their mothers as "submissive" or "defeated."

This is, in part, the kind of Good Girl I learned how to be. I identified with my father as the one whose work made him important in the family. Who wouldn't? It was obvious that the one who worked got attention, respect, even deference. The only problem was that work for my father, and later for his sons, was very much a substitute for relationships. And so I grew up thinking work was the only thing that could give me any value; I never trusted relationships.

In women at least, this is usually called fear of dependency. And if you're worried about turning into the kind of unhappy dependent woman your mother was, the description is accurate. But at bottom the fear is of rejection and of the unknown. If for most daughters the world of work is *terra incognita,* for the Desperate Achiever the world of pleasurable relationships is equally unknown, and equally risky. My father's philosophy seemed to be that if you worked hard enough, you could almost do without relationships altogether.

My brothers also still work longer hours than necessary, just to avoid the terrors of home and family—of relationships, feelings, demands. But this has always been an approved way for men to behave, and for my brothers it was easier to cope with marriage and family since those things, they had learned from our father, could be held at bay, kept subordinate to the demands of work while providing a refuge when work got to be too much even for them.

But a Desperate Achiever has learned that to relate to a man is surely to be swallowed up in his demands; our whole Identity Triangle taught us this.

The way out, the way to self-esteem, is to identify with Daddy as a son does—to be able to give ourselves the approval, vicariously, that he doesn't give. We identify with Daddy as a working man, because then we feel as important to ourselves as he is.

Except that we then remain daughters forever, submissive to Daddy's demands for ever-greater achievement, never rebelling, never saying, Enough!

I'm glad I identify with my father's stubbornness, his doggedness, his survival ability. You need all those things to carve out a career in Daddy's world. I have learned one thing, though: work can heal a lot of wounds, but it won't do as a substitute for life.

Reaching for the Top: Is Daddy Enough?

If Daddy is your ego ideal, if he holds the key to the Outside world, then the odds are you are going to start out your working life as a Good Girl.

If, like Holly Flax, you can succeed all too well in love by being a Good Girl—succeed, that is, at least to the point of attracting the sort of man who wants nothing more than a chronologically older version of Daddy's "ideal controllable little girl"—then you can also succeed all too well at work.

Good Girls make devoted secretaries, the ones who never burn the coffee. They've learned how to please Daddy, so they go on pleasing the boss in exactly the same way. It's easy. All you have to do is anticipate what he wants and interpret his needs—and what Good Girl hasn't learned that lesson? The fact that you can do this without constant reminders or instructions may pass for "independence," but it is actually a highly developed form of nurturing. Everything you do is in his name, as is your position in the corporation.

Good Girls can be found in the ranks of assistants of all kinds, from laboratory to financial. Daughters fall naturally into the role of aide, a job in which they can earn a lot of money screening calls and acting in the place of a boss, especially if he is a politician. Men do this sort of thing, too; but for them it is clearly a step on the ladder, their ultimate goal being to climb above the boss for whom they are currently serving as loyal "son." They are ambitious and feel competitive toward their boss.

Women are still less likely to be thinking so clearly in terms of ambition and competition. For us, the aide or assistant or Girl Friday role seems only too natural. It allows us to remain the Inside person, even Outside in the world. Why move on, when it is usually evident that we will have so much less power on our own than we enjoy under the protection of the boss's name and title?

Such a woman is simply Little Me transplanted to the office. She probably has no difficulty integrating love and work because she can play pretty much the same role in both. She may even marry the boss.

It's not generally realized, though, that even beyond the secretary/aide/assistant role, Good Girls do succeed: as corporate middle managers, as lawyers and entrepreneurs like Carolyn Rosenthal, as writers like myself. There are only two catches. The first is that, as we saw with Carolyn, achieving Good Girls even with the most supportive fathers in the world may have problems integrating love and work. The second is that conflicts between love and work may make it difficult for them to aim for the top.

Growing Up in the Identity Triangle

In the mid-seventies, when Hennig and Jardim interviewed over a hundred women corporate managers aged twenty-seven to fifty-eight, a pattern emerged. These managers remained relatively passive for ten years or so, during which time they focused on their skills and competence in the day-to-day job; many of them credited a boss or some superior with their advancement. Not until their early thirties did they begin to think of their work as a career, with any long-term goal.

Even then, the managers thought in terms of hard work, greater competency, greater self-assertiveness; in short, of personal qualities. They didn't think about the "organizational environment" or the politics they needed to play—the people they needed to influence, those who could be useful to them or whose notice they required.

Why this difference in the way in which men and women approach their work? The key lies in the ways boys and girls form their identities. Men have been learning to think about the "organizational environment" right from early childhood, when they first stepped into some nursery-school male dominance hierarchy and asserted their right to a place in it. A boy knows that some kind of position in the hierarchy is his by right of his sex; he has only to determine, through competition with his peers, what that position is.

This pattern continues through life. The institution with which the boy and later the man identifies is, obviously, a male dominance hierarchy. He is aware of the position of every man in it; he is accustomed to thinking about how to improve his own position through strategies of cooperation as well as competition. When he learns to play on the team, he learns how the team plays.

Women haven't learned all this. Not, as is often asserted, because girls don't play team sports. Team sports are just another form of the male hierarchy in action. The real reason is that *girls don't form their identities in a dominance hierarchy as boys do. Girls form their identities in the Identity Triangle.*

What this means is that girls are enmeshed in their relationships with the adults in their life—with Mother and Daddy—in ways that shape their future behavior as persons in the Outside world. Boys are significantly shaped by their relationships with their mothers and fathers too, but from an early age the masculine dominance hierarchy becomes an equally significant influence in their lives—and for the purposes of learning how to behave to get what they want in the Outside world, it may be the most important element. Maccoby and Jacklin, for example, found that while girls are far more obedient to the demands of adults than boys are, they are not willing to be directed or influenced by other little girls.

For boys, the reverse is true. They care very much about their position in the male peer group—the male dominance hierarchy—and are far less compliant toward adults than girls are.

No wonder Hennig and Jardim found that women corporate managers of all ages are not equipped with "a sense of the organizational environment," but think rather of "individual self-improvement" while they are "waiting to be chosen." We haven't spent our lives competing with other girls and women in dominance hierarchies, learning the arts of cooperating, of giving and receiving favors, of working with girls and women whom we dislike. We've been relating to Daddy.

Today, not many women follow the pattern of the Hennig-Jardim executives and tie their early careers to a protective boss. For one thing, women no longer stay with one company for their entire careers, as was common until a few years ago. Increasingly, women are adopting male patterns of moving from job to job in order to advance. Both Carolyn and Sally are doing this; neither of them is tied to a particular boss.

And very recently, a law student told me that she and her classmates feel strongly that they would not want their fathers (who were, as often as not, lawyers themselves) to run interference for them in the job market, as the fathers of the Hennig-Jardim executives had done. This is another clear sign of the changing times; women today want to prove they can do it on their own.

But will women ever really be integrated into masculine hierarchies? This is an important question, because the hierarchies are the power structure.

I remember a woman editor in a publishing house where I worked, the first in her subdivision to be promoted to full editor, who found that she was continually being excluded from the subdivision's informal editorial meetings. The men would forget to notify her, or would hold a meeting at a university club where women were not admitted.

There was no reason for this exclusion except that the men saw their meetings as masculine identity rituals that would lose their basic purpose if a female editor were allowed to intrude. Ironically, all the men respected this woman as an editor and admitted that her books were very successful. Still, the fact that she might have had useful ideas about departmental planning took second place to the assertion of masculine identity.

And she was helpless to change the situation. Isolated from the hierarchy, she had only two options: she could focus on her own work and do the very best job possible; or she could cultivate relationships with men higher up who might help her. In short, even when, as an adult, she might have begun to learn to negotiate the dominance hierarchy and to see the whole picture, she was forced back into the typical woman's pattern: a narrow focus on the job at hand and a reliance on attachments to men.

No wonder women who have achieved status in the corporate world may still fear the loss of their " 'queen bee' status" and have trouble welcoming younger women into the corporate ranks. Since they aren't really part of the hierarchy themselves, they have, essentially, nothing to welcome another woman to. There isn't any turf for women to share; they can only perceive a younger woman as a threat to their unique status.

While a male executive certainly perceives a younger man as a potential threat, he has many good reasons for extending his help. He may, at some point, want a protégé's support; and, as Daniel J. Levinson of Yale pointed out in his book, *The Seasons of a Man's Life,* if he himself had a mentor, he is likely to want to serve as mentor in his turn. This is like passing the power along from father to son—a male executive is, in the final analysis, welcoming a fellow male into the fraternity. The glue that holds the hierarchy together is the solidarity of masculine identity.

Women are just beginning to form support networks. It will be very interesting to see whether these networks will eventually serve as female versions of the hierarchies, into which older women can really welcome younger ones, or whether personalities shaped in the Identity Triangle will continue to turn women inexorably toward men as protectors. It is, after all, a consummate irony that many women in the corporate and political worlds today owe their advancement to government affirmative–action directives—government as Daddy, the ultimate boss, laying down the law to the corporations.

In the meantime, the hierarchies are still strange ground for women. For men, who bring to them a lifetime's experience in calculating their position in the group, in playing politics, in seeing "the whole picture," they are native turf.

Conflicts in the Identity Triangle

When the Hennig-Jardim executives started out, the idea of a company presidency or vice-presidency would probably have seemed either shockingly presumptuous or laughably naive; women didn't get that far.

Today, women feel much freer to choose career goals while still in college. According to the 1980 *Report* of the Brown Project, a survey of attitudes and experiences among 3,377 men and women undergraduates at six colleges and universities (Barnard, Brown, Dartmouth, Princeton, the State University of New York at Stony Brook, and Wellesley), 68 percent of the women wanted full-time careers, while 28 percent of them wanted part-time "careers." The undergraduates planned to go to business school, law school, medical school; they talked of entering highly competitive fields like international finance. Only 4 percent imagined themselves not working at all.

But even though women are free to plan careers today, they continue to have conflicts about how far they can, or should, go. "How ambitious," a twenty-seven-year-old law-school student muses at the very beginning of her career, "can I really be when I want to have children and take care of them? Can a trial lawyer realistically practice part time?"

The undergraduates in the Brown Project are more naive: the vast majority believe that they can take full- or part-time leaves of absence from their careers while their children are preschool age. When they enter the Outside world and discover that five-year leaves are simply not compatible with careers in international finance, their conflicts will become more acute. They, too, will come to the law student's question.

It is an important one, and the time/energy problems are real. It will take a great many women, insisting on their needs both as mothers and as serious professionals, to make a dent in the prevailing masculine patterns of work, career, and success. So far, feminism has yet to do more than give women a chance to prove they can succeed in the Outside world as well as men if they conform to the male pattern, which means remaining childless or turning their children over to other caretakers.

In the meantime, women have a bewildering array of choices to make: children now, or later, or not at all? Plunge into a full-time career or tread water until children are in school? What to choose that allows any alteration in the usual masculine pattern?

We still have to deal with the conflicts that arise from the fact that the masculine pattern and the feminine pattern are designed to take men and women into different worlds, in which they play different games and live by different rules. Marriage and motherhood, attachment and heterosexual femininity, make up a pattern that pulls us one way, while ambition and career, autonomy and self-assertion, and a traditionally more "masculine" style pull us in another. Do we act like women or men at work? Can we act like men in one part of our lives and like women in another?

This split in the patterns of the world we live in is a real one. Too often, though, we bring to it a split in our identities that only makes it harder for us to develop strategies to cope with the world.

The Hennig-Jardim executives had a strong, positive reaction when they found themselves stuck at the middle-management "wall," beyond which lay a vice-presidency. Their bosses had been promoted far beyond them, and they themselves had begun to feel that their nose-to-the-grindstone style was no longer satisfying. At this point, they took the "moratorium" I described in Sally Archway's bio and, as we saw, integrated into their identities the aspects of their heterosexual femininity (including dates, marriage, and motherhood, a more feminine style of dressing, and, more importantly, of relating to people) that they had forsworn in the first part of their careers.

Through the moratorium, the executives became "whole"; they grew up. One of them said her experience enabled her "to discover that I existed all by myself and that I liked that person and others did too."

Thirty years later, Carolyn Rosenthal says: "I have had to figure out who I was, as opposed to what everyone else was trying to make me, and to stand up and be who I am."

After the moratorium, the executives were able to have fuller, more emotionally and sexually satisfying lives, as Carolyn will be. But that was only one result. The second is more extraordinary: *for the first time they "saw themselves as capable of moving toward the highest management levels in their firms. . . ."* (Italics mine)

In fact, they all went on to become presidents or vice-presidents.

The question is, why? Why then, and not earlier—especially when they had had such supportive fathers and mothers? What had been holding them back before? And is their example of any use to younger women, who take career aspirations as their right?

Hennig and Jardim define the problem and its resolution in terms of roles and role conflict, but I believe the answer to all this lies in the Identity Triangle, and in its relationship to the world in which we live.

Before her moratorium, the executive quoted above had in a sense remained a Good Girl, like Carolyn, "stuck" in her attachment to Daddy. In the end, both she and Carolyn needed to move away from their fathers and back toward their mothers to complete their Identity Triangle, and, finally, their own identities.

Once through her moratorium, the executive, like her peers, could stand whole and individual, separate from both father and mother. By completing her Triangle she was, in effect, resolving all the old oppositions in herself—between father and mother, masculinity and femininity, autonomy and attachment, work and love.

And, as Hennig and Jardim point out, once she had resolved her internal conflicts, she, like her peers, was able to resolve what had seemed insurmountable barriers between the masculine and feminine patterns of life. She not only expanded her repertoire to include a social and private life; she was also able to include colleagues from work in that life, while at work she became more relaxed and feminine in her style, wearing makeup (apparently for the first time) and less businesslike clothes. She became, in short, the same person at work that she was at home, where her husband supported her success.

Only when they had all accomplished this integration of Inside and Outside were the executives able to reach for the top—and succeed.

It will be interesting to see whether Carolyn also becomes more overtly ambitious when she has worked through her "rebellion," her own special moratorium, and comfortably integrated her mother- and father-identifications. She hasn't yet really owned up very straightforwardly to ambition; she "sort of thinks" maybe she will make vice-president, but only because people, including her father, have been telling her for years that she could.

A daughter doesn't stop identifying with her mother just because she can't share the ego ideal her mother represents. She may, as Sally and Carolyn did, have to spend some time denying that identification; in more extreme cases she may, like the Desperate Achiever, deeply fear the dependency her mother represents.

But no matter how intensely you identify with your father as an achiever in the Outside world, if your mother offers a conflicting ego ideal, you are bound to have Identity Triangle conflicts. And, as Hennig and Jardim imply, the denial of a whole side of your personality results in a limiting of perspective—and so of your vision of a possible future. Until their moratorium, much of the executives' energy had been tied up in their conflicts; it was ultimately their dissatisfaction that impelled them to change their lives.

Once they did so, their "human skills" enabled them to succeed at the top. As they stopped focusing narrowly on achievement in the day-to-day job and began to see themselves as whole people, they began relating to their co-workers as people, too. When our energies are tied up in Identity Triangle conflicts, it seems, the result can be a rigidity, a limited ability to meet the complex demands of the top-management position, where an ability to "see the whole picture" and the flexibility to deal with other people and changing situations are much more important than simple technical competency.

The unhappy Desperate Achiever, on the other hand, may be too enmeshed in her conflicts to change. She was never given enough warmth and responsive tenderness to validate her core identity. Hennig and Jardim looked at one group of middle managers who, like the Desperate Achiever, had been treated as "sons" by their fathers: They couldn't change; they saw themselves in terms of a masculine role and they never developed those "human skills."

This group never got past the middle-management "wall." Subsequent studies have confirmed that, in general, women who feel compelled to deny their essential identities as women in order to assume a "male" role do not succeed at the highest levels in corporations.

Resolving Identity Triangle conflicts affects women's flexibility in coping with the earlier stages of their careers, too, as Sally Archway's bio shows. And the resolution makes a difference no matter what work or profession we choose. The corporate world is only one example.

Unfortunately, many women still seem to see an irreconcilable gap between their work roles and their personal lives as women: one is a man's role, the other a woman's. Women who try to behave in traditionally feminine ways fail in the work world, too—they can't see the large picture, they worry about being loved, and they rely too much on male authority.

What we need, it seems, is to be able to combine Dr. Henry Biller's definition of the personal characteristics of femininity—"a positive feeling about being a female" and "skill in interpersonal communication, expressiveness, warmth, and sensitivity to the needs of others"—with good old-fashioned masculine independence and assertiveness. Those people who can mix the styles that used to be split up between men and women are the ones who will succeed in the future.

Fame: The Conflict of Visibility

When I committed myself to a career in writing, I had to deliver real manuscripts to editors in the Outside world, my father's world. I couldn't sit in my room and write passionately in my journal, as I had been doing for years, or create poems that were never submitted to magazines, as I had also been doing for years. I had to go public, to be seen and judged. I had to become visible.

And this, it turned out, was to be a major conflict.

My father had, I was always told, two ambitions: to become a vice-president of the railroad and a general in the army. To achieve these would have made him, visibly, a success. He failed at both, rising only to director of research and colonel, respectively. Some of the reasons for his failure were certainly related to his difficult personality; he didn't really have the flexibility, much less the tact, to manage or command large numbers of workers or soldiers. (Men, too, can have their problems with these things.) He was by nature a man who was happier with objects than with people; I think he loved the trains, and the functional problems of making them run well or run better. His army service, in the Transportation Corps, had involved trains, too, which for him must have made a very happy combination. The Army, with its rigid rules and regulations, suited him well; nevertheless, he chose a civilian career.

It could be that his failure made me, in the end, more ambitious, like Carolyn Rosenthal. In any case, I acquired, secretly, the ambition to be a writer early in life. The problem was that I felt compelled to keep my ambition secret well into adulthood. It was all right to publish a few poems and stories in high school and college, but when I graduated it did not seem to me to be possible to say, "I am a writer. I will write."

So I spent years as an editor, then produced an anthology, and finally wrote my first "real" book. But it wasn't until some time after that that I began to define myself, publicly, as a writer. To say not only that writing is important to my identity, but that I intend to earn a living at it; to obtain through it whatever fame and fortune I can.

There was, of course, the problem of devotion, of my lingering guilt over "selfishness," my fears that I was, after all, nothing more than a Bad Girl. But there was something more: a lady does not *desire* fame, or even recognition. It is the same thing as notoriety to a daughter whose father believed you should only get your name in the paper three times. How can you advertise your books?

Recognition is what a man aspires to; visible success sets the seal on his masculinity.

Even when we have fathers who give us permission to think about careers, we often prefer to keep our goals private, to pretend (even to ourselves) that what we want is not really recognition, but other things—things that feel, perhaps, more feminine.

When Hennig and Jardim compiled data from questionnaires filled out in the 1970s by 3,000 women and 1,000 men, all middle-level managers in corporations around the country, they found that the women saw a career "as personal growth, as self-fulfillment, as satisfaction, as making a contribution to others" and, lastly, "as doing what one wants to do." Neither fame nor fortune were mentioned.

By contrast, the men defined a career as a chain of jobs which would lead to some kind of fame and fortune.

The women saw their career goals in personal terms; they alone would decide whether they had reached them. By this standard, I could have gone on writing in my journal and putting poems in a drawer. No one besides myself need ever know I was a writer.

None of this should be very surprising. As Inside people we were always supposed to be invisible in the Outside world, hidden under our fathers' or husbands' names, adjuncts or ornaments to their visible presence. Men have public names, and public reputations.

Not that women haven't always worked; but their work has often been invisible. Housework is the obvious example. Yet in the Outside world the typist, the secretary, the aide, the assistant are all hidden behind their boss's position and public reputation. So visibility, except in some traditionally feminine roles (actress, model), looks pushy and aggressive—unfeminine. And it makes us feel isolated; or worse. Women who win competitions are visible and may fear reprisal. Better to keep a man on the Outside.

Fortune: Conflicts About Money

I don't have an easy time with money. Younger women may be more at ease with it, but relative to men it can still cause problems. Money is connected to power, to authority, to status—all the things we have traditionally received through men.

Money, in fact, may be more of an issue today than sexuality.

Our problems with money are rooted in the fact that, in addition to its other functions, it is the ultimate symbol of masculine authority, the last icon of masculine superiority. To earn it in significant amounts is still, largely, a male prerogative, though one that is becoming increasingly threatened as women move into traditionally masculine fields. The masculine response, so far, has been to up the ante. If women generally earn 63¢ to every dollar men earn, corporate executive women earn only 37¢ for each dollar earned by corporate executive men. While women may start out in business and law on a roughly equal footing with men, in five to ten years they are falling behind.

The reason for this is that money has replaced most of the old symbols of male prowess. Men no longer have many opportunities to give public displays of their skills. Hidden away in offices, they can show their stuff to women and children (and to each other) only through money—by their superior ability to earn it, by their function as the financial support and mainstay of the family, by their power to dress up women and children to advertise their own success. But more and more women can now dress themselves, support themselves, and/or help support the family (when they aren't its sole source of support), so superior earning power stands alone, the last bastion of traditional masculine identity.

What all this means relative to Daddy's daughters is that almost all of us grew up with a man to whom money was an important aspect of identity. It was, ultimately, money that gave my father the authority to have the final say in family decisions, such as when we would buy a new car, how big a house we could afford, whether we could go to the theatre or a movie or a restaurant, take a vacation or buy a new couch. It was because he earned the money that we all moved whenever his career demanded it, that he could come and go as he chose and be late for dinner. In short, money means control. And, as females, we are the sex that Daddy wants most to be able, through money (if not through his ultimate weapons, size and strength), to control.

Furthermore, it is almost entirely through money that Daddy has, traditionally, been able to show his love for us. When Daddy gives us things (allowance, clothes, gifts), he is both showing us his love and showing the whole world how much he values us. It has always been so. In some primitive cultures, husbands pay a high price to a father to buy a bride. In others—and historically in much of the West—fathers have been expected to provide a dowry. The size and value of the dowry was an indication of the family's, the father's, social status and a measure of his success in the world, as well as of the value he placed on his daughter.

In Europe, many Jews lived in dowry cultures. Jews who immigrated to America adapted the idea of the dowry to the American custom, already well established, of dressing up daughters (and wives) to show off a father's success in business. So the Jewish American Princess was born, and given extra impetus by the desire of immigrants to show off their new success, as well as by the traditional Jewish pattern of placing children at the center of the family. But there have always been American WASP and Catholic and black Princesses, too.

Actually, being a Princess can have its advantages. Learning that she can get what she wants out of an adoring Daddy gives a daughter a sense of entitlement that will go far in helping her relate to men. Princesses usually manage their marriages very well. But when a Princess, or any other woman who has learned to equate Daddy's love with money, moves outside the role of receiver of Daddy's goods, she's in trouble.

If Daddy shows his love through money, and money is an important symbol of his identity, potency, power, and success, then when she provides for herself is she not somehow usurping his identity and authority? Even—final horror—symbolically castrating Daddy? (Consider the wives who agonize over a promotion for fear their paycheck will be bigger than their husbands'!)

Take Iris, the would-be television producer who had a generous father. When she made a stab at supporting herself, she found that it made her very nervous to spend money on her own pleasure because that was what her father had done for her. And, when she had to leave her husband in order to pursue the career she thought she wanted, she felt abandoned. Her father had taught her that she shouldn't do anything on her own, should let him provide for her. Is women's famous fear of success simply in part a conviction that unless we *let* Daddy control the money, we will be alone? Money is love. If we earn it ourselves, how can Daddy love us?

Let Daddy Provide may be the most lethal version of Let Daddy Do It.

Or consider the daughter who gets an M.B.A. and realizes that she is very likely to be earning more money as a young chit of a girl than her father ever earned in a lifetime of work as a small businessman. If a father gets his sense of masculine power from taking care of a wife and daughter, what's a daughter to do? Sons are expected to grow up and take care of themselves, but if a man can't take care of his women, he isn't a man at all. And these days, that means money.

The situation is worse if Daddy has retired, because he's lost his old place in the Outside world. He needs even more to be able to say, Let Daddy Provide. He sends her little checks in the mail. She doesn't want to take them; she wants to feel independent. And besides, she doesn't need them. But at the same time she feels a little guilty, a little lost, a little abandoned. It's a lovely feeling to be taken care of, after all; that's what Daddies are *for*.

Maybe Daddy starts telling her she's really still the feckless, self-indulgent, irresponsible daughter she always was when he was taking care of her. She resents the fact that he doesn't seem to respect her work. He wants her to be Little Me for him, but she wants him to approve of her new success. They aren't playing the same game at all.

There is a very tempting solution to this, and it's a version of the Secret Little Me: Why not go on playing Little Me for Daddy? After all, as one daughter told me, it's the only way she can find to be *close* to her father. The only link he recognizes. Money.

So even though she's grown up and married and she has a good job, she lets him slip her a check toward a vacation, or the new car.

And yet she feels sad. It's tough to be a grown-up working woman and find out that your father, instead of asking you what you think should be done about the high interest rates or who the next governor will be, tells you you're still the same extravagant girl you always were, and that's the only way he loves you.

Masculine oneupmanship. No wonder we're doubtful about pressing onward, about acquiring a real ambition. Little Me offers all the proven rewards; Going Too Far offers only risk.

Carolyn Rosenthal thinks her father has given her permission to earn money, so she doesn't have to feel selfish or guilty or worry about Going Too Far.

For Sally Archway, money may be secondary to the other satisfactions of her career, but her father always advised her to go first class. Dr. Archway taught her something about money when he made her pay for a semester's tuition that was wasted as she dropped out of college and then changed schools altogether. She took this as a sign that he expected her to deal responsibly with her own life, and found that it did make her take herself more seriously. Fran Nobile, on the other hand, was allowed to remain the feckless daughter when she dropped out of college for a semester and her father never mentioned the cost, thus ensuring his own position as the powerful provider. Fran has kept a good deal more Little Me in her than Sally Archway.

Not Going Too Far was usually a specialty of our mothers, who were generally more tied down by Let Daddy Provide than we have been.

And yet they had been educated far beyond the level of any other group of American women in history. Many of them had worked, had even proven their competence on some professional level before marriage and children pulled them into the old roles of Good Girl and Little Me.

So they were not really prepared to be simply submissive to Daddy.

In effect, they were torn between their restlessness under the old roles and their inescapable dependency on Daddy's money; and more often than not, this inner tug-of-war led to a form of covert conflict called:

Getting Around Daddy. It's important to understand Getting Around Daddy because, as a form of covert warfare, it has been responsible for most of the accusations that women are more "manipulative" than men, who are supposedly more straightforward, sincere, and honest in their dealings with other people, especially women. The man who had legal authority and financial control over a woman could afford to be very straightforward when he told her what he expected. In the face of the combined power of state, religion, society, and economy, women had only one possible way to carve a little space for themselves: collusion. Getting Around Daddy. A practical strategy applied in a game in which he held all the aces.

Getting Around Daddy—which men have also called manipulation, or treachery—has been a common pattern that daughters have learned from both mothers and fathers.

It may involve social freedom, as it did when Callie Opal's mother lied to her husband so Callie could go to the beach with a group of boys and girls. But by far the greatest number of stories I have heard involve money. If Daddy earns it and so, ultimately, controls it, then the only way mothers and daughters can get it or control it is to manipulate Daddy.

The game takes many, many forms. The most straightforward is waiting until Daddy is in a good mood to ask for something you want. A mother may do this for her daughter, and nobody suffers.

But usually the game gets more tangled. Daughters become pawns, and it's hard to tell whether Mother or Daddy is villain or victim. Let's take two specific examples.

Game #1: One woman I interviewed recalled what happened when, as an adolescent, she wanted a new dress for a dance. Her mother told her Daddy didn't want to spend the money. She was crushed, felt that Daddy was the bad guy; worse, he was rejecting her. What's more, she noticed that when he wanted something for himself he bought it, even if her mother objected. For a new car, he would overrule Mommy.

But now, years later, this woman has decided that her mother never even asked her father about the new dress; that she was just using him as a cover for her own cheapness, and as an excuse to be mean to her daughter: "My mother gave the impression that it was all him, that if it were up to her, she would do so many nice things. She made me believe it was his fault she was not more generous to me. I believed it because I saw he was cheap. I had seen him give five dollars to my aunt when she asked for twenty-five for a pet charity."

So now she feels betrayed by her mother, and Daddy has moved from the role of villain to victim.

This same daughter also learned directly from her father how to manipulate him. If this sounds odd, consider that Daddy may not *want* his daughters to learn to be direct and straightforward. Not only is such directness a masculine style, it may well be a masculine prerogative, based as it is on a sense of possessing the right to make a demand and the power to back it up.

Daddy wants the pleasure of a daughter's flirtation. He likes having her use coyness and indirection; it flatters him.

So this daughter learned to sit on the arm of his chair (having picked the right moment, when he was mellow), put her arm around him, smile, kiss him, and then present her demand.

"Daddy," she would say, "I want a new sweater. Mommy doesn't want me to have one, but I don't have as many as she thinks I do, and I don't have as many as my friends do, and it's really important, and I saw a bargain . . ."

Girlish chatter. From a man's point of view, this argument, being entirely personal, has nothing to do with logic. From a man's point of view, his daughter is manipulating him, using her "feminine wiles."

But that's not necessarily how a daughter sees it. She knows Daddy wouldn't respond to a straightforward demand.

"Daddy used to tell me," says this woman, now a wife and mother who can afford to buy her own sweaters because she manages a dress shop, "how smart I was, what a good arguer I was. If I were a boy, he'd say, I'd make a good lawyer.

"But I wasn't a boy, so it wasn't enough for me to be smart. I had to be flirtatious, too, and give him the adoration, the caring. I had to nurture him."

Learning to Get Around Daddy, to manipulate him, is in fact just one more lesson in femininity, an essential part of Let Daddy Provide.

And if you did it right you could, like the Appleman sisters, get your father to give you what your mother had refused. Maybe even the new dress.

Except that, like Carolyn Rosenthal, this daughter had learned early never to ask for anything she didn't already know she could have. Carolyn knew she could have what was in her uncle's store, which gave her a pretty wide selection. This daughter's criterion was much more personal: "I never asked for anything I thought he would give me a hard time about."

The essence of Good Girlism. We learn it with money as with everything else. Read the right side of the menu and order what you estimate Daddy is willing to pay for, or can afford. Don't even *ask* for a new dress if you think he'll give you a hard time.

In this family's version of the game, it was ultimately the daughter who was the victim. But maybe the mother herself had learned never to ask, even for the sake of her daughter, for something she couldn't have. Maybe she didn't even feel she could refuse her daughter by herself, she had to invoke her husband's authority. Having to Get Around Daddy makes mothers sneaky.

Game #2: "When I was twelve," says a forty-year-old mother, a social worker, "I wanted heels to go to a Bar Mitzvah. My father said I was too young for heels. My mother took me to get a pair anyway. When we got home, she said, 'Stick them in the back of your closet.'

"So on the day of the Bar Mitzvah I trotted down in my heels and my father said, 'What is this?' To me. So I was in trouble with my father; I was stuck with the argument because she couldn't handle it herself. I told him Mommy bought them for me—I was miserable. So my father asks my mother, 'How come?' and my mother says, 'She wanted them.'

"So I felt sick. And my mother was the nice guy and my father was the bad guy. Why didn't they have that fight behind closed doors and let me wear my heels?

"So even though my mother basically ran the show at home, I saw my father as much more powerful than she was. Sure, she was in charge of all the child-rearing things; I'm sure he never knew anything about how much allowance I got. Because I'm just like her. Last month I called up my friends, took a poll, found out how much nine-year-olds were getting this year, and set a new allowance. She worked the same way.

"But she couldn't deal with his power. Why should she have to hide from him? She was an adult. I know now that if I have to hide how much I spent on something, if I have to lie to my husband, I feel like a piece of shit. But my mother used to tell me all the time, 'Don't tell your husband; charge it. Maybe he won't notice.' "

She leans forward, intense. Her finger stabs the air for emphasis as she speaks:

"The message she passed on to me is that to confront a man, a husband, directly is a very dangerous activity. You don't do that—you go around the back door. You go get the heels, you slide them in the closet, and maybe he won't notice when you walk out in them. Maybe he's so busy working he won't even see them.

"Behind all this was the message that my father's disapproval was too terrible to endure. You couldn't withstand it; that level of arguing and haranguing and criticism would reduce you to tears—or to nothingness."

* * *

These daughters grew up feeling determined to learn how to earn money and, thus armed, to be more direct about their own financial needs. Without the first step, economic independence, their mothers could not take the second.

Yet because the choice in the first place was often between self-supporting spinsterhood and economically dependent wifehood, women have had very good reason to devalue their own efforts and despise their economic independence.

My own mother, as soon as she married, gladly gave up what probably quite rightly seemed to her the bleak life of a legal secretary; she never felt very sure of herself in a world where she had to establish her own position, her own identity. She was pleased to hook up with the ready-made identity of wife to my father.

My stepmother had worked for twenty years before she married my father, but she still felt basically the same way my mother had. From her point of view—and it is impossible for me not to sympathize with it—a position as upper-middle-class wife was far superior to that of single, middle-aged working woman. In those pre-feminist days, there were slim grounds for such a woman to stand on, let alone find a little height, a little status, for comfort. She had the wit and the energy to earn a living for herself, but nothing she did on her own could give her that inner sense of self-assurance with which a woman could face the world and say, "I have a husband, therefore I am somebody!"

This, of course, was a lesson first learned from Daddy. It was only my generation that began to admit to ourselves (our mother's generation noticed but couldn't admit it) that smiling for Daddy didn't give us everything we wanted.

But although I understand and sympathize with both my mother and stepmother, I still bear a grudge against both of them for refusing to collude with me against my father.

My father wanted me to learn to practice self-denial; there was no getting around him at all. It was the same for my mother and stepmother. I think he felt aggrieved by his family's continual need for money, as if we were somehow going to devour him. So his way of using his power to give or withhold money and goods was, generally, to withhold. He had done this to my mother, I have been told (although not by her), from the beginning of their marriage; he did it with everyone else in the family for as long as I knew him.

He liked to give certain things—the Whitman's Sampler on the weekend, a bottle of sparkling wine for dinner on special occasions. The giving of allowances was accomplished with enormous ceremony once a week after dinner, when we children's peccadillos were weighted against our need for some spending money. He liked to be in complete control. He didn't like to be asked to give, to respond to needs. It wasn't only the bike. Once when I was eight or nine I asked him for an eraser; he offered to sell me one for fifteen cents.

I felt, like any daughter, rejected. When you are little, Daddy spends money on you to show his love. When you get older, having men spend money on you is supposed to be your compensation for giving up the ability to earn it for yourself.

I certainly learned that my father was supposed to earn and control the money; I got the giving up part but not the compensatory masculine generosity.

The odd thing is that my father had always insisted I have jobs; it was part of learning the value of a dollar. I began babysitting at eleven, and in high school I worked variously as day-camp counselor, mother's helper and, during Christmas and Easter vacations, salesclerk in a florist shop. When I was thirteen, he took me to the bank to open my first checking account. But through all this he assumed that my ability to earn some of my own spending money would have no effect whatsoever on my obligations as a dutiful daughter. It didn't mean I could become independent— only that I wouldn't have to ask him to give me any money.

This same logic applies all too often when grown women work today. Wives contribute to the family income, but Daddy's salary is still the crucial one, the one that gives the power of decision-making, of control.

It's not surprising, then, that so many of us never outgrow the feeling that, in relation to money, we are perpetually Little Me. No wonder we feel abandoned when we have to provide for ourselves, devalued if we have to earn our own living, and full of self-doubt about the real worth of our own efforts.

It's not so much that we are dependent on Daddy as that we don't believe we are worth anything if we are independent.

Part Five

CHAPTER SEVEN

Seduced and Abandoned:
Losing Daddy to Divorce or Death

Trying to Kill the Doll
Judy Stampler

*J*udy Stampler is small, delicately made, and precise. Until you talk to her for a while it is easy to assume that she really is the sort of Dresden-doll figure she has been taken for all her life.

There was a time when she cultivated that image because it was safe: a generalized Smile for Daddy. But she is not really like that at all. At twenty-six, she is fighting gamely for control over her life: for work that she feels is satisfying and at which she is successful, and for a relationship with a man, ditto. She would love to have children.

She has to fight harder than most of us for these things because she is starting from a slippery base. Her father left her twice, at the two moments when a daughter needs a father most. When she was four and a half, her mother, Rose, divorced him. When she was fourteen, he died.

Her mother remarried very soon, so Judy did grow up with a father figure around the house. And until her own father died, he would visit once or twice a month and drive off with her for the afternoon.

But basically, Judy still feels that she was rejected by her father and that, partly because of that rejection, there is no place where she really belongs.

We have become more psychologically sophisticated since Judy was a child. We now know that when you are very young, you are likely to think your father left you, even if it's your mother who moved out with you and divorced your father. And you will believe that it is your fault, because you're Bad, or not pretty enough, or maybe even not smart enough. Even sophisticated teenagers can have such feelings; a four-and-a-half-year-old, whose feelings are still entirely raw, unmodified by experience, can be overwhelmed by them.

After the divorce, Judy's first reaction was that nobody loved her.

At five, she went on a crying jag one day, hysterical with grief for herself. She told her mother no one loved her. Her mother said the sort of thing parents used to say to children. Not, "I still love you, and Daddy still loves you," but, "How can you say that? How can you even think it?"

Which of course made Judy feel even more guilty because it meant that even her feelings were wrong. Bad.

It wasn't that Judy's mother didn't love her. It was just that Rose, like many parents of that generation, simply had no idea how a child would feel. No one had made any allowance for her feelings when she was growing up, so the whole idea of considering a child's feelings would hardly cross her conscious mind.

Rose herself is a warm, feckless, trusting woman, who always believed that a man would take care of her. Irv, Judy's father, was her second husband; she met her third while Judy was only two, which might have explained why Irv used to accuse her of running around.

When Judy got a little older, she began to worry that her looks had offended her father. "I remember one day when I was eight and he was coming to pick us up, crying to my mother that I wasn't pretty enough and I couldn't see him. I became hysterical—my hair wasn't right, or whatever. Something very physical. I wasn't good enough to see him that day and he might reject me."

Her mother did her best to help Judy with this problem, which was reassuringly concrete and feminine: "She set my hair for me every night because she knew I couldn't deal with it otherwise. I think I compensated [for feeling rejected] by trying to be pretty, but of course I was scrawny and gangly and gawky like every other eight-year-old. So there remained all this leftover stuff—'You're so scrawny, who would want you?' At this point I'm trying not to care, because it doesn't matter."

Patterns of feeling that are reinforced by the people around us when we are small have a way of lingering, of forming a basic mood that permanently colors our sense of ourselves.

Certainly, to become doll-like was both a way of compensating for and an expression of Judy's own feelings of helplessness about controlling adult comings and goings. If she were pretty, passive, and doll-like, might her father, this time, stay? What else could she do, anyway? She certainly couldn't risk a show of temper, Go Too Far; that might send him away forever.

"I can't remember," she says, "going to him for anything. I can only remember trying to look pretty enough when I saw him so it might be as painless an experience as possible."

If threats of rejection by a father who lives with you are enough to make you a Good Girl, once you really feel you've actually been rejected, you may become so Good all you can do is try to be perfect. For Judy, too, force was an additional factor in her early life with her father. Irv had a violent temper. One snippet of memory that survives from that time is of his "coming into the house with a gun, after my mother, and my mother calling the police."

He was, as she called him later in extreme understatement, "volatile."

There must have been other such times, and Judy remembers that, typically, she would sit very still on the couch. "I would feel helpless and then not feel anything at all. I blocked it out. I remember just sitting there wishing, 'Please make it stop.' "

It is not surprising that one of the great longings of her life has always been for calm.

Irving Stampler came from a clannish, possessive family that had never liked or even accepted Rose. The most possessive of the lot was Irv's sister, Judy's Aunt Kara. She adored Irv, and Judy is convinced that she had a hand in breaking up his marriage to Rose.

Rose was an only child and her parents were dead, so Irv's family was the only network of relatives Judy had. When he went away, for all practical purposes they went too. Although she did see them while her parents were divorced, after Irv died, they "disowned" her. She has never seen any of them since.

In a way, both Irv and his family actually rejected Judy at birth. She was the second daughter, and the family, with the exception of Irv, had been hoping for a boy. Irv simply had not wanted another child, and he had told Rose that whatever its sex, this child would be hers, not his.

The family, or at least Aunt Kara, liked Judy's sister Kara, perhaps because of her name. "If my sister and myself were in the same room," Judy remembers, "Aunt Kara would say how wonderful my sister looked and how terrific it was that she was finally getting Cs and not flunking out. No one cared at all that I was getting straight As, or what I looked like. I was just scrawny or skinny. If I said I did this or that in English class, my aunt would tell me about some contest she had won when she was my age.

"I don't remember my father ever defending me," she adds a little sadly. "I think he probably should have."

When Irv took her to his family on holidays, his parents would pretend she wasn't there. They would speak Latvian, and the only words she could distinguish were the names of her mother and Herb, the man Rose married six months after she divorced Irv. "There was a lot of gossip, a lot of dirt."

With all this, it's not surprising that Judy has an image of an ideal father, and it's the opposite of Irv. What she would like to have had, she feels, is "balance. I needed a calmer environment than I had. Since I was rejected along with my mother, what I needed from my father was a person to balance that and to take all the conflict and the tension away. To accept me. Perhaps by having a father there who loved me . . ."

She doesn't finish the sentence.

Judy has always had to provide her own balance, since most of the world around her was out of control and took no notice of her except as a pawn in its own quarrels. And when she was very young, her only way of remaining calm and in control was to hide or to sit very still. She hadn't, after all, had a chance to learn how to manage other people to get what she wanted; she only knew how to manage herself. As a small child she was the only person over whom she could exert any control.

The problem, though, is that this kind of early training can put you at a big disadvantage when you grow up. You aren't used to pitching in and defending yourself when you're attacked, for instance. You've trained yourself, instead, to withdraw. To block everything out.

"I react," says Judy, "very strongly to situations where I feel I don't belong, or someone's going to reject me. I become passive. I feel it's out of my control because, as a child, everything was out of my control for years. I was probably too frightened to do anything about it. I couldn't side with either one, because if I did, I would lose it all."

Today her tendency is to back off from any confrontation, even when it could mean losing her job as a sales representative at the major record company where she now works. Recently, the sales manager, an irascible man who took over the job shortly after she was hired, called her on the carpet. He was, says Judy, literally screaming at her; he told her she wasn't aggressive enough, wasn't selling her share. She would ruin the record of the office.

"Here was a man who was rejecting me straight out. He saw the facade, thought I was too sweet, thought I wasn't a sales-type person at all and what was I doing in this position? Someone else chose me; he didn't want me.

"I couldn't answer him. Had I had a different family background, I would have told him off, put myself back in the position I should have been in. But I was afraid because I had been rejected."

She hadn't actually been fired, but she started looking for a new job anyway. Which brought up the whole conflict between work and love all over again.

Judy is ambitious. Not always the thing for a Good Girl to be, perhaps, but she had some very special motivation. "I always felt I had one foot in quicksand because of my family, and I wanted to get out of it."

Education was the way to do that, "to get entirely clear." (This phrase "to get out of it" or "to get clear of it" comes up again and again in the interview, as though Judy still feels too close to that quicksand.)

Judy was the first person in the family to go to college. Irv's mother never learned English. His father helped run a small family export-import business that had never done well enough to provide more than a bare living for three brothers and their families. Irv had quit high school to go into the business, and as his father and uncles got older, he gradually took over and built it into a considerable success.

Judy thinks Irv's frustration about his lack of education and opportunity helped make him such an angry man.

"I think the fact that I did go to college would have pleased him. I think he was a very intelligent, frustrated man. I don't think he was a reader, but I think he was a rather smart businessman. If anything, I think he was overly sensitive. He was musical; he was always buying albums and singing. And he wrote. He was always writing or doodling or singing. I had the feeling he had a lot of frustrated talents and was caught in the business."

Her father, it turned out, had left her almost exactly enough money to make it through four years of college. "I was thrilled," says Judy. "I thought I was very, very lucky."

Education was important for another reason; she was never really confident of being smart, any more than she thought she was pretty. No one told her she was smart, and although she knew on one level that she was—she did get straight As—on another level, without that confirmation from someone who mattered, she would always have doubts. Even her mother never really praised her, and they moved so often after her father died and Herb's business started doing badly that she was continually having to adjust to new schools.

But Judy graduated from college with honors, and managed to spend a year in Europe—another family first.

In college, she was happy for the first time in her life. She discovered dance and art. In her senior year, a teacher told her she would hate to see her "just get married" because she was so creative. "That," says Judy, "was the best compliment I've ever had."

She misses all that terribly. And selling does not, in fact, excite her at all. "I like the power in this job," she says, "and some of the people, but I've never felt quite as good as I felt in school when I was drawing and dancing and feeling creative. I have a terrible fear of losing that forever."

She is single, she has learned how to earn a good living, she is still young. Why not try a new field, perhaps teaching, or even commercial art?

She has a lot of reasons why not. For one thing, if she changed her field, she would have to start all over again, take a cut in salary and probably a lower-level job. She doesn't really feel she can afford it.

"Part of me is saying, 'I'll stay in sales and try to make a lot of money and I'll be totally self-sufficient.' And the other side is saying, 'Perhaps I should go backward a bit and try to do something that makes me feel good.' "

But if she risks doing something creative, she runs up against her fears of rejection: "It's easier for me to do things to be accepted than to go plowing into an office with something to show, saying, 'Look how talented I am, I've put together this portfolio,' or whatever." They might just tell her she's crazy, that she's not really talented at all.

On the other hand, she is worried that people will see only the pleasing facade, the doll: "What I want is to be recognized as a very intelligent and talented individual. When an interviewer told me he didn't think the job I was applying for would be intellectually stimulating enough, I was delighted."

Yet she is unable to break through the passivity and demand to be seen, or heard, in the way she wants to be. She has to hang back and hope someone will see behind the facade she keeps throwing up to ward off the rejection she is sure will come if she Goes Too Far.

And she is always afraid of being poor.

She wanted to get an M.F.A. from a prestigious school (Columbia maybe, or Radcliffe) right after college, "something that would break me completely out of it." But there wasn't any money left and she felt she had to go to work. Now, several years later, she says: "I sometimes get resentful, and I think, why won't someone help me? I want to go back to school and get a master's degree, but I'm afraid to take out loans, afraid of being poor."

What a bind! She's ambitious, but she's afraid to assert herself. She doesn't like selling, but she's afraid to take the risks that come with trying something else. Better not to rock the boat. Better to stick with what you know, even if you aren't entirely happy with it. And better, too, to hang on to Daddy in the only way you can—by identifying with him and arranging your life to match the pattern of his.

Which is exactly what Judy is doing.

She has taken in the whole thing. Irv's frustration at never being able to develop his talent; his inability to break out of work he didn't much like but at which he did well financially; even his line of work. Export-import is, after all, essentially sales. But Irv was good at it, while Judy does not, so far, seem to have been conspicuously successful—a fact she may not want to admit. So even though she is single, she feels she can't afford to change fields, can't afford to start over again as an assistant in a field with more future.

"Conscious or unconscious signs of increased identification with the absent parent," writes Dr. Lora Heims Tessman in *Children of Parting Parents,* her study of the effects of death and divorce on children, "constituted one of the most frequent findings in encounters with the children of the divorced or deceased. One way of attempting to maintain a sense of intimacy with the parent, guarding against feelings of loss, was to become more like him as he was perceived by the child. . . ." And in connection with work and creativity, she goes on to point out that "working creatively or working at all was valued in relation to the image of that parent."

To change fields, then, or to take up a whole new direction as a free-lancer, is for Judy neither a calculated nor indeed a calculable risk at all. It bears the freight of the enormous losses of her childhood and adolescence. For if she breaks out of her frustrating but financially secure sales work, she risks losing her father a third time.

It is the images we carry inside us that are the hardest to separate from because the parting seems too final. Especially when the person behind the image is in reality already gone, so that our image is all we have left.

Judy's may be the ultimate conflict between love and work.

When it comes to love itself, though, the potential for loss is equally great.

Now that Judy is older and sometimes talks things over with her mother, Rose tells her that Irv really had loved her a lot. He used to carry her around, and besides, she had been such a sweet, good child, who couldn't love her?

But when Rose sent Judy a photograph of her father holding her in his arms, she didn't feel anything. She just stared at it. Nevertheless, she does have some poignant sensual memories of him:

"My father had big, round, royal-blue eyes. He was overweight, but I remember his hands, and his ears. His hands were beautiful. I remember his fingernails; they were very shell-like, and I remember him doodling, and his ink pen.

"Most of my memories of him are in the car, because he would pick me up and drive me and sing to me, so I would see his ear. Just before he died, I had a dream in which he lost his ear."

Sometimes, on these trips, he would take Judy to an amusement arcade he owned. On other Saturdays, though, he would use the time for business: "He would leave me in the car while he went off and took care of something. It was painful for me because I didn't come first. He would say, 'Well, we have to stop by the business.' I felt abandoned."

No comparison here to the companionable trips to the clinic that Sally Archway took with her father. Irv made no attempt to include Judy, to give her a sense of access to his world. She got the worst of it from both points of view—in work and in love.

She developed a chronic case of father-watching. "I would look at friends of mine with supportive fathers, fathers who hugged their daughters, and not know how to deal with my envy. I remember coming home and telling my mother about these wonderful Daddies. My best friend had a very domineering father and her Daddy was everything to her. I would observe.

"I desperately wanted a Daddy who would be emotionally supportive and demonstrative. But basically I was afraid of my father. The most endearing thing I remember him doing was patting me on the knee once when we were in the car."

For a while Herb, whom she called "Uncle Herb" after it was made clear to her that this man who appeared to stay six months after Irv left was not really her father, took up the slack.

Judy's sister (with whom she never got along, and who didn't like Herb) had been sent to live with Irv, who had remarried. "That was probably the best time in my childhood. My life was very calm, the way I wanted it to be. I was an only child, and I would go places with my mother and Herb. They would take me to the movies.

"Herb was like a father, and I would talk to him about my math. I don't recall having a demonstrative relationship with him, where I would crawl into his lap, but for that period of time he was there."

This relationship with Herb may have been an important anchor for Judy, even though she thinks that, on the whole, he was not a real father figure and that, in the end, he disappointed her almost as much as her father had. Unfortunately, her adolescence coincided with Herb's decline as a businessman. They were chronically hard up and moved around a great deal. "Herb went from being a very gentlemanly, smooth, sophisticated man to being rather gruff, not taking care of himself. My father died from strokes and sugar diabetes. He wouldn't take care of himself. Herb also became overweight and started not taking care of himself. I lost respect for him. He would buy me a car to show me he loved me, then the car would be repossessed. He could only show love in terms of money."

So in her relationships with men Judy is full of conflicts, too. She dated a little in high school but felt afraid of boys; she didn't think they really liked girls. In college she had two successive long-term relationships, both based on security rather than love. One was the first male, she believed, who had ever really accepted her. That lasted a year. The second she found boring, but his family had money and that counted for a lot. Herb thought she should marry him.

Her feeling was, and is, that "I would like to get married, but I'm in no great rush to make any mistakes."

After all, she has been disappointed by both the men her mother married in her lifetime. As far as she could see, her mother's philosophy didn't work at all. You can't rely on a man to take care of you.

Yet the wish to be rescued is there. Herb blew up at her for turning down the rich boyfriend: "He was saying, 'I love you'—I never knew he loved me—'and because I love you, you're perfect, and because you're perfect, you will marry this wealthy Jewish man from a good family. So what if you're bored sometimes?'

"My reaction was, 'The hell with you! I'm going to find someone to take me completely away from all this.' "

To get her clear of everything.

For a while, she found someone who could do that—a wealthy Canadian businessman, sophisticated, urbane, part-French. He could take extremely good care of her, and he seemed to be the demonstrative man she had always wanted. But this immediately brought out her fear of dependency. "It made me feel too vulnerable. I don't like having my hand out. I felt as if I were using him. I like contributing; I don't ever want to find myself begging."

It also made her feel helpless, as she had felt as a child. When she learned the Canadian was divorced, and had a six-year-old daughter, she found herself identifying with the daughter.

The conflict is tremendous. She is terrified of being poor, so wealth is enormously seductive. She'd like a man who would be proud of her, who valued her for her own achievements, as her father never did. She wants a kind of father figure, like the Canadian, but when she feels vulnerable, she fears being overwhelmed by his power. Even so, she has a wish that is rather like Alicia Appleman's—to be supported by a man who will urge her to paint.

Will she ever manage to create this neat synthesis of achievement and dependency?

Rose wasn't a terrific role model: she worked off and on, but she was always dependent on men. "She always felt," says Judy, " 'Why should I work here? I pay my maid that much!' She was very spoiled. I don't want to be dependent like that."

Especially since Judy could never depend on the men Rose depended on.

Rose's proclivity for walking out on a relationship worries Judy, too. She fears she has inherited the same trait. When she left the Canadian, she says, she felt as if she had betrayed him. He was looking for a mother for his daughter; she had "played little girl, to try and be accepted, and then left. It was what my mother did—I just left, instead of trying to stay and work it out."

Of course, there was a third reason why she left the Canadian. Dr. Tessman observes that adolescents and young adults who have lost their fathers may go on repeating the loss. Paradoxically, this is a way both of hanging on to them and of obsessively reliving the painful experience. It happens, perhaps, when a child never has a chance to grieve, to work through the first love and so "give it up" along with the lost parent.

Irv had never been generous or kind. Of the Canadian, Judy found herself thinking, "How could this man do that? He must be wrong." She had no pattern for this kind of relationship. She had several patterns for leaving; she followed them.

* * *

Growing up, separating from strong internal images, is a lot more difficult when the model for those images is no longer alive. But Judy is working hard at it, with a little help from a therapist.

Actually, she has been trying hard all her life, starting around eight. At the same time she found herself slipping into the "doll" role to ward off rejection from her father, she was also trying to find another way. "I remember at seven or eight I didn't want to be sweet and good anymore. It wasn't getting me anywhere. My sister was more of a problem child and she was getting more attention than I was."

She first began to get angry in high school, when Herb and Rose "expected me to get straight As in school, be popular, do well—but never helped. They never listened. I went through one whole year without showing them my report card, and they never noticed. I began to feel I didn't want to please them anymore."

But she was still "afraid to walk out of the house without makeup on. That was my one thing to try for, to be accepted.

"Lately, though, I've been working a lot on trying not to fall into the doll-like role, trying not to be passive. Trying to be assertive."

The most important thing is killing the doll.

A large part of her strength and support came, all along, from Rose, who after all, was always there. "I was very, very close with her. Even when I was young, she would tell me all her problems. She took care of me; she was my friend."

And it was feckless, dependent Rose who pushed her daughter not to follow her own path: "She always told me to do whatever I wanted to do, and to be independent, because her parents had never let her make up her own mind. It took."

So Judy is strong, and now she feels she is beginning to integrate her anger—at her father, at Herb. An anger that Good Girls can't allow themselves because it inevitably leads to rejection.

"Since I've said I refuse to be a doll, I'm finding that my relationships with males are definitely improving. I'm saying I want more than that. I can accept my femininity with its un-doll-like side; I also want someone I can accept as masculine, with his doll-like side."

Now she's beginning to enjoy men more as equals. "If they want me, they're going to want me," she says firmly. "That's a big barrier I've crossed. I don't have to play any role with them. And I probably have more male friends than I've ever had in my life because I feel that way."

But she still worries about the effects of her father's lack of support on her future, because she wants to be successful. "I see other women who don't feel as insecure in business situations as I do, and who can deal with the men around them a lot better than I can, and not take it all so personally. When the sales manager yells at me, I take it personally. A woman with a stronger father image would be able to go into a situation and say, 'Yes, I can do it.' I say, 'I want to do it, I will try to do it.' But in my mind, I think that perhaps I can't do it. Perhaps I'm trying to get myself into a place where I don't belong: the world of men.

"But I still think I want to do it, to get myself into a situation where I'm there and my opinions are finally there. Whereas I think other women probably always thought that their opinions were valid, because there was always somebody there saying, 'My smart little girl, and my this and that.' I think it would be wonderful to get into a situation where I say, 'My opinions are valid, damn it, and you're going to hear them.' "

She is beginning to say goodbye, finally, to Irv.

She has kept his old opera records all these years, and one night recently she was listening to them with a new man she feels hopeful about. He watched her listening for a while, then said, "You really loved your father a lot, didn't you?"

"No one," said Judy to me, "had ever asked me that. I just looked at him and I said, 'Of course I did. He was my father.' There is never going to be another one. I'm the same blood—it's all there. How can I not have the strong feeling and the strong loss when the person who made me is gone, and that's the only one there will ever be?"

The "Good" Divorce

Peter Backlin

*P*eter Backlin has a prosperous car dealership in a Philadelphia suburb that contains a mix of working-, middle-, and upper-middle-class families. He falls somewhere between the last two categories. He is living with Alice, the woman he plans to marry as soon as his divorce from his first wife, Betty, comes through. Alice's son from her previous marriage lives with them. Peter's son is in college; his daughter, Angie, now thirteen, divides her time between her father's house and her mother's, a couple of miles away.

The Backlin ménage is, in short, a typical suburban family.

Peter knew from the moment the idea of separation from Betty came up that he was neither going to desert his children nor have to ask to see them once a week. He coaches Angie's softball team, makes sure she is getting into the right programs at school, and worries about her skin problem.

The deal he and Betty have finally worked out, without benefit of a lawyer, is that each "has" Angie three days a week; the remaining day is "open," meaning either parent is free to make plans with Angie, or she with them. She has her own room in each house; on the "open" night, she chooses where to sleep. It is her responsibility to keep her engagements straight, since Peter and Betty aren't on the best of terms at the moment. But one of the deals they made fairly early in the separation was that they wouldn't try to use the children to get at each other. If Angie says she has a date with her mother, Peter doesn't push it.

However, this arrangement was not the first one Peter and Betty tried. Originally, they came up with what they thought was the ideal way to spare the children the most pain: the children would stay in the house where they had grown up, and Peter and Betty would take alternate six-month turns as live-in parent. They rented an apartment for the live-out parent, informed the children, and eased slowly into the six-month schedule with six-week and three-month stints.

"For both of us," says Peter, "the goal was to say to the children that this separation was an item between Betty and me, and had little to do with them. We hoped that this living arrangement would be the best way to make this statement to the children, but we found it had exactly the opposite effect. Each time there was a moving in and a moving out, they felt abandoned by both of us. The month before and the month after the changeover, the anger and hostility were incredible."

Peter is a placid man, who smiles easily and often. He slouches comfortably on the chintz couch. He is wearing sneakers, blue jeans, and a sweatshirt; later that afternoon he and Angie have a date for a league softball game.

He says the divorce has finally made him grow up.

He and Betty had been "the perfect suburban couple" when Angie was born: "We had a house, two cars, and two children, a boy and a girl." Peter loved his work, his wife, his home. He loved seeing Angie breastfed; he even helped with diapers and night feedings. "I was thirty-two; it was the first time in my life that I could say I experienced joy. It looked like all the promises that had been made to me were going to come true."

The joy lasted for five years. Then, as the story always says, things began to fall apart.

Peter now believes that one of the big problems in the marriage was that both he and Betty wanted to avoid confrontations with the kids and with each other. They wanted everything to be "quiet and nice," to look good on the surface, a little like Holly Flax's parents. And even when Peter "was beginning to realize that the promise that had been made to me really wasn't so terrific," that maybe maintaining the image of the ideal family wasn't what he wanted to do with his life, he couldn't yet do anything to risk breaking the facade; "I didn't want anyone to be angry with me because I wanted to keep this whole act together." It isn't, after all, that easy to come to terms with the gap between expectations and reality.

But the act finally broke up anyway, and he and Betty, a newly fledged psychologist, went their separate ways.

Everything was set up for the kids to have as positive a divorce experience as possible: both parents remained in town and on tap. Angie and her brother could drop into Peter's office any time to say hello, cadge a few dollars, or use the bathroom. Peter found he was extremely successful as sole live-in parent, playing a dual father/mother role.

What is the result?

"I would say that Angie was mad at me, and is still mad at me, for changing her life."

He has tried to talk with her about it, but Angie doesn't like to discuss things that make her feel uncomfortable. She was certainly as painfully eager to avoid an interview with me as were virtually all adolescent daughters of divorced parents I ran across. And I don't blame her. Your identity is confusing enough in adolescence, without having the Identity Triangle come apart on you. A thirteen-year-old has enough difficulty just trying to keep her own act together.

So how did Peter handle Angie's anger?

At first he tried reasoning. "I started out with, 'Please understand, it had nothing to do with you. It's not your fault. Both Mommy and I do love you. I'm here, my office is here, I'm here in the apartment or I'm living with you.' "

Now he's changed. "I let it be. Less is more. It comes down to, 'I don't live at home. I'm sorry that you're having difficulty with it, but that's the way it is.' "

Of his first tack, he says, "It was all true, but it had nothing to do with what she was prepared to believe. I think she believes that we ruined her life. But I have come to terms with that. If it were true, which it isn't, I needed to choose myself, and she has got to accept that. My trying to reason with her and make her feel not angry isn't going to work. She's going to have to come to terms with whatever it is she's feeling. Maybe I can help her, if she'll let me. But if she won't let me, it's really her problem that she's gotta come to terms with.

"That's not an easy thing to say. My stomach turns over, because I would like to take charge of myself and her and everybody's feelings, so everybody goes smiling off into the sunset. But it just doesn't work that way."

What Peter has discovered is that adolescents are conservative, self-centered—and need firm rules. At least, he has discovered the part about rules with Angie. His son, he says a bit sadly, was already wrapped up in his own life of sports and girlfriends at sixteen, and he had seen very little of him since the breakup.

First, there is the question of conservatism. Peter knows, for instance, that there was talk when he and Alice moved in together, even though he is living "as a married man, and on this block alone there are three or four other couples doing the same thing."

With the kids, "any change is automatically not good. Once I began to date Alice," who had grown up in the same town but whom he hadn't known, "it turned out our kids knew each other." All the kids had problems with that. And the fact that divorce has now become quite common "doesn't make any difference in terms of its acceptability. I think kids are very parochial: 'It's terrific for Ruthann, but. . . .' Is it any different," he muses, "than when a kid says, 'You mean *my* parents have *sex?*' "

Which is of course the universal and quite necessary self-centeredness of children. "I find," says Peter, with no judgment in his voice, "that children are extraordinarily selfish, and really only want to deal with the thing as it affects them. They're not interested in the fact that you're unhappy, that's of no interest. They want to know, 'How does it affect me? Am I going to get my allowance? Am I going to be able to go to college?' Those are the discussions I had with my son, and his response to the whole thing has also been anger. Annoyance that his life has been upset."

Dealing with all this has helped Peter become, he thinks, a parent in the true sense of the word. He has, for instance, become firm. There are now clear rules, and a lot less nagging on his part or whining and arguing on Angie's.

He has also become a conveyor of feelings. He has stopped behaving like a passive American male when it comes to such Inside things. For example, "I've begun to tell the kids what I feel. They might want to know why I did something, and I might say, 'Gee, that is really not your affair.' But I will tell them how I feel about it." Then he asks them how *they* feel. "It's a very slow process, because I spent all those years running away from the confrontation. But that's okay, too. It's even okay *not* to tell me how you feel."

He seems to be a very relaxed man.

It's a good thing he has learned to accept anger, because besides being angry at him, Angie "hates Alice. Alice is a threat; she is replacing her mother."

He thinks this is a very female response. He has known women "who felt replaced when they found out their ex-husbands had girlfriends." But he doesn't believe men feel the same way. He tells me that when Betty went out for a while with his best friend, "I never felt replaced. I felt sadness at the loss of him." (Of course, the fact that the friend was "lost" suggests that some kind of feeling of replacement was going on, but I don't voice this.)

What I do mention is that daughters often fantasize replacing their mother if she's gone; becoming, in effect, their father's wife. I felt this way when my own mother died. I was nine, and I fully expected to take over all her chores—the laundry, the cooking, the bedmaking. I was quite crushed when my three older brothers callously did these things, expertly heating frozen chicken pot pies and french-fried potatoes. And when my father got a housekeeper, I refused to speak to her. I spent a lot of time hiding in the closet in my bedroom.

Peter is interested in this idea. "When I was growing up," he says, "I just wanted to get out of the family and be like my father as soon as I could. And my father was never around, at least not emotionally." He doesn't think it would have occurred to him to feel jealous of a new domestic arrangement. As a son, he was already oriented toward the Outside world.

In any event, the situation with Alice and Angie has progressed to the point where "Angie's getting comfortable enough to be angry with Alice now." For instance, "Alice has been very outgoing. Angie's reaction is, 'She's just trying to be nice to me so I'll like her.'"

Actually, right now Peter is more worried that Betty isn't really available to Angie in the way he thinks she should be, particularly as Angie is moving into adolescence.

Although on the whole he doesn't believe mothers and fathers are different with daughters, at least not if they do the kind of full-time parenting he has done, there is one exception: "female-type things." And now that Angie's getting older, "There are certain things I can't do for her. Menstrual problems. General girl-type problems: clothes, boys, lipstick, stuff like that. She has bad skin; kids can be cruel. I can help her only partially."

One of the first difficulties he encountered with her when he took on his first sole-parenting stint was that Angie, who loved shopping, "didn't want to go shopping for camp. She had tantrums; it went on for days. Finally she told me she didn't want to go into the dressing room by herself. I couldn't go in with her." So he called Betty, who took her shopping the next day.

Even before the separation, Peter was doing a lot of parenting because Betty was in graduate school getting her Ph.D. And he thought he had learned what it meant to be a parent because he seemed to have all the responsibility. But when he really took over sole parenting, "the big discovery was that up to that point I was still helping. I was a feminist, so my wife went to graduate school, but I really wasn't responsible for the kids. I was always helping out, and I was a terrific person. I was the perfect husband. Then I became responsible. That was the big difference."

Part of it was "the nitty-gritties: 'Did you do your homework?'" Partly it was simply having to be at home. But the main thing, he found, was "being available. Not necessarily at three o'clock after school. But there has to be some time, many times a week, when you are available, totally and exclusively."

And now he doesn't think Betty is available enough. In fact, he feels that in some ways Betty really wanted "out" of family obligations. At the moment she is very busy with clinic work, professional obligations, and all the socializing-cum-business that is typical of any profession. She says it's quality, not quantity, that matters.

The funny thing is, he sympathizes with the way she is feeling about her work: "I understand what Betty is going through from when I was twenty-five and thirty and beginning to hit the highs of my career. It's intoxicating. But our situations are different. As far as the kids went, I was doing what I was supposed to do; I was helping out. I was off the hook."

After the separation, "my response was to bring my children into my social life, to set up housekeeping in the same community, and start living just the way we live—being a family. I would probably not live here if the kids weren't here."

Now he worries about Angie. How will she deal with adolescence, with the areas where he can't help her? He worries that if her skin doesn't clear up she will have problems with dating, and that will affect her relationships with her friends, who are important to her. She is seeing a specialist.

But he finds hopeful signs, too. Angie is "beginning to blossom." She was always shy about speaking up, now she's becoming a leader. "As a parent now, I can participate in that blossoming. I can enjoy it, maybe help fertilize it a little bit."

With his son, he says, again a bit sadly, "It's too late for me. He's going to have to come to terms with whatever he has to come to terms with the way I did, at thirty, when my skin was one size too small for me."

I ask Peter about sons and daughters and competitiveness. He thinks his relationship with his daughter is much less conflicted than that with his son. "My son and I are much more competitive—or he is certainly more competitive with me. And that creates problems with us. Angie is not competitive with me; she is only concerned about whether I look good. She talks about my silly clothes, or she says I don't comb my hair right, or I wear designer jeans so I'm a fag. My appearance is very important to her."

He has coached his son's baseball and basketball teams, as well as Angie's softball team, and he found that both children wanted to be treated with special favoritism (which he leans over backward to avoid). But there is a vast difference between boys and girls on the playing field: "Coaching boys was really a pain in the ass, because boys are so damned competitive that it's really not fun. The girls are terrific. They go out there, and they are just as competitive, and they want to win just as badly. But when they make a mistake, they laugh about it. And when they lose, they get upset, but it's not a thing where they can't go to school because they're embarrassed. It's over. That's been my experience."

There might even be hope for Angie's relationship with Alice. Recently, Alice and Peter were standing in the kitchen after dinner, hugging, and "Angie just walked right into the middle of it. We took her right in and we all hugged each other."

Seduced and Abandoned:
Losing Daddy to Divorce or Death

*D*ivorce has become so common in America that the odd child in some suburban schools is the one with both parents. Recently, one such teenage daughter, angry at her mother, yelled: "Why aren't you divorced like every other mother I know?"

There were a record 1.18 million divorces in 1979, two and a half times the number in 1959, when Judy Stampler's mother was divorcing Irv. It has been estimated that 40 or 50 percent of the children born since 1970 will spend part of their childhoods with one parent, usually their father, missing or only occasionally available. Even though nearly 10 percent of single-parent families today are headed by fathers, and shared custody arrangements like Peter Backlin's are becoming more common, most fathers still tend to drift away after divorce. The psychologist E. Mavis Hetherington of the University of Virginia, an authority on father-absence and its effects on children, reported in 1978 that after two years, only about 41 percent of one group of middle-class preschool children saw their fathers as often as once a week.

Three quarters of the mothers of those children will remarry, but not immediately. It used to be that a woman divorced in order to remarry, as Rose did; today, more and more divorced women spend time as the heads of their families, acting as father and mother both.

For some, this can be an exhilarating as well as a difficult period. While the demands on their time and energy are immense, they may also learn for the first time that they are competent to support themselves and their children. Necessity can help them overcome conflicts about taking on a "man's role" in the Outside world and in the family, and their daughters may actually benefit both from this new image of their mothers as strong, competent people and from the absence of traditional reciprocal identification patterns. A 1977 study by Janet G. and Larry L. Hunt found that father-absence seems to "release" girls to achieve in high school. If there is no Daddy around to say Let Daddy Do It, daughters may not worry as much about Going Too Far.

Yet Henry Biller points out that one reason people are interested in fathers today is because the growing numbers of fatherless families have made us aware of the problems those families face. The children of divorce are vulnerable to overprotective mothers, psychological problems, delinquency, and other difficulties.

Which view is closer to the truth? It turns out they both may be. Divorce or death is traumatic for an entire family; how a child will be affected by living for some time without Daddy, though, depends on a complex web of social, economic, and psychological factors. Growing up without Daddy is in one respect just like growing up with him—everything depends on what happens in the Identity Triangle.

After a stressful marriage, divorce can be a relief for everyone, and some fathers report better relationships with their children afterward than before. Children from intact homes can be vulnerable to psychological problems and delinquency, and overprotective mothers can be found anywhere, just as incestuous or remote fathers can. In fact Henry Biller has observed that technically present but emotionally absent fathers are responsible for more child neglect than divorce.

As divorce has become "normal," our attitudes toward it have changed. Twenty years ago, divorced women were still called "divorcées," a word that contained equal implications of glamour and scandal. A divorcée was probably "fast," or promiscuous, and in an era when most women were economically dependent on their husbands, she represented a threat to them and an object of fantasy to their husbands.

The children of divorce were invariably seen as victims of "broken homes"; their mothers, those same divorcées, were considered to be helpless to take care of themselves or their children. Without a man's status, income, and authority, the family was doomed.

Today, few young women, at least, face life after divorce without some work experience. Divorced women are no longer divorcées, and their children are no longer automatically seen as victims. We know that the adaptive powers of every human being are enormous, and that even under the best of what used to be called normal circumstances no child develops exactly like another. If the children of divorce regularly turn up in studies of delinquency, they also turn up in disproportionately high numbers in studies of genius—and, in general, they frequently become successful people.

Our attitudes toward divorce have changed so fast that studies of the effects of losing a parent have hardly begun to catch up. Many of them are wildly contradictory. One, for instance, shows that the daughters of divorce suffer cognitive damage—they don't think as analytically as girls with fathers—and even acquiring a stepfather doesn't help. Another, however, shows just the opposite—girls with stepfathers actually do better, in some areas, than girls with their own fathers.

Children test differently at different ages and at different stages after the divorce. Hetherington, for instance, found that preschool children were deeply troubled a year after divorce, but in another year girls, at least, were practically back to normal. Cultural factors count, too. Whether a family is black, white, or Hispanic; Catholic, Protestant, or Jewish, urban, suburban, or rural; working class or middle class; accepted patterns of behavior for men and women and fathers and mothers will help determine how individual family members react and adapt. If a father is very powerful in the family, for instance, as has been true traditionally in Hispanic cultures, his absence may cause serious problems. Working-class families, too, may be particularly hard hit, since traditional working-class sex roles are more rigid than in the middle class, and fathers are more likely to be the main source of access to the Outside world. Fatherless working-class children have shown lower IQ scores than those with both parents.

We really need to look at the whole person. It may be that the clinical records of psychoanalysts and other therapists will in the end provide the most sensitive barometers of the complex reactions daughters can have to divorce, as well as their equally complex adaptations to changes in the Identity Triangle.

In *Children of Parting Parents,* Dr. Tessman analyzed the responses of a number of children she saw over many years, in some cases into adulthood. In her view, divorce or death is, first and foremost, a loss. Children react to their loss in ways characteristic of their age and of their own unique needs. Their parents are crucial in helping or hindering their adaptation, but, whether well or badly, they do adapt. They often grow up to become highly successful adults.

Another way to look at it is that a daughter who loses her father loses one corner of her Identity Triangle: the Outside, masculine corner, inhabited by the person she first identifies with excitement, independence, autonomy, and (in the past) with work. He is the man with whom, in reciprocal identification, she shapes her own particular heterosexual femininity, the man with whom she first falls in love and experiences heterosexual erotic excitement. Since she both loves and identifies with her father, it is not surprising that her efforts to cope with his loss will mobilize the same elements—love and identification.

Dr. Tessman finds that almost all children combine elements of a "quest" for their lost parent with attempts to identify with him; in these ways, they try to repair their loss. Girls might search for a lost father in lover or husband, or find themselves reliving a painful loss over and over again. On the other hand, they might identify with Daddy's role as Outside man, and go on to their own success in the world. Through divorce or death, the Identity Triangle can be altered in ways that help as well as hurt a child, or that compensate in some areas for hurt in others.

Losing Daddy at Five or Under

One of the few facts on which most studies seem to agree is that at five or under children are particularly vulnerable to damage from the loss of a father. July Stampler's story shows how this can work.

At four and a half, Judy was at the height of her love affair with her father. When Irv left her life, she felt tremendously rejected—she had, in effect, been seduced and abandoned. It didn't matter to her that Rose was the one who walked out; children under five can't make such a distinction yet. Regardless of the reality, they are likely to feel, as Judy did, that they were responsible—that Daddy left because they weren't good enough or smart enough or pretty enough.

As Dr. Tessman points out, much depends on what kind of relationship a child had with her father in the first place. Four- and five-year-olds have intense fantasies about their absent fathers; she mentions one whose fantasies of a good father made it easy for her to adjust to a loving new relationship with a stepfather. She applied her fantasies to him and so expected (and luckily got) good things.

Even before the divorce, though, Judy had been subjected to a lot of conflict between her parents and Irv had been violent. Her fantasies must not have contained many images of a good father; she couldn't make an untroubled transition to her stepfather.

A common reaction to conflict or loss is to become afraid of dependency, of the need for closeness with parents and other people. When they don't get the right kind of emotional support after a loss, small children may become afraid of intimacy, a fear that can last their whole lives. Dr. Tessman describes how children of two or three can become hyperactive, quietly watchful or precociously mature as a way of warding off intimacy.

In addition, children of all ages need "emotional permission" to continue loving an absent parent, and to grieve for him. The child who isn't given this permission suffers the most damage, because until she works through her grief she can't really let her father go.

We have seen how all this operated in Judy's case. The watchful little doll, sitting on the sofa, must have seemed precociously mature, and in some ways she was. She had learned a method of self-preservation in the midst of chaos: to be perfectly controlled was, after all, a way both of blocking other people out and of ceasing to need them. She had been rejected by Irv at birth because she was the wrong sex. When he left, she wasn't allowed to express her grief. So she has hung on to Irv by identifying with him, all these years.

There were other things, too. Rose and Irv were no more friendly after the breakup than before; Judy probably felt conflicted, maybe even guilty, about loving her father and wanting him to love her. Especially since his family's rejection of Rose and herself made one line of loyalty—Judy and Rose versus Irv and his family—perfectly clear. She *owed* Rose loyalty. But how could she reject her father?

And if she felt, somehow, that it was her fault Irv had left her, and sorry for him at the same time because her own mother had walked out on him, she repaired her guilt by identifying with him as a kind of waif, just like herself. Right after the divorce, she remembers, she visited him "in the big empty house that was left to him and I saw him sleeping in a small bed with his feet hanging out. I thought my mother didn't leave him enough, that she left this poor man deserted in a bed with his feet hanging out."

Such compassion surely enabled her to deny the rage—and the guilt over it—she must have felt all along at this man who threatened her mother with a gun and made her own life terrifying.

It might have been easier for Judy if Irv had disappeared from her life; she might have been able to make a clean break with him and form a stronger attachment to her stepfather. As it was, she must have felt very torn. No wonder she still has a conflict between her longing for a loving relationship and her need to control the situation.

The Fantasy Daddy

In a little girl's fantasies, Daddy is a powerful figure. But as we grow up, we gradually begin to perceive him as a real human being. With luck, by the time we are grown up, our image of him has been scaled down to something closer to human size, although to some extent he remains forever a powerful person in our fantasies because he started out so much larger than life.

But if Daddy isn't there, he can't become a real person for us. He goes on being what he started out to be: a fantasy, an image in our minds. And the fantasy can be terrifying.

Even the ordinary, neglectful but nominally present father, such as a workaholic, may not be involved enough with his family to become a real person for a child. Such a father, writes the psychoanalyst Marjorie Leonard in her important article on father-daughter relationships, may seem to the child to be a "punitive and cruel" authority figure. A twelve-year-old daughter of divorce who was struggling to deal with her complicated, contradictory feelings about her father, herself, and her mother wanted her father to be powerful. But in her fantasies he had "a frightening aspect of cruelty and violence," which made it hard to identify herself as a feminine person who might have a relationship with such a man: "To be feminine was to be lost . . . to be exposed to possible injury. . . ."

This girl's parents had divorced when she was nine, but they had separated several times since her birth and, like Judy Stampler, she had witnessed a lot of conflict. Also, like Judy, her Identity Triangle problems were acute. She was, literally, afraid to grow up and become a woman.

Fantasies like this are formed at a very young age and unless a child is helped by concerned adults they have a way of hanging on, so that even when we meet men who might contradict the image, our fantasies color our view of them. And the younger a daughter is when her father leaves, the wilder and larger-than-life her fantasy father-image is likely to be.

My father, after all, became in my three-year-old fantasies God, Santa Claus (but a cruel, judgmental Santa who was waiting to see whether I was bad or good), and a fighter pilot, one of those men who shot down other planes and killed people.

When a father dies, fantasies can combine with the quest for him to produce fantasies of suicide, reunion with the dead. Dr. Tessman suggests that suicidal fantasies are usually engendered by a very deprived relationship; for instance, with a rejecting or very remote father. Workaholics, perfectionists, and autocrats would seem to fill the bill. A deprived child feels angry; if Daddy dies, she feels guilty (he left me because I was angry). Suicide then becomes self-punishment as well as a reunion. Children can have suicidal fantasies at four or five. If these aren't worked through, they can linger in the unconscious and lead to actual suicide at any age.

Sylvia Plath, whose autocratic father died when she was ten, wrote an angry poem to him in adulthood after the breakup of her marriage with Ted Hughes. When she killed herself shortly afterward, it could have been at least partly a compulsion to repair her abandonment by her husband with a reunion with the original male in her life, Daddy.

On the other hand, a dead father can become, in fantasy, a perfect being—so perfect that a girl despairs of ever being good enough for him, or of finding a man to live up to his image. Marjorie Leonard describes the feelings of a daughter who had never known her dead father. She had "an exalted and idealized image of a father for whom she was constantly searching; an image against which all others were doomed to fall short."

The dead are commonly idealized by surviving adults, as well; a widow who never remarried could hang on to her own image of a perfect husband and communicate that to her daughter. This girl wasn't even allowed to mention her father to her mother: she had no information at all with which to modify her fantasies. We need both love and information if we are to cope with loss and replace fantasies with reality.

How Can You Learn to Love a Man if Daddy Isn't Around?

If Daddy, or a reasonable substitute (a stepfather, a much older brother, or a male relative) isn't on hand during our most formative years, we may have problems breaking out of that intense, symbiotic relationship with Mother and learning to relate to a man. If heterosexual femininity is a learned identity, the product of thousands of small, subtle, intimate interactions with a male parent starting at birth, then without him the learning process can be impaired. The psychologist Tess Forrest goes so far as to suggest that in such a situation men can seem forever strangers: instead of pleasure, a relationship will provoke fear and anxiety.

In reality, of course, virtually no child grows up without some kind of male figure to practice on, whether it is a teacher, a minister, or the boy down the block. Even so, a girl who doesn't get that important validation at three or four or five could have greater-than-usual problems at times when other girls or women also have problems, as in early adolescence. In a 1972 study, Hetherington found that girls whose parents were divorced before they were five and whose mothers had never remarried tended to be extremely "boy crazy." They hung around the boys at a community center the way Callie Opal hung around her father when she was a small child.

Callie just wanted to be with her father; these girls just wanted, more desperately than the other girls their age, to be with males. For Callie, such hanging around was appropriate at four or five. But the teenagers seem to have been reduced to a kind of helpless begging for attention, to the point, apparently, of occasional promiscuity.

Hetherington's subjects were white, Midwestern, working-class girls who had grown up, for the most part, in strict religious traditions— Catholic, Lutheran, or Baptist. Their mothers disapproved of their fathers and let their daughters know it. It's not surprising that the girls were hungry for male attention, even to the point of confusing sex with love, as so many "promiscuous" girls do. It's also not surprising that they proved to have low self-esteem. Given the messages from their mothers, their own desires for male attention must have seemed like betrayal. Given their religious backgrounds, their sexual urges must have seemed nothing short of Bad. Nevertheless, their need for closeness overcame their inhibitions.

Two other women I interviewed who had lost their fathers before they were five and who had had difficult, stressful family relationships in general (the mother of one remarried twice; the other's mother never remarried) spoke of using sex as a way to keep a man close, or simply to have a moment of closeness. One spoke of picking up men in bars; the other of her inability to say No to sex—not because, like Blaise, she had no will of her own, but because she couldn't bear to deprive herself of a few moments of closeness, and the feeling of being held and cherished by a man. These were women in their twenties, another vulnerable period, when most women are, however unconsciously, engaged in the process of selecting a mate. If these women had never received the validation they needed to feel secure in their heterosexual femininity, it could be very difficult for them to be selective.

At least one study, by Seymour Fisher, claims to have found that women who lost their fathers very early in life have problems with orgasm. Since we now know that many factors can interfere with orgasm, this seems too sweeping a conclusion. But one element in the Fisher study makes good common sense. He ties problems with orgasm to fears of losing control, and says they both stem from the lack of a secure, trusting father relationship in early childhood. Orgasm represents the ultimate relinquishing of control, and we have seen, for example, how Judy Stampler's problems with her father have led to a great need for control. Judy, too, finds herself hesitant to "let go" enough to come to orgasm in sex.

On the other hand, it is possible to create a situation in which you can feel sufficiently in control overall to allow yourself to experience orgasm; paradoxically, this could be during a "one-night-stand." If you feel you are leaving or throwing the man out in the morning or right after sex, you don't have to worry about rejection.

Coping: Older Children Deal with Daddy's Loss

Children of seven or eight are still vulnerable to guilt if their relationship with their father was difficult, and to loyalty conflicts if their parents are in conflict. Like Judy Stampler, they too can develop what Dr. Tessman calls "pseudo-independence," which is really withdrawal, an attempt to distance themselves from intimacy.

But on the whole, older children are better able to cope with loss than younger ones. For one thing, as Dr. Tessman points out, by eight or so they can understand that Daddy needed to leave Mother, not themselves. And if a child feels secure in her relationship with her mother, she can adapt to life without her father; by ten, she can comprehend that, in reality, she won't ever be reunited with a dead or absent father.

A woman I'll call Arlene managed very well indeed. As the oldest daughter of a wealthy San Francisco businessman, Arlene was used to a lot of comfort; there were chauffeured limousines to take her and her little sister to school, ponies to ride, a boat in the Bay. She was eight when her mother finally had enough of her father's philandering and divorced him.

Arlene found herself in the middle of the divorce because her parents became involved in a bitter, two-year custody fight. She remembers that she loved the drama of the courtroom, and the lavish gifts her father sent her.

But the adultery charge stuck, so Arlene's mother got custody. And her father disappeared from their lives. Within a year, her mother had sold their large townhouse and moved the children to a small farmhouse in Marin County (this was in 1943). Within another year, her father had ceased to pay alimony; Arlene's mother went to work as a commercial artist. She was an indomitable woman. She turned her ladylike hobby, watercolors of landscapes and still-lifes, into a career. She sold children's book illustrations to Eastern publishers and learned to do public relations and advertising brochures. Between that and the chickens they kept, the family scraped through.

Arlene says she never felt abandoned—how could she, when her father had fought so hard to keep her? Still, there was one detail about the divorce that was unusual: Arlene was the one who found the letter from her father's mistress that gave her mother the proof she needed to initiate divorce proceedings. Arlene doesn't really want to talk about this, but it makes you wonder whether she didn't, on some level, feel a bit guilty about the divorce. And perhaps she felt betrayed as well, since eight-year-olds are still very much attached to Daddy. In any event, she coped with her loss by identifying very strongly with her father.

As the oldest child, Arlene very quickly became her mother's right arm. After school, she took care of her sister, three years younger, who missed their father very much. Arlene fed the chickens, and by twelve was selling surplus eggs house to house on her bicycle. As a teenager, she cooked when her mother had a deadline to meet.

As she describes it, she became the family "father figure." She was the strong one, the dependable one, the independent one. And she was ambitious. By fifteen, she knew just where she was heading: into a career, and, ultimately, back into money. She disliked being poor; her childhood memories of plenty were always beckoning.

Arlene was popular in school, but she kept her distance. She knew she would take her time about picking a man. She would never go through what her mother had.

She spent two years at Berkeley, but she was impatient to get out into the world. At nineteen she landed her first job, as a secretary to an advertising vice-president, at a firm for which her mother had done a lot of work. Her mother moved into the city so Arlene would have a place to live.

From then on, Arlene worked her way up. She evaded marriage for another eight years, which was unusual for that time. But she wanted to make sure she married at the top. So she brushed off the middle-management types who wanted a suburban housewife, and kept going. At twenty-five, she was the youngest account executive in her firm, and the only woman. Her boss, who became her mentor, kept promoting her. Maybe he had a soft spot for her mother, or maybe it was for her. At any rate, she became very successful.

And when she did marry, it was to the thirty-nine-year old president of a small, independent, but fast-growing advertising firm. He was divorced, but she knew she would hang on to him. He had a lot of money, he was smart, and he was successful. She got back her chauffeured limousine—every day it takes her from their townhouse to the downtown agency in which they are now partners. And on the weekends it drives them up to Marin County, where the enlarged and restored Victorian farmhouse still sits, next to the swimming pool and tennis court they added.

And if gossip sometimes mentions her husband, that's the price of any man's wealth and success. Her own daughter has grown up with both wealth and a father and is now at Yale. Arlene feels entirely fulfilled.

Dr. Tessman describes a girl who was able to turn her grief at the loss of her father into an identification with the useful, positive aspects of his personality; Arlene was able to do very much the same thing.

In a way, she went even further. She was able to repair her Identity Triangle by both becoming her own father and marrying him. In marrying a successful man and hanging on to him, she has made up both for her mother's loss and her own—and, not incidentally, assuaged any guilt she may have felt about having precipitated her parents' divorce. In her family role after the divorce, in her ambition, and in her own early success, Arlene "became" her own father. And by continuing her career in partnership with her husband, she has remained true to herself, the girl and woman determined never to be vulnerable to the blows her mother suffered.

If too many daughters are raised to Smile for Daddy and to Let Daddy Do It, if girls are too often indulged by loving fathers while being denied the chance to identify with them as people who can succeed in the Outside world, then the strong tendency for children to increase their identification with an absent parent could sometimes work to the advantage of girls who lose their fathers to death or divorce.

Of course, the effectiveness of such an identification would be modified by age and by the kind of relationship a girl had with her father before the separation. Judy Stampler, too, is ambitious, and she has been working steadily to "get clear" of her difficult past since high school. She strongly identifies with her father, the absent parent. But in her case, identification has been complicated by extreme conflicts in her Identity Triangle. She seems to be suffering from what Dr. Tessman calls "ego-alien identification." As we saw, she identifies with many aspects of her father that aren't really "her"—his frustrated creative urge, his occupation of buying and selling. As a very small child, she wasn't able to be as selective about her identifications as Arlene.

Even so, Judy has succeeded to a large extent in her ambitions. She has "gotten clear" of the family turmoil by becoming the first in her family to graduate from college and move into the white-collar world.

A woman I interviewed whose father had been very supportive and encouraging toward her as a child but who died when she was an adolescent, thinks that his death enshrined his support and approval permanently in her psyche. She doesn't even really know, she points out, whether he would have approved of her ultimate decision to go to a music conservatory and become a pianist. No matter. The support and approval were there for her to draw on, and will be for the rest of her life.

When Gail Sheehy looked at the lives of eight women leaders, she found that four identified strongly with a beloved father or father figure who died or left the family by the time they were twelve or thirteen. One never knew her father. Some had strong mothers, able to cope with raising a family on their own; like Arlene's mother, they provided an anchor in their corner of the Identity Triangle. For two, Jane Fonda and Gloria Steinem, identification with their fathers allowed them to cope with less strong mothers. Rosalynn Carter had to take on heavy responsibilities at home while her mother worked; like Arlene, she married a man with whom she could have a real working partnership. All these women, Sheehy points out, seem to have been motivated by the desire to avoid being trapped in the same vulnerability and insecurity as their mothers. Like Judy Stampler, they all wanted to "get clear."

It is striking how much this pattern resembles that of Sally Archway and Carolyn Rosenthal. They, too, identified with their fathers and determined never to be trapped in the role of Inside woman. Even when a father is lost, it seems, a loving relationship with him can be transformed into the elements of an identity that can take a woman far beyond most women's limits. And—as Sheehy also suggests—in some circumstances it may be the loss that ultimately counts for most.

Dr. Robert S. Weiss, of the University of Massachusetts, thinks that adolescents in single-parent households benefit from having to grow up "a little faster." They become more like a "junior partner" in the family than a child; they share in household responsibilities and in decision making, as well as becoming parent figures for younger children. They trade off security for growth and increased feelings of competency and self-esteem. Even younger children can take on more responsibility than they otherwise might, although they also need more direct nurturing.

This picture doesn't fit the adolescent daughters of Hetherington's study, who were found to be more dependent on adults—especially women—than were daughters with fathers at home. But their strict religious, working-class, small-city backgrounds may have been responsible; their mothers may simply not have been able to admit them to any kind of real "partnership." The mothers seem to have felt victimized, by their ex-husbands and by life in general. They all felt they had very little control over their lives. Arlene's mother, by contrast, took vigorous control of her life and expected her daughter to share responsibility. Ironically, divorce or death could give a daughter the chance to grow up.

Adolescence can be a difficult time for the daughters of divorce, as Hetherington's study shows. It is a tricky period, at best; but as Peter Backlin's story illustrates, coping with a drastically altered Identity Triangle can make it much harder. Just as she is entering adolescence, and so feels a heightened awareness of her father, Angie has to cope with feeling jealous of a new stepmother. Her mother, too, plans to remarry soon, so a stepfather is in the wings. Angie's Identity Triangle has doubled.

But Peter is working hard to make Angie feel loved and included. He is the father who does not disappear after divorce, but feels an intense commitment to his children. There is a hint of conflict in his disapproval of his wife's way of handling Angie, and Angie's skin problem could certainly be a response to the new complications in her Identity Triangle. But the fact that Peter is paying attention to these problems augurs well for their eventual resolution.

During early adolescence, children are struggling with very intense feelings toward themselves and their parents, in what is almost a reprise of their feelings at three, four, and five. But they are older; while a daughter needs Daddy's validation of her heterosexual femininity, for instance, she also needs to begin to move beyond him, toward boys her own age. She needs to be able to feel he is strong and protective. But she also needs to begin to scale him down a little, to see him as less godlike and more human than she perhaps did as a very small child.

When an adolescent loses her father, Dr. Tessman points out, she may become depressed both because of the separation and because her image of her father, still idealized from her childhood, is suddenly devalued. How could this loved man do such a thing?

She may devalue Daddy partly out of her hurt feelings, and partly out of the need children of all ages have to devalue a parent in order to separate themselves. Small boys do this with their mothers, and then compensate by creating an image of a highly valued, idealized mother figure.

When a daughter loses a father, she may do the same thing—both devaluing him and, in compensation, idealizing him.

Hetherington found that her young adolescent subjects devalued their absent fathers; this seemed to go along with their low self-esteem. At the same time, they seemed to idealize the men and boys at the community center. (They weren't helped by their mothers, who also devalued the fathers.)

Arlene, Judy, and Hetherington's teenagers show how, for girls, the quest for a lost father and identification with him can overlap, as their ego ideal becomes enmeshed with their search for a love relationship. This meshing of ego ideal and relationship is, as we have seen, a common problem for women. Arlene's story shows how, at best, it can become a triumphant solution to conflicts in the Identity Triangle.

Part Six

If He's Not My Prince, How Can I Be a Princess?

Learning to Live with a Fallible Daddy

If He's Not My Prince, How Can I Be a Princess?

Learning to Live with a Fallible Daddy

A group of women met one afternoon in a suburban living room to talk about our fathers. Two of us had just turned forty; the rest were in our mid- to late thirties. All of us were what they used to call "career women," although two had spent fifteen or twenty years as full-time wives and mothers before going to graduate school and launching full-time careers. One of us had recently separated from her husband.

We found out very quickly that we were all intensely curious about each other's father relationships. We had all discussed our mothers often over the years, sharing our feelings about them with friends and sometimes with friends' mothers. Continual reassessment of our mothers seems to have been, since we were small girls, part of the process of identification and growth.

But our fathers were more remote in our lives and we had not discussed them as much. It was as if each of us had made a separate peace with her father, and so with the world of men. None of us had wanted to look too closely at the terms of this peace before.

Now we are ready to. We are Out There in Daddy's world. If we've separated from a husband, we are ready to look very closely at the man who was probably the prototype of the man we've just left behind. Our children are grown into adolescence and we are now the age our parents were when we began to experience them most intensely.

We are as old as our parents! As old as Daddy was when we formed the image we may still carry around, in which he is a giant and we are little girls, or he is a bewilderingly attractive and repressive older man and we are confused adolescent daughters.

We are finally able to begin to see that we are as big as he is.

It seems that before we can let go of Daddy, we have to have something with which to replace him. Not someone exactly, although that can be part of the process of growth. But the someone (boyfriend, lover, husband) who replaces Daddy may also fill his role as authority and Outside man in our lives.

What we need is some sense of ourselves. Or something of our own.

It seems to me that women very often don't begin to assert themselves until they hit their mid-thirties. It's as though we need to have that validation of our heterosexual femininity that a husband and children provide. Once we have it, have lived with it and made it part of ourselves, it's as if we feel complete and ready to set out on our own. We don't have to worry so much about Going Too Far because we've already gotten the things we were afraid we'd lose before: the husband and the children. Attachments. We're free, now, to concentrate on work, having accomplished love.

Or maybe we've been exclusively Daddy's Girls, and kept our love and performance in some job or career for him, or his fantasy image inside us. Somehow—maybe because we've reached a plateau in our jobs, some measure of success and self-confidence—we're restless now. Maybe Daddy has become old, or died. Our old self, protected inside by Daddy and therefore self-sufficient in the world, like a ten-year-old at the height of an efficient and competent girlhood, doesn't fit any longer. We itch. We are ready to burst out of our girlishness, our secret love affair with our fathers, grow into our own adolescence and through it into adulthood. We are ready, finally, for another man.

If we've carried around with us all these years some gigantic fantasy image of an absent father, an image that makes it impossible for us to relate to real men in the real world, we may be ready at last to let go of it, to trust ourselves a little and take our first steps into reality.

Options and Images

On the other hand, there may not be anything magical about the mid-thirties period. That may just be a pattern generated by earlier patterns, such as growing up before there were options for moving Out or In. Before women could change their lives.

Options are the crucial element in all this. When you married for life, and had no reliable means of birth control, you had no options. When you were considered to be an unmarriageable spinster by twenty-five, and were stuck in some small town, you had no options.

Our mothers' generation—the mothers of the women in my little group, certainly those of older women, and even many of those of younger women—did not, on the whole, have real options. Wives did not, as a rule, enter the job market or start graduate school at thirty-five or forty. Marriage was still pretty much for life.

Things have changed with dazzling speed. Today, there is no such thing as a spinster, and a woman of thirty-five or forty, or even forty-five, fifty, or sixty, is still alive, attractive, and more young than middle-aged, if youth is measured by vitality, interest in life, and the capacity for change. The women in my little group all consider themselves at the top of their form. They are operating with more self-confidence, energy, and direction than ever before, and they all feel sexier than they ever have in their lives.

When Freud declared that by thirty women became rigid, apparently incapable of change, he was correctly observing the effects of a life without options on late Victorian Viennese women. Unfortunately, he didn't use a sociological perspective. He attributed the problem to an inherent flaw in the female psyche generated by—what else?—lack of a penis.

It was during the nineteenth century that masses of middle-class women began living entirely private lives, deriving their identity from their husband and children. This enforced relativity continued right through the 1950s and even the 1960s, and it remains an ideal among many people today. It means that women have no clear reference point by which to measure their own capacities. When we began having fewer children we couldn't even gain self-esteem as the "mother of many sons." And husbands as well as fathers had a stake in keeping us firmly enmeshed in Little Me and the Good Girl. A forty-year-old wife and mother with no job experience would think very hard before asking for a divorce. Better to keep on being a Good Girl.

The whole idea of becoming your own woman is still a fairly radical one. Even today, in most countries a woman by definition belongs to her father or her husband. She does not possess herself.

In the West, the suffragist movement of the late nineteenth and early twentieth century created recognition of women as citizens. This meant we were officially defined as individuals who could have equal power with men to determine, through the ballot, the selection of people who would have the authority to run things Outside, in the world.

Such power was unprecedented. In primitive tribes, ruling councils have almost always been male, although there have been tribes in which older women have gained considerable power as behind-the-scenes advisers. In more complex cultures, citizenship, as defined by the right to vote, had always been bestowed on males alone.

Contemporary feminism has continued the process begun by the suffrage movement—the recognition of women as individuals, as citizens—but on the Inside as well as the Outside. So, for instance, the slogan, "The personal is political," was coined to signify that feminism intends to extend the rights granted to all citizens in a democracy to women within the institutions of marriage and the family. (Contrary to the assertions of conservatives and various religious groups, the aim of feminism has not been the destruction of the family but its democratization.)

So the options, and the growth, may both be coming earlier for women today than they did for my generation.

Any crisis or transition period in our lives can force us to redefine ourselves, our parents, and our relationship to them. Most of us go through several such points; the transitions to adolescence, to young adulthood, to marriage and motherhood. In a sense, we are all continually redefining our identities and our images of our parents.

Yet crises or life changes in themselves are not enough. My father died when I was twenty-six, but I carried around his image (and my internal relationship to him) substantially unaltered until my late thirties. Writing this book has finally begun to place him for me as a person separate from me, and myself as a person who at last belongs to myself and is no longer part of him.

Letting Go of Daddy: The Process

What does it mean, to let go of Daddy?

It means, on some level, that we challenge him—or the image of him we have carried around with us all these years.

Maybe, while we are young and Daddy is alive and well, he simply carries too much power, too much authority for us to challenge him. We aren't ready to assert our own identities, or to look for validation of our own power, our own authority. A husband can help. One woman I interviewed has found that with her husband's support she is finally able to say No to her father, a man who has always demanded a great deal of attention and consideration from his daughters.

Or sometimes Daddy is enough for us; while he's alive, we don't need another attachment.

In *The Seasons of a Man's Life,* Daniel J. Levinson describes the mixed feelings of the younger man, or "mentee," toward his mentor: while he "feels admiration, respect, appreciation, gratitude and love," he also, to some extent, feels "resentment, inferiority, envy, intimidation."

For someone like Carolyn Rosenthal, a father is the first and perhaps the most important mentor. I believe that for many, if not most, daughters, our fathers are mentors in one way or another, especially if we are moving out into the world and our mothers were Inside women.

Even if we did not have the kind of superdaddy Carolyn had, we make our father our mentor by identifying with him as the person who works, who has authority, who knows how to function in the world. He was also our mentor in heterosexual femininity, as we molded ourselves into the image of femininity he found pleasing. This double-barreled mentoring, combined with the enormous power of a parent, makes it very hard for us to grow beyond our fathers.

Daughters certainly do feel the kind of ambivalence toward a father that the young man feels toward his mentor. Possibly the more so, the more passionately we are attached to him.

But we have far more at stake than the young man in denying our negative feelings. A big part of our identity is bound up in our relationship with this man, Daddy. His regard feeds our self-esteem, his power our sense of competency. If he isn't perfect, what will happen to us?

If he's not my Prince, then I can't be a Princess.

We don't want to be angry with him, and we certainly don't want to feel disappointed in him. If we feel intimidated by him at times, in the end this may simply give our relationship with him more value as an identity before the world. The man who intimidates us will surely also intimidate the world on our behalf.

If Daddy fails us, rather than getting angry with him we are more likely to turn against ourselves, to believe the fault is ours because we aren't lovable enough, not perfect enough.

I certainly did this. By failing to believe in me, my father was an immense disappointment to me, but I was terrified to admit it. Instead, I identified with his doubts, and felt acutely that I was a disappointment to him because I had failed to live up to the image he had of what he wanted and needed in a daughter.

I couldn't admit I was disappointed in him for failing to be what I wanted and needed in a father, even though it is a father's responsibility to be what his daughter needs, not the other way around.

I wouldn't admit that Daddy was fallible.

"You don't want to give them any kind of pain," said Carolyn Rosenthal of her parents, "because their lives are predicated on our being terrific. . . . You would cause them pain if you didn't live up to their expectations. It would be a significant disappointment."

Now Carolyn is angry at her father. Her expectations of him, it turns out, were every bit as high as his of her. She is disappointed in him. She felt, all these years, that his eyes were on her, making her special, encouraging her to succeed. Now she finds that it wasn't really *her,* or not her as she now perceives herself. Now she feels that by being a success she was in a way just serving him, catering to his needs.

She feels betrayed.

Every mentor relationship is designed to end at some point. The young man enters it in order to have an ally and a model for his own growth. Both mentor and mentee understand from the beginning that at some stage the younger man will need to give up his mentor in order to become his own man.

This, of course, is a quite different pattern from the usual father-daughter relationship. Usually, a daughter is given by her father to another man, her husband. She is never meant to grow beyond Daddy and become her own woman.

When and if she does this, her experience may be similar to the one Levinson describes, in which in the process of letting go of his mentor, a young man again has strongly mixed feelings: "bitterness, rancor, grief, abandonment, liberation and rejuvenation. . . ." The mentor seems now to have become like a "tyrannical father or a smothering mother."

These are the feelings Carolyn Rosenthal is experiencing.

Carolyn was allowed to be arrogant, to be aggressive, to be strong and argumentative, and still be feminine. All this was the gift of her father. How special must Daddy be, to be able to give her all that?

Especially when so much of the rest of the world would disallow it.

Now she has begun to see that the warm spotlight of her father's gaze is too small for her. Inside it she feels fuzzy, blurred. Her father can't see *all* of her. She feels angry.

This anger at our fathers leaves us panicked. The more so, the more closely we identify with him.

If he is less than we want him to be, smaller than god-size, then what does our identification with him mean?

If our ability to function in the world, our sense of access, our self-confidence are all, we believe, bestowed as gifts from Daddy, ours by right of association with him, then if he no longer has the power to give them to us, will we still possess them?

Almost, we would deny our own powers, our own identity, to keep Daddy on his pedestal.

Fear of Anger

There are other reasons why we are afraid to feel angry at Daddy.

In the process of becoming Good Girls, we learned to fear a father's anger. We were also afraid of it for the simple reason that he was so much bigger and stronger than we were, or ever would be.

And then we learned early, most of us, that Good Girls don't get angry. You can't smile prettily if you're angry. "Wipe that frown off your face," my father would say. "You'll never catch a man that way."

Yet anger is a strong separating emotion. It can, for instance, lead a Good Girl to assert herself. The child who is allowed to feel her anger and express it learns more about who she is as a person separate from other people.

The child who is coerced into Smiling for Daddy all the time is the more easily going to be confused and intimidated by him, to see his power as overwhelming and to confuse his will with her own. We saw this in the dilemma of Iris, the television producer.

To some extent, most of us are overwhelmed by our fathers. We learn indirection from our mothers and fathers both, and we find that getting around Daddy is much more effective than an angry demand for justice. We not only become doubtful of our right to self-assertion; we learn early that direct self-assertion doesn't get us what we want as often as indirection.

And then there is our fear of our own anger, of that ancient, powerful earth-mother anger we fear we inherit with our femaleness.

We fear our own anger because we carry around with us the memories of what seems to be the immense, destructive power of a woman's rage. When we were infants and small children, this was how it felt to us. As we grow up and identify with that same mother who was inevitably at least occasionally angry with us, we fear we carry within ourselves the same capacity for annihilating other people.

This is the anger that men (who also recall it from infancy) have personified as Medusa, who turned men to stone with a frown. A hero saved mankind from Medusa by cutting off her head and taking it to Zeus, who later gave it to Athena, that archetypal Daddy's Girl, to hang on his shield, which she carried. (So a daughter allies herself with Daddy over and against Mommy and uses a mother's wrath in the service of Daddy.)

In fact, we are much more likely to be paralyzed by our own anger than to paralyze any man with it. It is the strength of anger turned inward that binds us into Good Girlism and, worse, into depression and self-doubt.

The earth-mother anger is part of the earth-mother power that women are supposed to possess. This "power" was, for our mothers, the only compensation they had for Little Me. Indeed, Mrs. Ramsay is the flip side of Little Me. They go together. And it is possible that our mothers may have been the last generation of American women to assume the curious dual role of eternal, dependent daughter to the godlike, all-powerful male and—flip!—the eternal, all-powerful earth-mother to the helpless husband/son. (For the classic depiction of this schizy state from a woman's point of view, read *Diary of a Mad Housewife,* the novel by Sue Kaufman.)

Many of our mothers were skilled at stepping from one role to the other without any apparent break, but the strain of the contradiction at the heart of their situation told in the confusions and mixed messages they passed on to us.

That strain, and those mixed messages, may have been not the least of the many forces working in my generation to produce the eruption of anger that was shaped into feminist consciousness—and feminist consciousness is only, really, an assertion of female selfhood. Letting go of Daddy.

The contradictions in our mothers' lives, and their own confusion, were graphically illustrated by the ways they interpreted Daddy to us.

For instance, one of the women in our little group remembers her father as more emotional than her mother. "He was the one who would cry, or laugh—who would be touched by things. My mother would always say, 'Oh, that's just him. He's not as strong as we women; we can take it much better.'"

This is the classic wife as earth-mother, one-upping Daddy, who has been reduced to the status of little boy.

On the other hand, this same mother had no illusions about her own power in the Outside world. "It's a man's world," she would tell her daughter, "and don't you forget it."

This is the equally classic wife as Little Me, the eternal daughter, resigned (if only partly) to her political and economic dependency on Daddy.

In a static culture, in which things don't change from one generation to the next, or a stable culture in which the rate of change from generation to generation is slow enough to be fairly easily absorbed and integrated, the contradiction in such an interpretation would be useful and even necessary. As long as women had few options, a daughter would need to pay attention to both sides of the message as she assumed her own place in the grownup world.

But in America, and in postindustrial cultures generally, daughters have become critical of the whole set of assumptions that generations of women have lived by. They see clearly that the earth-mother power their mothers claimed, that ancient strength and endurance of women, was no real power at all.

Still, we fear our anger, and men fear it. And for us the ultimate fear is that if we are angry rather than smiling, we will be isolated. Separation feels too complete, too final.

Yet until we do separate from Daddy, let him go, we can't really recognize our own strengths.

We can't, for instance, develop a sense of our own internal authority; become, in our own lives, our own authority. Without this internal authority—call it self-confidence, if you will—we have a hard time assuming any authority in the Outside world: at work, say.

As long as we're Good Girls, we can't claim our own feelings. Especially our anger, the anger that Carolyn Rosenthal finds is a releasing mechanism. As she is experiencing her own anger, she is asserting her own identity, including her own sexuality. There do seem, often, to be corollaries between these things.

Authority, anger, self-assertion, sexuality; it seems at first a list of unmatched items. Authority is a trait or an attribute, anger is a feeling, sexuality a psychobiological aspect of the species, and self-assertion an act.

The first item, authority, has always belonged to Daddy. The last three are all Bad Girl traits.

But we need them all to feel, and be, whole.

To claim our anger does not mean we become perpetually angry—that is a state in which anger controls us. When and if we get through that and learn to harness the energy of our own anger, we can recognize our own power and assert ourselves.

To experience and assert our own sexuality is to assert ourselves, since sexuality is so essential an aspect of self.

To assert ourselves is, simply, to claim our place in the universe.

To assume internal authority is to become, in a way, our own father and mother. To take responsibility for ourselves.

And if Daddy is our chief mentor, we have, finally, to leave him behind if we are ever to own ourselves.

The Integration

When the young man breaks with his mentor, writes Levinson, and the smoke has finally cleared, the anger and bitterness fall away. He "may take the admired qualities of the mentor more fully into himself. . . . The internalization of significant figures is a major source of development in adulthood."

Daddy's double messages may have kept us from internalizing him, rather than the mirror image he has shown us of the feminine person he wants us to be.

But if we don't internalize Daddy, we will never go beyond him.

That, ultimately, is what going beyond him means. We don't step off into darkness and isolation. Rather, we take the parts of him we admire and want to keep, and integrate them into our own identities. Daddy becomes part of us, instead of the other way around.

Even when a father like Jack Rosenthal allows his daughter to identify with him and adapt his qualities to a feminine identity, it seems she may still have to go through a separation process, a sorting out of who she is and who he is. This process is bound to be accompanied by disappointment and anger, but only after we have gone through it can we be said to have integrated Daddy into our own identity. To have become our own woman.

When Iris the would-be television producer returned to her husband, it looked like defeat for her dreams of separateness and growth; but in reality it was part of the growth process. She and her husband have worked out a compromise in which he accepts her need to pursue her career during the week, and she accepts his need for a close family life by devoting weekends to him.

Their teenage daughter, meanwhile, is moving increasingly off on her own, as teenage daughters will. One direction in which she is moving is to the city, where she has enrolled in dance classes. Before her mother's temporary defection, "the city" was for her, as it is for most suburban children, a foreign and frightening place. The fact that her father's insurance agency was in the suburbs had further located her sense of place firmly outside the city. Doubtless it had also made him feel more threatened by his wife's forays into the city than he might have been if he worked there.

In this case, Iris's insistence on broadening her own identity beyond home and family has opened up her daughter's horizons and increased *her* sense of options for the future. The husband and father, on the other hand, was a conservative force in all this, resistant to change.

If you were brought up, as I was, with the traditional notion (one that still permeates sociology and psychology) that man is the adventurer, the risk-taker, while woman is the conservator of values, the homebody who fears all change, this observation is startling. In fact, women have been the risk-takers and change-agents in this society for some time now, while Daddies always, within the family, have been the conservatives. They have been the conservators of the values of the larger society, the layers down of the law. That is part of their role as anchor.

And, of course, this role has been one of the things that makes it so hard for us to let go of them.

Getting to Know Daddy at Last

One of the good things that can happen when we grow up is that we finally establish a relationship with Daddy.

This isn't always possible. In my small group, it proved too late for all but one of us. When we were younger, our fathers were working; and then we moved away to college, to marriage, to new lives. Now we are ready to get to know them at last. But our fathers have all died too young, of heart attacks, of cancer, as fathers so often do in America. They were older than we are now but not, we suddenly realize, so much older. My father was sixty-three, an age far away for me but not out of sight.

Jess still has her father, a gentle, feckless man, a scholar. He and her mother live in Arizona and recently, while she was visiting them, she got into a fight with her father for the first time in memory. Her own fight. She is thirty-eight; she has two teenage children and has just gotten her Ph.D. But she had never had a fight with her father because her mother always intervened to deflect the anger and smooth things over.

This time her mother said, "Sh-sh-sh—don't start with your father." But Jess did, anyhow. She and her father actually raised their voices to each other.

The reason for the fight wasn't important, some ancient, never-acknowledged tension about which one of them was habitually late, but the confrontation gave Jess a new sense of power. Of her own power as a woman, able to express her anger with her father at last, with this man who had been kept out of reach by her mother, who owned him and who defined him to Jess as weak and vulnerable, a man of whom not much was to be expected.

He had not been good at earning money. Jess's mother had done that, but she hadn't been able to focus her considerable talents in any satisfying way. She held a succession of jobs, each of them temporary, filling in until Jess's father would at last make a success and she could quit work and be what she ought to be, a wife and mother.

The trouble was, Jess's father never did do what, as a man, he was supposed to do. So, says Jess, "My mother was humiliated because she had to be so aggressive. She used to tease him. I was mortified. He was a very emotional man, he cried easily. He always felt he had a right to those feelings, but my mother disapproved; she thought he was weak." So Jess, through her mother, learned to see her father as "very emotional, weak, temperamental and selfish, exactly the way women are usually portrayed."

Now she is moving away from the image of a man who was bound to disappoint, of whom her mother had said, "Whatever a man does surprises you because you expect less." And she is finding that "my father had a little more substance than I thought. He writes poetry, he's a romantic, he speaks several languages."

Leaning toward her mother's side of the Identity Triangle, Jess had made sure to marry a workaholic who would earn a lot of money.

Yet this daughter of a working mother and a "disappointing" father is finding, now that she has launched herself on a full-time career and shows every promise of success, that it is her view of her father that has changed. Jess's mother, trapped and unhappy in the old role, the one that says the man must be the provider and the woman dependent, could only be dissatisfied with her husband. Jess, having finally grown out of Little Me and discovered that she is capable of a serious professional career of her own, can accept her father for his charming qualities, and see his serious, scholarly side as well.

She couldn't do this until she herself became a scholar, certified complete with Ph.D. Then, having crossed over, so to speak, into her father's world, she could see him with more sympathy.

This is the opposite of Carolyn Rosenthal's process: she started out on her father's side of the fence, and has only begun to see her mother later in life. She is also beginning to have a more realistic view of her father; he had to be brought down from his pedestal.

Interestingly enough, her mother, whom Carolyn wished not to be like, had herself put Carolyn's father on a pedestal. A woman of intelligence, energy, and talent, she withdrew completely from Carolyn's discussions with Jack. In this family she was the scholar and the less "worldly" person.

Carolyn's mother only blossomed, apparently, in a setting away from her family. With her husband, she never did manage to grow beyond Little Me; the shadow of her father, of the years in which the pattern of deference to him became ingrained, was too strong.

It was natural for someone in our small group to observe very early in our discussion that we really couldn't talk about our fathers without talking about our mothers. Someone else pointed out that if we had started the evening talking about our mothers, our fathers might never have come up at all.

Real intimacy between fathers and daughters may be difficult to achieve. Most men only become intimate with their wives, their sexual partners. And then again, many men don't have a lot of intimacy in them. They are far too passive, emotionally, far too conditioned to the patterns of the masculine world, where a kind of emotional neutrality, an emphasis on the surface of things-as-they-are, a focus on process in the real world rather than feelings makes for an easy geniality but not a lot of depth.

And yet, as we get to know our fathers, we also get to know ourselves. I am finding my father in the only way left to me—recollection from a new vantage point. But the recollection has itself changed me, forced me to see both him and myself in a new way.

Perhaps most importantly, it has made me accept him. This is something I spent half a lifetime saying I would never do, because I assumed that to accept my father, with all his rigidity and rage, would mean I would become just like him.

In fact, I was more like him while I resented him, worshipped his power, and refused to accept the fact that I was disappointed in him.

I so much wanted him to be my hero, but it turns out he wasn't even a very nice man. And yet I loved him. And love him still. Our attachment was passionate—perhaps the more so for the contradictions in him, the weakness that made him reject me, but also, in the end, made him more human.

He was a powerfully seductive man, and he lied to me. The world is not the way he said it was, and I am not the person he tried to make me out to be.

And yet. When I think of him standing there in the photograph on the teak deck of that motorboat, in his Al Capone hat and his pinstripe suit, part of me wants to be his dizzy blonde, perched on the rail, with my stockings rolled at the knees.

And part of me has become very much *his* ideal, the tough-minded American pragmatist.

I will always answer to certain smells: Mennen Skin Bracer and a good briar pipe. I will always be susceptible to the sensual pleasures of men's shoes, of pigskin wallets, of gray felt fedora hats and gray flannel vests.

Because I was, when all is said and done, a Daddy's Girl, I will always be different from women who were Mother's girls, who were never taught to shoot a rifle by their father or never filled his pipe when they were little girls. My natural empathics are with men. I am more at home around large-bodied males in tweeds and corduroys than around small, feminine women.

My brothers, too, are implicated in these tastes, and yet they each bore, one way or another, the stamp of my father.

Wallets and vests are superficial items, easily sentimentalized. They don't quite cover the gaps, the failure to understand, the arbitrary dicta, the sometime brutal rejections.

Here is a different kind of father, a newer one. His daughter is four years old: "I have always tried to be straight with her, I tell her. If I'm saddened by something she does or says, I tell her. It's a nice give-and-take kind of thing. She'll ask, 'Are you serious at me?' I'll say Yes, and tell her. She'll listen, and there'll be a little negotiation.

"I didn't know she would have this capacity. My parents were always threatening me. My father was a punisher. He was a hitter."

I will never know whether my father made such discoveries with me. I doubt if he did, because he belonged to a generation, and was of a temperament, that was more concerned with maintaining the right image, and a proper distance between the sexes and the generations. So there will always be sadness at the core of my feelings about my father, as well as an edge of anger. Some things shouldn't be forgiven.

But if I don't forgive him, how can I ever forgive myself?

The edge of his judgments still preys on me. Because of him, there are areas of femininity that may forever be uncertain ground for me.

And yet, because of him I will survive. He had what my Pennsylvania grandmother would have called backbone. He kept on driving forward, even in the defeat of his dreams. So I add a certain gallantry to that image in the photograph, and I begin to flesh it out to someone I can live with, since he will, after all, live on in me.

"She's a really sensuous little beast," the young father tells me. "Everyone says it about her. I and everyone else thought if I had a daughter, she would be a tomboy. I was a laborer before I went to college, although

I never really fit in with the macho pattern. I don't mind doing dishes but I never saw myself taking my daughter to the shoe store to buy little white shoes. Kids should wear kid clothes. So I take her to the shoe store and she says, 'Daddy, I want those,' and we come home with Mary Janes. What are you going to do?"

My father loved to see me in Mary Janes. I hated them. I wanted to be a boy. Yet I remember flirting with him, and loving every minute of it.

What contradictions we contain!

"I never felt all that attractive until she was born," says the father of the four-year-old. "People are always saying how pretty she is, and that she looks like me. It's flattering." He had worn a beard, out of shyness, for fifteen years. One day his daughter said, " 'My Daddy doesn't have a face, he has a beard.' So I shaved my beard." That was the same year he was accepted into a difficult postgraduate program and received a grant as well.

For him, the birth of a daughter began a period of growth, of self-discovery, because he has been able to identify himself in her.

My father feared that self-knowledge; his fear made him reject me rather than grow.

For that, I can feel sorrier, at last, for him than for myself. I am one of the lucky ones. I've had a chance to grow, and some stubborn seed in me, from whatever ancestor—maybe my Norwegian grandmother, who got on the boat at seventeen to come to America—has urged me on to take the chance.

My father's death was not pretty. After he collapsed on the street one bright July day, he was tied up with tubes at every orifice and laid on a table in the intensive-care unit. Summoned from the beach, I came resentful and frightened to his side in a bright purple and orange summer dress my stepmother thought a scandal. I didn't think he should have interrupted my summer romance. As always, he was upstaging me.

I spoke to him, briefly. He looked at me, but I don't know whether he saw me. Every so often his body twitched. The tubes breathed.

I walked back to their apartment slowly, through side streets, looking in the windows of herbalists and apothecaries and palm readers, looking for some sign of my feelings.

He died that night, of a second massive coronary aneurysm. I helped choose the coffin, walked my stepmother back up the aisle after the funeral, where I was astonished to find how many friends he had had. Men came from the railroad, from his old army unit, from his Masonic Lodge. In his last years he had not, I thought, been very sociable; here was a whole lifetime of sociability with men that had been hidden from me.

I was suddenly proud to have been his daughter.

It was years before I knew what I felt. Mainly, I thought, I felt lingering anger at him, and relief that he was gone. I agreed with Virginia Woolf, who once remarked that if her father hadn't died she never would have written anything.

But now I know what frightened me that day in the intensive-care unit. My father was helpless. The look he gave me contained, I think, frustration and rage at his condition. That impatience may have been responsible for the second aneurysm.

It has taken me nearly sixteen years to be able to recognize that my father was helpless, and to accept it. With the acceptance, writing this, I have cried, for him and for myself and for all the chances that were missed between us.

I have also had a recurring image, or fantasy, while writing this book—one that although certainly "unfeminine" is, I think, healthy.

My father and I are in a boxing ring, going at it head-to-head toe-to-toe, and I am holding my own.

It is an exhilarating image, because it means I am as big as my father and I am questioning the validity of his authority. I am challenging him. I am the young challenger, at last.

Other women have told me that as they became ambitious and more self-confident, they discovered in themselves feelings of competition with their fathers. Knocking the old man off, as a son would.

Except not as a son would.

In order to have the fantasy, I have to see myself as a person who is as strong as my father. Of course I would not be physically as strong as he if he were alive and in his prime. But in the image lies the conviction that a woman, myself, can be as strong as any man in character, in strength of will and purpose.

Boxing is a supremely aggressive sport, and it is appropriate that my image of asserting myself against my father's authority—which was, for me, always arbitrary and overpowering—should be such an aggressive one.

Some readers may have trouble accepting this image because it is so "unfeminine." But then, so was working up a sweat by jogging in gym shorts and a T-shirt until a few years ago.

It is too bad that the idea of standing up for yourself, of holding your own, should still be considered in any way "unfeminine," that femininity so much still suggests compliance, submission, obedience.

I think the father of the four-year-old, who shaved off his beard so his daughter could see his face, will raise a daughter who is both feminine and tough enough to do whatever boxing she needs to do for herself.

And I like to think that at the end of my fantasy boxing match, my father and I will hug each other, and flirt a little, and he will take me out for lunch. And after lunch he will sip his favorite Benedictine-and-Brandy and smoke a fine Havana cigar.

Notes

CHAPTER ONE

13 Simone de Beauvoir, *The Second Sex*, trans. and ed. by H. M. Parshley (New York: The Modern Library, Knopf, 1968), 287.

13 Part of it comes, quite simply, from his scarcity: See Michael E. Lamb, Margaret Tresch Owen, and Lindsay Chase-Lansdale, "The Father-Daughter Relationship: Past, Present, and Future," in Claire B. Kopp, ed., *Becoming Female: Perspectives on Development* (New York: Plenum Press, 1979), 89–112 (hereafter cited as Lamb, *et al.*, 1979).

13 "As a rule his work": De Beauvoir, *The Second Sex*, 287.

17 ... the symbiotic bliss of the first few months of life.... : For this and all references to symbiosis and the separation-individuation process, see Margaret S. Mahler, Fred Pine, and Anni Bergman, *The Psychological Birth of the Human Infant* (New York: Basic Books, 1975).

17 The things that make our mother physically different from our father.... ; He came and went frequently.... : The importance of the father's difference from the mother, as perceived by the infant and toddler, was first suggested to me by Dr. Sylvia Brody in an interview on June 10, 1980, and also by Dr. John Munder Ross in an interview on June 13, 1980 (hereafter cited as Brody, int. and Ross, int.). The father's lesser comprehension of our cries, however, is my own observation.

17 ... more likely to roughhouse with us: See Lamb, *et al.,* 1979.

18 ... to trust ourselves and our independence: This concept was suggested to me by Dr. Lora Heims Tessman in two telephone interviews on June 8 and August 10, 1980 (hereafter cited as Tessman, int.).

18 De Beauvoir, *The Second Sex*, 287.

18 Unable to identify.... : The daughter's dilemma of identification was partly articulated by Ross, int.; the central importance of the daughter's alliance with her father as a means of separating from her mother is my own insight, interpretation, and conclusion, based on the whole range of my research.

CHAPTER TWO

21 *Santa Claus Is Comin' to Town:* Haven Gillespie and J. Fred Coots (Leo Feist, Inc., copyright 1934, 1962).

22 He would set up little temptations.... : Martha Saxton, *Louisa May: A Modern Bi-*

ography of Louisa May Alcott (Boston: Houghton Mifflin, 1977; all citations to paperback ed., New York: Avon, 1978), 101.

22 "Give up your want to Father's. . . .": Madelon Bedell, *The Alcotts: The Biography of a Family,* Vol. 1 (New York: Clarkson N. Potter, 1980), 80.

22 "Louisa required authoritative measures. . . .": Saxton, *Louisa May,* 100.

27 "Family members must adapt. . . .": Leonard Benson, *Fatherhood: A Sociological Perspective* (New York: Random House, 1968), 19.

28 Fathers: A Brief History: Except where specified, most of the information on primates and other animal species in this section comes from William E. Redican, "Adult Male-Infant Interactions in Nonhuman Primates," in Michael E. Lamb, ed., *The Role of the Father in Child Development,* Wiley Series on Personality Processes (New York: John Wiley, 1976), 345–385. (Hereafter cited as Redican.) See also William E. Redican and David M. Taub, "Male Parental Care in Monkeys and Apes," in Michael E. Lamb, ed., *The Role of the Father in Child Development,* 2nd ed. (1981), 203–258. (These editions are hereafter cited as Lamb, 1976, and Lamb, 1981.)

28 Except where specified, some animal data and the post–hunting-hypothesis information on evolution and primitive man in this section comes from Mary Maxwell West and Melvin J. Konner, "The Role of the Father: An Anthropological Perspective," in Lamb, 1976, 157–184. (Hereafter cited as West–Konner.) See also Mary Maxwell Katz and Konner, "The Role of the Father: An Anthropological Perspective," in Lamb, 1981, 155–186. The bottom line of fathering. . . . : list derived from Redican and West–Konner.

29 . . . book after book assured us. . . . : See, for example, Robert Ardrey, *African Genesis* (New York: Atheneum, 1961; all citations to paperback ed., New York: Dell, 1967); Lionel Tiger, *Men in Groups* (New York: Random House, 1971); and Lionel Tiger and Robin Fox, *The Imperial Animal* (New York: Holt, Rinehart & Winston, 1974; all citations to paperback ed., New York: Dell, 1974).

29 Betty Friedan, *The Feminine Mystique* (New York: W. W. Norton, 1963).

29 Eleanor Emmons Maccoby and Carol Nagy Jacklin, *The Psychology of Sex Differences* (Stanford, Calif.: Stanford University Press, 1974), 352.

29 From observations of baboons. . . . : See, for example, Ardrey, *African Genesis;* Tiger and Fox, *The Imperial Animal, passim.*

30 . . . the all-male group is a dominance hierarchy: See Ardrey, *African Genesis,* 13 and *passim;* Tiger and Fox, *The Imperial Animal,* 43ff.

30 . . . dominant females . . . defer to . . . adult males: See Jane van Lawick-Goodall, *In the Shadow of Man* (Boston: Houghton Mifflin, 1971; paperback ed., New York: Dell, 1972), 133.

30 "sexual selection": See Ardrey, *African Genesis,* 130; Helen E. Fisher, *The Sex Contract* (New York: William Morrow, 1981); Tiger and Fox, *The Imperial Animal,* 114, and Redican.

30 . . . size, strength and weapons. . . . : See Redican.

31 . . . to suit the requirements of different environments. . . . : See West–Konner.

31 . . . our cousins, the apes, are also large. . . . : See Redican.

31 . . . the rhesus macaque. *Ibid.*

32 Jane Goodall, *In the Shadow of Man,* 192, 194, 118, 199ff, 193.

32 West and Konner: See note at beginning of this section.

32 So were the ancient tribesmen. . . . : These conclusions are my own.

34 Freud . . . decreed that women and the family represented instincts. . . . : Sigmund Freud, *Civilization and Its Discontents,* International Psycho-Analytical Library, ed. Ernest Jones (London: The Hogarth Press and the Institute of Psycho-Analysis, 1957), 73.

34 Talcott Parsons declared that women are "expressive.". . . : See Talcott Parsons and R. F. Bales, *Family, Socialization and Interaction Process* (Glencoe, Ill.: Free Press, 1955), *passim.*

36 Alexis de Tocqueville, *Democracy in America*, ed. J. P. Mayer and Max Lerner, trans. George Lawrence (New York: Harper & Row, 1966; first published 1835), 525, 568.

36 Frances Trollope, *Domestic Manners of the Americans* (New York: Knopf, 1949; first published 1832), 156.

37 de Tocqueville, *Democracy in America*, 565ff. Trollope, *Domestic Manners*, 156, 138. Harriet Martineau, *Society in America*, two volumes in one (Paris: Baudry's European Library, 1842), Vol. II, 157, 148.

38 Harriet Martineau, *Society in America*, 156.

38 Edith Wharton, *The Custom of the Country* (New York: Scribner's, 1913), 207.

40 Saxton, *Louisa May*, 14.

Blaise

57 I received many ideas for interpretation from Judith Herman and Lisa Hirschman, "Father-Daughter Incest," *Signs* 2:4 (Summer 1977), 735–756.

57 The tension between them gets expressed. . . . : Brody, int.

58 Tiger and Fox, *The Imperial Animal*, 146.

59 Susan Brownmiller, *Against Our Will* (New York: Simon & Schuster, 1975).

60 One current rationalization for incest. . . . : See, for example, James W. Ramey, "Dealing with the Last Taboo," SIECUS Report VII:5 (May 1979); Benjamin de Mott, "The Pro-Incest Lobby," *Psychology Today* (March 1980).

Abby and Calvin Bartlett

65 "desexualized affection": Marjorie Leonard, "Fathers and Daughters," *International Journal of Psycho-Analysis*, 47 (1966), 323–334.

CHAPTER THREE

page

74 "the boys will be very interested. . . .": Ross, int.

74 A daughter's heterosexual eroticism. . . . : Tessman, int.

75 "add the father to her repertoire": *Ibid.*

75 "inner-genital," "active loving exuberance": *Ibid.*

76 . . . all men . . . want . . . sons: Ross, int.

76 "on his own history. . . .": *Ibid.*

77 points out Dr. Tessman: int.

77 . . . to "avoid or disparage" her. . . . : Ross, int.

77 In studies, homosexual women have described. . . . : Henry Biller, "The Father and Personality Development: Paternal Deprivation and Sex-Role Development," in Lamb, 1976, 89–156. See also Henry Biller, "The Father and Sex-Role Development," in Lamb, 1981, 319–358 (hereafter cited as Henry Biller in Lamb 1976, and "Father and Sex Role").

77 Recent evidence also shows. . . . : *New York Times* (Jan. 26, 1982).

77 "In general," writes Henry Biller: In Lamb, 1976, "Father and Sex Role," Lamb, 1981.

78 Not incidentally, the kind of fathering. . . . : Ross, int.

78 "Fathers exhibit themselves. . . . : Ross, int.

79 David Finklehor, *Sexually Victimized Children* (New York: Macmillan, 1979): two peak periods. . . . : 60; 530 women college students. . . . : 42–43; Nearly one-fifth. . . . : 53; *over half of those by adult men.* . . . : 55; less than a tenth. . . . : 53. Other estimates of sexual abuse. . . . : See Florence Rush, *The Best Kept Secret: Sexual Abuse of Children* (Englewood Cliffs, N.J.: Prentice-Hall, 1980), 4–5.

79 Eighty-three percent of the boys' experience. . . . : Finklehor, 58.

79 . . . a little over 1 percent. . . . ; "three quarters of a million. . . .": *Ibid.*, 88; 39 percent of all the incest. . . . : 89; . . . *almost half of these brothers.* . . . : 55; . . . *not one* of Finklehor's college men. . . . : 93; "For girls . . . the family. . . .": 88.

On incest: See also Judith Herman, *Father-Daughter Incest* (Cambridge, Mass.: Harvard University Press, 1981).

80 Indeed, as scholars have begun to point out. . . . : Ralph Blumenthal, "Did Freud's Isolation, Peer Rejection Prompt Key Theory Reversal?" *New York Times* (Aug. 25, 1981); Florence Rush, *The Best Kept Secret,* 80–103.

80 . . . male dominance is a big factor: Herman and Hirschman, "Father-Daughter Incest."

80 . . . one kind of bond. . . . : Fox and Tiger, *The Imperial Animal,* 145.

80 The dominance of males over females. . . . : *Ibid.,* 146.

Fran Nobile

89 One survey of successful men. . . . : Jane Adams, *Making Good: Conversations with Successful Men* (New York: William Morrow, 1981), 71.

89 George Gilder, "Playboy Interview," *Playboy* (August 1981).

96 . . . this reliability, this trust: Henry Biller in Lamb, 1976.

97 He wanted her to retire from all that. . . . : See Letter #28, Nov. 15, 1883, in *The Letters of Sigmund Freud,* ed. Ernstl Freud, trans. Tania and James Stern (New York, Basic Books, 1960), 74–76.

Holly Flax

101 Children . . . become more like the parent who is more dominant: E. Mavis Hetherington, "A Developmental Study of the Effects of Sex of the Dominant Parent on Sex-Role Preference, Identification, and Imitation in Children," *Journal of Personality and Social Psychology,* 4 (1966) 119–125.

105 She did instead what studies have shown is common. . . . : See Lamb *et al.,* 1979.

Steve, Alicia and Patty Appleman

115 . . . as an analyst pointed out to me. . . . : Dr. Marjorie Taggart White, personal communication.

The Pygmalion Syndrome

121 Walter Toman, *Family Constellation,* 2nd ed. (New York: Springer, 1969), 129, 132.

122 Ann Roiphe, "Daddy's Girls: Women Who Win," *Vogue* (October 1980).

124 Virginia Woolf, *To the Lighthouse* (New York: Harcourt Brace, 1927; all citations to Harvest paperback ed., New York, Harcourt Brace); "the whole of the effort of merging and flowing. . .": *Ibid.,* 126.

124 "wedge-shaped core of darkness. . . .": *Ibid.,* 95ff.; ". . . the thigh bones, the ribs. . . ": 137, Mr. Ramsay comes upon Lily. . . . : 225ff.; "an odd-shaped triangular shadow. . . .": 299–300.

CHAPTER FOUR

page

131 *The Identity Triangle:* Psychoanalysts have been writing about the importance of Daddy as the Outside man in a triangle, beckoning a child away from Mother and out into the world, for a number of years. More recently, they have come to see him as an important figure of identification for girls as well as boys. Some psychologists, too, have seen the early importance of the father as an exciting other person. T. Berry Brazelton: presentation at the 12th Annual Margaret S. Mahler Symposium, Philadelphia (1981).

131 Dr. Ernest Abelin has been developing his theory of early triangulation for many years; his ideas are summarized by Dr. John Munder Ross in "Fathering: A Review of Some Psychoanalytic Contributions on Paternity," *International Journal of Psycho-Analysis*, 60 (1979), 317–327 (hereafter cited as "Fathering"). See also Ernest L. Abelin, "Triangulation: The Role of the Father and the Origins of Core Gender Identity During the Rapprochement Subphase," in *Rapprochement*, eds. R. Lax, A. Burland, and S. Bach (New York: Jason Aronson, 1980; hereafter cited as "Triangulation").

131 Dr. Phyllis Greenacre, cited in John Munder Ross, "Paternal Identity: The Equations of Fatherhood and Manhood," in Toksoz B. Karasu and Charles W. Socarides, eds., *On Sexuality: Psychoanalytic Observations* (New York: International Universities Press, 1979), 73–97. See also Ross, "Fathering," for a review of Dr. Greenacre's other writing on the subject.

In addition, Dr. Margaret Mahler wrote about the father as the "knight in shining armor" in an unpublished manuscript (1966) cited by Dr. Abelin in "Triangulation." See also Margaret Mahler, "Aggression in the Service of Separation-Individuation: Case Study of a Mother-Daughter Relationship," *Psychoanalytic Quarterly*, L:4 (1981), 625–638, for an important statement about a daughter's selective identification with her father in the early Triangle.

To my knowledge, Helene Deutsch is the only person who has written about the lifelong tendency of girls and women to form relational triangles. This was first brought to my attention by Dr. Nancy Chodorow in *The Reproduction of Mothering: Psychoanalysis and the Sociology of Gender* (Berkeley and Los Angeles: University of California Press, 1978). See Helene Deutsch, *The Psychology of Women*, Vol. I (New York: Grune & Stratton, 1944).

131 The full-fledged toddler begins, explains Dr. John Ross. . . . : Ross, int.

131 The concept of "disidentification" I first found in Abelin, "Triangulation."

133 "It does seem, for whatever reason. . . .": Ross, int.

133 The need to enjoy Daddy, says Dr. Ross. . . : *Ibid.*

133 *But does he also validate our autonomy?*: See Margaret Hennig and Anne Jardim, *The Managerial Woman* (New York: Doubleday, 1977; all citations to paperback ed., New York: Pocket Books, 1978), 75.

134 reciprocal identification: See Lamb, *et al.*, 1979. Lamb and his colleagues described this idea as "reciprocal role learning." See also Biller, "Father and Sex Role," in Lamb, 1981.

134 This is not a brand-new idea, but it reemerged. . . . Lamb, *et al.*, 1979.

134 Helene Deutsch, *Psychology of Women, passim.*

134 A little later . . . we are mothering dolls: See Abelin, "Triangulation."

135 . . . his "controllable ideal little girl": Tessman, int.

135 Dr. Lamb writes of a 1974 study. . . . : This and the reference immediately following from Lamb, *et al.*, 1979.

135 By two, for instance, most boys choose. . . . : *Ibid.*

136 He describes a father. . . . : John Munder Ross, "The Forgotten Father," in Marie Coleman Nelson and Jean Ikenberry, eds., *Psychosexual Imperatives: Their Role in Identity Formation* (New York: Human Sciences Press, 1979), 261–303.

136 "We have seen that children of both sexes. . . .": Deutsch, *Psychology of Women,* 251.

136 "In learning situations. . . .": Lamb, *et al.,* 1979.

137 *Heterosexual Femininity*: Dr. Miriam M. Johnson, "Fathers, Mothers and Sex Typing," *Sociological Inquiry,* 45:1 (1975), 12–16. The detailed expansion of the concept of heterosexual femininity that follows is entirely my own. See also Johnson, "Sex Role Learning in the Nuclear Family," *Child Development,* 34 (1963), 319–333.

138 Helene Deutsch has pointed out. . . . : In *Psychology of Women.*

139 Girls who grow up without fathers don't have trouble with this aspect of femininity. . . . : E. Mavis Hetherington, "Effects of Father Absence on Personality Development in Adolescent Daughters," *Developmental Psychology,* 7 (1972), 313–326. See also E. Mavis Hetherington, "Girls Without Fathers," *Psychology Today* (February 1973), 47–52.

146 Colette: Robert Phelps, ed., *Colette, Earthly Paradise* (New York: Farrar, Straus, 1966).

146 This might well be one explanation for women's "fear of success". . . . : Matina Horner, "Fail, Bright Women," *Psychology Today* (February 1973), 47–52.

146 Mothers who work, and who enjoy work . . . and studies have shown. . . . : See Lois Wladis Hoffman, "Changes in Family Roles, Socialization, and Sex Differences," *American Psychologist* (August 1977), 644–656.

147 A large study of preschoolers and their fathers. . . . : Norma Radin, "The Role of the Father in Cognitive, Academic, and Intellectual Development," in Lamb, 1976, 237–276. See also Norma Radin in Lamb, 1981, 379–428.

147 Dr. Lamb, who reports the same study. . . . : Lamb, *et al.,* 1979.

147 In 1981 the *New York Times.* . . . : Rochelle Semmel Albin, "Has Feminism Aided Mental Health?", *New York Times* (June 15, 1981).

148 Rosabeth Moss Kanter, *Men and Women of the Corporation* (New York: Basic Books, 1979), 184.

148 And, in fact, a 1979 study of depression. . . . : J. Conrad Schwartz and David C. Zuroff, "Family Structure and Depression in Female College Students: Effects of Parental Conflict, Decision-Making, Power, and Inconsistency of Love," *Journal of Abnormal Psychology,* 88 (1979), 398–406.

CHAPTER FIVE

page

153 Robin Morgan, *Going Too Far: The Personal Account of a Feminist* (New York, Random House, 1977).

153 But, according to Maccoby. . . . : Maccoby and Jacklin, *Psychology of Sex Differences,* 353–354.

153 L. Kohlberg and R. Kramer, "Continuities and Discontinuities in Childhood and Adult Moral Development," *Human Development,* 12 (1969), 93–120.

153 Freud claimed. . . . : As described by Ross, int.

154 Nancy Chodorow, *The Reproduction of Mothering;* see note p. 000.

155 If this sounds strange, consider that retired widowers. . . . : Joel Greenberg, "Married People and Widows Found to Outlive Widowers," *New York Times* (July 31, 1981).

156 Jane Adams, *Making Good,* 34–35.

156 Gail Sheehy, "Introducing the Postponing Generation," *Esquire* (October 1979).

164 Edith Jacobson, *The Self and the Object World* (New York: International Universities Press, 1964); and Helene Deutsch, *Psychology of Women.* Both cited in Lora Heims Tessman, *Children of Parting Parents* (New York: Jason Aronson, 1978), 77.

167 a spinster became, in English law. . . . : See *The American Heritage Dictionary of the English Language* (Boston: Houghton Mifflin, 1978).

167 "that sisterhood called disappointed women": Saxton, *Louisa May,* 307.

168 Ralph Waldo Emerson, "Self-Reliance," *Essays: First Series.* Vol. II (Boston, Houghton Mifflin, Riverside Edition, 1903).

168 He, too, had a daughter—but she was devoted to him: *Ibid.,* 352.

Sally Archway

175 Hennig and Jardim, *The Managerial Woman,* 100.

177 *Ibid.,* 101ff.

177 . . . her father did not *expect* her to be . . . a winner: See *ibid.,* 103.

177 This distance, this mutual autonomy. . . . : See Lamb, *et al,* 1979.

185 But once you have achieved your ego ideal. . . . : I am indebted for this entire idea to Hennig and Jardim. They discuss resolution of the conflict between work and private life in terms of roles, whereas I have applied my concept of the Identity Triangle to similar situations and discuss resolution in terms of identifications with Mother and Father. The use of the term "ego ideal" in this context is also my own. See Hennig and Jardim, 164ff. Also 106, 127–128, 131.

185 . . . embodied the image of the nurturing . . . woman: *Ibid.,* 105.

185 . . . like asexual "automatons": *Ibid.,* 170.

185 "moratorium": *Ibid.,* 169. See 164ff. for full discussion, 165 for what conflict meant.

186 . . . half of them married widowers. . . . : Ibid., 173.

Carolyn Rosenthal

192 . . . feeling entirely secure in their fathers' affections. . . . : *Ibid.,* 125.

193 . . . saw their mothers as rather vague figures, too: *Ibid.,* 105.

CHAPTER SIX

page

201 This entire chapter draws principally on the work of Margaret Hennig and Anne Jardim in *The Managerial Woman.*

201 . . . a highly specialized group. . . . : Hennig and Jardim, 100.

201 . . . an earlier study by Margaret Hennig and Barbara Hackman Franklin. . . . : *Ibid.,* 99.

202 Several studies have shown that when a mother works. . . . : See Hoffman, "Changes in Family Roles," L. W. Hoffman and F. I. Nye, *Working Mothers* (San Francisco: Jossey-Bass, 1974).

202 Sandra Schwartz Tangri, "Determinants of Occupational Role Innovation among College Women," in M. S. Mednick, ed., *Women and Achievement: Social and Motivational Issues* (New York: Halsted Press, 1975), 255–272.

202 And an Israeli study has shown. . . . : Cited in Marjorie Lozoff, "Fathers and Autonomy in Women," in Ruth B. Kundsin, ed., *Women and Success: The Anatomy of Achievement* (New York: William Morrow, 1974), 103–109.

203 Hennig and Jardim's executives had a great many such conflicts. . . . : Hennig and Jardim, 170ff.
206 But what if . . . he takes us with him into his world?: *Ibid.*, 105.
207 The Hennig–Jardim executives had also been welcomed. . . . : *Ibid.*, 99ff.
207 Their first jobs were, in effect, privileges. . . . : *Ibid.*, 149.
207 . . . each woman's boss became a "sales agent". . . . : *Ibid.*, 157.
208 "I really have to thank Jim. . . .": *Ibid.*
208 "read what you like": Leon Edel, *Bloomsbury: A House of Lions* (Philadelphia: Lippincott, 1979), 91–92.
209 . . . confirmation that we have what it takes. . . . : The idea of confirmation was suggested by Jane Adams, *Making Good,* 37ff. See also Hennig and Jardim, 106, 117, 165.
209 . . . a father's attitude can be crucial. . . . : Hennig and Jardim, 165 and *passim.*
210 Jane Adams, *Women on Top: Success Patterns and Personal Fulfillment* (New York: Dutton, 1979), cited in *Making Good,* 255.
210 When she turned to successful men. . . . : Jane Adams, *Making Good,* 37ff, 42.
210 *The Tools of Success*: see Hennig and Jardim, 109, 117.
211 Jane Adams reports. . . . : *Making Good,* 44.
212 Tessman, int.
214 Marjorie Lozoff, "Fathers and Autonomy in Women."
214 Jack Block, Anna von der Lippe, and Jeanne H. Block, "Sex-Role and Socializations Patterns: Some Personality Concomitants and Environmental Antecedents," *Journal of Consulting and Clinical Psychology,* 41:3 (1973), 321–341.
215 Is Daddy Enough?: Phrase suggested by Marjorie Lozoff, "Fathers and Autonomy in Women."
216 . . . when Hennig and Jardim interviewed. . . . : 21ff.
216 "organizational environment": *Ibid.,* 26.
216 Men have been learning to think about the "organizational environment." . . . : See Hennig and Jardim, 45, 79.
216 Maccoby and Jacklin, *Psychology of Sex Differences,* 353–354. See also Hennig and Jardim, 78–79. Hennig and Jardim develop a very similar idea here, but the idea that the Identity Triangle is central to girls' identity is my own.
217 "a sense of the organizational environment," "individual self-improvement," "waiting to be chosen": Hennig and Jardim, 31.
218 " 'queen bee' status": Hennig and Jardim, 177.
218 Daniel J. Levinson, *The Seasons of a Man's Life* (New York: Knopf, 1975), 97.
218 *Men and Women Learning Together: A Study of College Students in the Late 70's: Report of the Brown Project* (Providence, R.I.: Brown University, 1980).
219 . . . and discover that five-year leaves are simply not compatible. . . . : Memo on the Brown Project, Felice N. Schwartz, President, Catalyst, New York City.
219 Their bosses had been promoted far beyond them. . . . : Hennig and Jardim, 166ff.
220 "whole": *Ibid.,* 174.
220 "to discover that I existed. . . . : *Ibid.,* 173.
220 *"saw themselves as capable of moving toward the highest management levels.* . . . : *Ibid.,* 174.
220 . . . they all went on to become presidents or vice-presidents: *Ibid.,* 177.
220 . . . the executive, like her peers, could stand whole and individual. . . . : *Ibid.,* 174.
220 . . . once she had resolved her internal conflicts. . . . : *Ibid.,* 170ff. Hennig and Jardim discuss conflict resolution in terms of roles, but not specifically in terms of identifications with Mother.

221 . . . the denial of a whole side of your personality. . . . : *Ibid.,* 174–175.

221 . . . much of the executives' energy had been tied up in their conflicts. . . . : *Ibid.,* 180.

221 Hennig and Jardim looked at one group of middle managers. . . . : *Ibid.,* 178ff.

221 "human skills": *Ibid.,* 178ff.

221 Subsequent studies have confirmed that. . . . : See Patricia Kosiner, "Socialization and Self-Esteem: Women in Management," in Barbara L. Forisha and Barbara H. Goldman, *Outsiders on the Inside: Women and Organizations* (Englewood Cliffs, N.J.: Prentice-Hall, 1981), 31–41.

222 Women who try to behave in traditionally feminine ways. . . . : Kosiner, "Socialization and Self-Esteem."

222 "a positive feeling about being a female": Henry Biller in Lamb, 1976.

223 data from questionnaires. . . . : Hennig and Jardim, 31.

223 "personal growth, . . . self-fulfillment. . . . : *Ibid.,* 33.

223 the men defined a career . . . the women saw their career goals in personal terms. . . . : *Ibid.*

224 37¢, 63¢: from a survey by Heidrick & Struggles, Inc., cited by Patricia O'Toole, "Hers," *New York Times* (May 21, 1981).

225 So the Jewish American Princess was born. . . . : See Lesley Tonner, *Nothing But the Best: The Luck of the Jewish Princess* (New York, Coward, McCann & Geoghegan, 1975).

Judy Stampler

240 Tessman, *Children of Parting Parents,* 80.

240 *Ibid.,* 76.

CHAPTER SEVEN

page

All references to Dr. Tessman in this chapter are from Tessman, *Children of Parting Parents.*

252 E. Mavis Hetherington, Martha Cox, and Roger Cox, "Play and Social Interaction in Children Following Divorce," *Journal of Social Issues,* 35:4 (1979), 26–49.

252 There were a record 1.18 million divorces in 1979. . . . : Figures taken from the National Center for Health Statistics, reported in "Divorces Reach a High of 1.18 Million in a Year," *New York Times* (June 11, 1981).

252 It has been estimated that 40 or 50 percent. . . . ; Even though nearly 10 percent of single-parent families. . . . : Estimates from Henry Biller, "Father Absence, Divorce, and Personality Development" in Lamb, 1981, 489–552 (hereafter cited as "Father Absence").

252 Three quarters of the mothers of those children will remarry. . . . : Sar A. Levitan, "The U.S. Family," *New York Times* (July 27, 1981).

252 Janet G. and Larry L. Hunt, "Race, Daughters and Father-Loss: Does Absence Make the Girl Grow Stronger?" *Social Problems,* 25 (1977), 90–102.
Henry Biller, "Father Absence."

252 Biller in Lamb, 1976.

253 studies of genius. . . . : See Norma Radin in Lamb, 1981.

253 Many of them are wildly contradictory: See Michael Chapman, "Father Absence, Stepfathers, and the Cognitive Performance of College Students," *Child Development,* 4 (1977), 1155–1158.

254 Hetherington, "Play and Social Interaction."

254 Cultural factors count, too: See Norma Radin in Lamb, 1976, and Lamb, 1981; Henry Biller, "Father Absence."

254 Fatherless working-class children. . . . : Biller, "Father Absence."

254 Children react to their loss. . . . : Tessman, 492ff.

254 elements of a "quest" . . . attempts to identify with him. . . . : *Ibid.,* 45ff, 89ff.

255 One of the few facts on which most studies seem to agree. . . . : See Biller, "Father Absence"; also Tessman, *Children of Parting Parents.*

255 . . . one whose fantasies of a good father. . . . : Tessman, *Children of Parting Parents,* 515; Dr. Tessman describes how children of two or three. . . . : 493ff; Children of all ages need "emotional permission." . . . : 505, 510.

256 Judy probably felt conflicted . . . about loving her father. . . . : *Ibid.,* 495.

256 Marjorie Leonard, "Fathers and Daughters."

257 Dr. Tessman suggests that suicidal fantasies. . . . : Tessman, 513.

257 Sylvia Plath, "Daddy," *Ariel* (New York: Harper & Row, 1963).

257 Marjorie Leonard describes. . . . : In "Fathers and Daughters."

258 Tess Forrest, "The Paternal Roots of Female Character Development," *Contemporary Psychoanalyst,* 3 (1966), 21–28.

258 Hetherington, "Girls Without Fathers."

258 Hetherington's subjects were white, Midwestern. . . . : See Louise Hainline and Ellen Feig, "The Correlates of Childhood Father Absence in College-aged Women," *Child Development* 49 (1978), 37–42.

259 Seymour Fisher, *The Female Orgasm: Psychology, Physiology, Fantasy* (New York: Basic Books, 1973).

259 Children of seven or eight are still vulnerable to guilt. . . . : Tessman, 497; "pseudo-independence": 514; . . . by eight or so they can understand. . . . : 496; . . . by ten she can comprehend that, in reality. . . . : 514.

261 Dr. Tessman describes a girl. . . . : *Ibid.,* 472ff.

262 "ego-alien identification": *Ibid.,* 495.

262 Gail Sheehy, "Hers," *New York Times* (Thursdays, Dec. 6, 1981–Feb. 7, 1982).

262 Dr. Robert S. Weiss, "Growing Up a Little Faster: The Experience of Growing Up in a Single-Parent Household," *Journal of Social Issues,* 35:4 (1979), 97–11. See also Richard A. Kulka and Helen Weingarten, "The Long-Term Effects of Parental Divorce in Childhood on Adult Adjustment," *Journal of Social Issues,* 35:4 (1979), 50–79; and J. S. Wallerstein and J. B. Kelly, *Surviving the Breakup: How Children Actually Cope with Divorce* (New York: Basic Books, 1980).

263 Hetherington's study. . . . : Hetherington, Cox, and Cox, "Play and Social Interaction."

263 When an adolescent loses her father. . . . : Tessman, 499–500.

263 She may devalue Daddy. . . . : This interpretation is my own.

264 Hetherington found. . . . : "Play and Social Interaction."

CHAPTER EIGHT

page
269 When Freud declared. . . . : See Sigmund Freud, *New Introductory Lectures on Psychoanalysis,* trans. James Strachey (New York, W.W. Norton, 1964, 1965, Norton paperback ed.) 134–135.

270 Levinson, *Seasons,* 100.

272 *Ibid.,* 100.

275 *Ibid.,* 101.

Index